International Political Economy Series

General Editor: **Timothy M. Shaw**, Professor of Commonwealth Governance and Development, and Director of the Institute of Commonwealth Studies, School of Advanced Study, University of London.

Titles include:

Francis Adams, Satya Gupta and Kidane Mengisteab (*editors*)
GLOBALIZATION AND THE DILEMMAS OF THE STATE IN THE SOUTH

Susan Dicklitch
THE ELUSIVE PROMISE OF NGOs IN AFRICA
Lessons from Uganda

John Harriss, Kristian Stokke and Olle Törnquist (*editors*)
POLITICISING DEMOCRACY
The New Local Politics of Democratisation

David Hulme and Michael Edwards (*editors*)
NGOs, STATES AND DONORS
Too Close for Comfort?

Gordon Laxer and Sandra Halperin (*editors*)
GLOBAL CIVIL SOCIETY AND ITS LIMITS

Staffan Lindberg and Árni Sverrisson (*editors*)
SOCIAL MOVEMENTS IN DEVELOPMENT
The Challenge of Globalization and Democratization

Laura Macdonald
SUPPORTING CIVIL SOCIETY
The Political Role of Non-Governmental Organizations in Central America

Kurt Mills
HUMAN RIGHTS IN THE EMERGING GLOBAL ORDER
A New Sovereignty

Michael G. Schechter (*editor*)
THE REVIVAL OF CIVIL SOCIETY
Global and Comparative Perspectives

Hans Peter Schmitz
TRANSNATIONAL MOBILIZATION AND DOMESTIC REGIME CHANGE
Africa in Comparative Perspective

J.W. Wright, Jr (*editor*)
STRUCTURAL FLAWS IN THE MIDDLE EAST PEACE PROCESS
Historical Contexts

International Political Economy Series
Series Standing Order ISBN 0–333–71708–2 hardcover
Series Standing Order ISBN 0–333–71110–6 paperback
(*outside North America only*)

You can receive future titles in this series as they are published by placing a standing order. Please contact your bookseller or, in case of difficulty, write to us at the address below with your name and address, the title of the series and one of the ISBNs quoted above.

Customer Services Department, Macmillan Distribution Ltd, Houndmills, Basingstoke, Hampshire RG21 6XS, England

Transnational Mobilization and Domestic Regime Change

Africa in Comparative Perspective

Hans Peter Schmitz

Assistant Professor of Political Science
Maxwell School of Citizenship and Public Affairs
Syracuse University

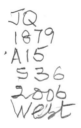

palgrave
macmillan

First published 2006 by
PALGRAVE MACMILLAN
Houndmills, Basingstoke, Hampshire RG21 6XS and
175 Fifth Avenue, New York, N.Y. 10010
Companies and representatives throughout the world

PALGRAVE MACMILLAN is the global academic imprint of the Palgrave Macmillan division of St. Martin's Press, LLC and of Palgrave Macmillan Ltd. Macmillan® is a registered trademark in the United States, United Kingdom and other countries. Palgrave is a registered trademark in the European Union and other countries.

ISBN-13: 978–1–4039–8538–5 hardback
ISBN-10: 1–4039–8538–3 hardback

This book is printed on paper suitable for recycling and made from fully managed and sustained forest sources.

A catalogue record for this book is available from the British Library.

Library of Congress Cataloging-in-Publication Data
Schmitz, Hans Peter, 1965–
    Transnational mobilization and domestic regime change : Africa in comparative perspective / Hans Peter Schmitz.
        p.   cm. — (International political economy series (Palgrave Macmillan (Firm)))
    Includes bibliographical references and index.
    ISBN 1–4039–8538–3 (cloth : alk. paper)
    1. Democratization—Africa.   2. Human rights advocacy—Africa. 3. Kenya—Politics and government.   4. Uganda—Politics and government—1979–   5. Comparative government.   I. Title. II. Series
    JQ1879.A15S36 2006
    320.96—dc22   2005056594

10   9   8   7   6   5   4   3   2   1
15   14   13   12   11   10   09   08   07   06

Printed and bound in Great Britain by
Antony Rowe Ltd, Chippenham and Eastbourne

Contents

List of Figures and Tables

Figures

Tables

Preface and Acknowledgments

Transnational human rights mobilization plays an increasingly significant and visible role in shaping global institutions and domestic political change. This book traces the effects of global norms and transnational activism in challenging authoritarian rule and shaping subsequent processes of democratic reforms. The results confirm some of the earlier claims in the literature, but challenge an unbridled optimism about the role of transnational mobilization. External actors are more effective in challenging authoritarian rule than in positively contributing to subsequent democratic reforms. This may not be surprising, since the building of democracy is a more complex process than bringing down a repressive regime. But the book also shows how certain types of transnational activism have distinct negative effects on democratic change.

Vertical networks with international activists 'uproot' domestic leaders and develop into a long-term liability for local groups, distracting them from building effective coalitions at home. Transnational activism not only strengthens domestic allies, but also provides a host of mobilizing opportunities for an embattled regime. Arguments based on national sovereignty resonate domestically and provide a powerful rejection of external interventions. Mobilizing donor governments creates a powerful challenge to authoritarian rule, but rivaling strategic and commercial interests make donors unreliable partners in the long run. Human rights pressures on donors translate into demands for multiparty rule, which is far from creating conditions for sustainable democratization. In sum, the domestic translation of international norms faces challenges, which require greater attention by scholars and policy makers alike.

I have received tremendous help in the research for and writing of this book. Most importantly, I thank the many individuals I met in Kenya and Uganda who made this project an utterly enjoyable and unique experience. As I was shuttling between embassies, NGO headquarters, and newspaper offices, my interview partners patiently answered my questions and generously shared their perspectives. A list of interviewees is included in the back of the book. Many of the individuals I met in both countries went far beyond their duty and invited me to their homes or provided me with office space and transportation. Everyday life experiences and interactions played a significant part in shaping the results of this research. In place of many others, I mention Albrecht

Bossert of the Konrad Adenauer Stiftung in Kampala and his family who provided me with temporary shelter and took me to the northern town of Gulu to see firsthand the difficulties of human rights work. I also want to thank the researchers and activists at Amnesty International (London) and Human Rights Watch (New York) who took the time for interviews and discussions on the human rights issues in Kenya and Uganda.

The Deutsche Forschungsgemeinschaft funded some of the initial field work, allowing me to spend more than nine months to conduct interviews in Kenya and Uganda. I have also received institutional support from the Human Rights Program at the University of Chicago and the Moynihan Institute of Global Affairs as well as the Political Science Department at Syracuse University. My thanks go to my academic mentors and friends for their continued investment into this project. Thomas Nielebock, Frank Schimmelfennig, and Frank Adler taught me skills and perspectives beyond the nuts and bolts of research and writing. There are too many to name who have commented on parts of the manuscript or on related work. Audie Klotz, Mitchell Orenstein, and Sidney Tarrow have given extensive feedback and helped to improve my arguments. Amy Mehringer read and critiqued the entire manuscript. I also thank Timothy Shaw, Jennifer Nelson, and anonymous reviewers at Palgrave Macmillan for their immense help and dedication.

Syracuse, New York
September 2005

Acronyms

ADF	Allied Democratic Forces
ACR	Africa Contemporary Record
AI	Amnesty International
CA	Constituent Assembly
CP	Conservative Party
DCF	District Consultative Forum
DDG	Democratic Development Group
DP	Democratic Party
FBIS	Foreign Broadcast Information Service
FORD	Forum for the Restoration of Democracy
HRW	Human Rights Watch
HSM	Holy Spirit Movement
ICJ	International Commission of Jurists
ICRC	International Committee of the Red Cross
IGG	Inspector General of Government
IMF	International Monetary Fund
IPPG	Inter-Party Parliamentary Group
KADU	Kenya African Democratic Union
KANU	Kenya African National Union
KBC	Kenya Broadcasting Corporation
KHRC	Kenya Human Rights Commission
KY	Kabaka Yekka
LC	Local Council
LRA	Lord's Resistance Army
LSK	Law Society of Kenya
MP	Member of Parliament
NCCF	National Constitutional Consultative Forum
NCA	National Convention Assembly
NCC	National Consultative Council
NCCK	National Council of Churches in Kenya
NCEC	National Convention Executive Council
NDP	National Development Party
NEC	National Executive Committee
NPC	National Political Commissar
NRC	National Resistance Council
NRM/A	National Resistance Movement/Army

OAU	Organization of African Unity
PLO	Palestine Liberation Organization
RC	Resistance Council
RPF	Rwandan Patriotic Front
RPP	Release Political Prisoners
SDP	Social Democratic Party
SPLA	Sudanese People's Liberation Army
UHRC	Uganda Human Rights Commission
UN	United Nations
UNICEF	United Nations Children's Fund
UNLA	Uganda National Liberation Army
UNLF	Uganda National Liberation Front
UPDF	Uganda People's Defense Forces
UPM	Uganda Patriotic Movement
UPC	Uganda People's Congress

1
Introduction

During the past decades, non-governmental organizations (NGOs), intergovernmental organizations (IGOs), and bilateral donors have made human rights and democracy a major goal of their external interventions in Africa and elsewhere. Transnational NGOs such as Amnesty International (AI) began in the 1960s to report on human rights conditions around the world, pressuring reluctant donor governments and multilateral agencies to monitor the domestic conduct of aid recipients. The end of the Cold War and the global diffusion of democratic governance in the early 1990s further pushed human rights and democracy to the center of many aid programs.

Like many other African nations, Kenya and Uganda have been for some time subject to those external interventions. Human rights NGOs have long mobilized against repression and built alliances with domestic dissidents. More recently, donor governments have pushed for press freedom, multipartyism, and a more independent judiciary, while multilateral agencies increasingly view 'good governance' as a prerequisite for economic development. As a partial result of those external pressures, Kenya re-introduced multiparty politics in 1991 and experienced its first peaceful electoral change of leadership in late 2002, while the Ugandan government led by Yoweri Museveni agreed to hold the first multiparty elections since 1980 in 2006. After almost 40 years of continuous post-independence rule, the Kenya African National Union (KANU) and President Daniel arap Moi were ousted by the National Rainbow Coalition (NARC), which represented both long-time adversaries of Moi and recent high-profile defectors from KANU. In Uganda, the National Resistance Movement (NRM) established a 'no-party rule' after winning a brutal civil war in 1986. Twenty years after taking power, the NRM and its leaders have reluctantly

1

agreed to the re-introduction of multiparty rule in exchange for constitutional changes designed to allow Museveni to run for an extra-constitutional third term as President. Like many other African nations, Kenya and Uganda have implemented significant political reforms since the mid-1990s, but cannot be assumed to move toward democracy in the future. They have taken distinct paths of regime change, which point toward interactions of external and domestic factors shaping current processes of regime change.

A comparison of regime change in Kenya and Uganda reveals important lessons about the external promotion of human rights and democracy. Building on recent scholarship on transnational activism (Burgerman 2001; Keck and Sikkink 1998; Risse, Ropp and Sikkink 1999), this study demonstrates that NGOs play an important role in challenging authoritarian rule and pushing donor governments as well as IGOs toward a more proactive role against repressive regimes. NGOs focusing primarily on human rights violations have an impact on the politics of democratization because they effectively mobilize domestic and international pressure against authoritarianism. In this perspective, cross-border mobilization aided by new technologies empowers domestic movements in their struggle against repressive regimes. Activists adopt distant causes, create transnational networks, report human rights violations, and generate what Margaret Keck and Kathryn Sikkink have termed the 'boomerang pattern' (Keck and Sikkink 1998: 12–13), designed to circumvent unresponsive governments and mobilize global support for deserving local causes.

While this study confirms some of the promises of transnational activism expressed in the literature, it also demonstrates that such external interventions do not necessarily contribute positively to the long-term consolidation of democratic governance. External actors play a more significant and positive role in confronting repressive regimes than they do in contributing to the long-term consolidation of democratic governance. Once significant political reforms are under way, external actors frequently lack the tools to effectively support further reforms and subsequently undermine domestic pro-democracy activism.

Building democracy presents different challenges to outsiders and requires more attention to domestic conditions than simply challenging authoritarian rule. The role of external actors changes markedly after a successful challenge to authoritarian rule, and principled mobilization can produce significant unintended negative effects on democratization by (re-) empowering ruling elites and weakening allied domestic activists. While transnational mobilization may be well intentioned and principled on the outside, it becomes part of a political struggle on the inside as domestic actors instrumentalize those interventions for political and personal gains. In challenging the conventional wisdom on transnational activism, this comparison shows how external interventions can undermine rather than strengthen the domestic bases for democracy and provide significant strategic opportunities to elites opposed to regime change. Challenged leaders frequently bolster their position by framing external interventions as 'neo-colonial' and denouncing domestic allies of transnational networks as unpatriotic and without a democratic mandate.

Meanwhile, domestic activists become distracted by the vertical networks build by external allies and neglect the effective coalition-building at home. Increasing external financial support for domestic civil society primarily created a new class of urban-based NGO professionals, whose principles and interests did not necessarily overlap with their external partners or the economic and social needs of the large majority of Kenyans and Ugandans. While political leaders primarily relied on popular support from the rural areas, the most visible parts of civil society were concentrated in Nairobi, thus exposing a urban–rural divide (Orvis 2003). Donor funding for civil society also increased competition on the domestic level as well as dependency on outside support.[1] It burdened local NGOs with annual reporting requirements and frequently emphasized short-term project execution rather than capacity-building or coordination among civil society actors (Ngunyi, Kithinji and Matsvai 2004).

Understanding these domestic conversions of external interventions requires an integration of recent transnational scholarship and the comparativist literature on democratization. Yet comparativists have been reluctant to give outside forces and in particular transnational non-state actors much credence in shaping domestic regime change.[2] With a few exceptions (Huntington 1991; Pridham and Vanhanen 1994; Remmer 1995; Schmitter 2001; Whitehead 2001), comparativists remain skeptical about the systematic effects of outside forces on democratization. This study shows that transnational interventions are not just 'shifting winds of change that blow in intermittently from abroad' (Bratton and van de Walle 1997: 32), but represent sustained and continuous efforts affecting processes of domestic political change.

Following the recent 'third wave' of democratization (Huntington 1991), scholars of democratization have shifted attention away from a traditional focus on structural 'requisites of democracy' (Lipset 1960) to the role of elites and negotiated transitions (Karl and Schmitter 1991; O'Donnell and Schmitter 1986; Przeworski 1991). This agency-centered emphasis on the choices of elites presents opportunities to integrate external factors into the study of democratization. Rather than explaining the emergence of democracy primarily based on economic development, a focus on the politics and process of democratization gives domestic and external actors a more visible role in shaping regime change.

Most states in the world face regular criticism of their domestic governance by transnational activists. Domestic dissidents frequently call on outside support for their cause(s), especially if they fail to get redress from their own governments. The domestic issue becomes transnationalized and (re-)framed in terms of universal human rights principles.[3] Transnational activists mobilize by building networks with domestic activists and like-minded Western donors, which pressure the accused government into compliance. As the mobilization returns to the domestic level, it offers opportunities for activists and governments alike to manipulate the political struggle for control. Keck and Sikkink's model reduces governments to objects of mobilization, while portraying an identity of principles and goals among domestic and international activists. Those assumptions do not hold true in many cases, especially where governments play a much more active role in resisting external pressures and where civil society is divided along ethnic, social, or political lines and remains frequently only united by a common enemy.[4] The 'boomerang pattern' presents but one and certainly the most optimistic form of interaction across the international–domestic divide (Tarrow 2005). Figure 1.1 represents a modified and more complete version of the 'boomerang pattern.'

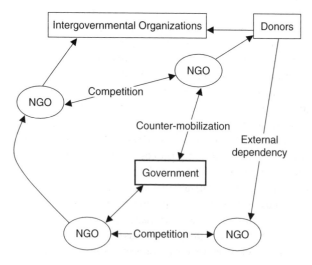

Figure 1.1   Transnational activism for human rights and democracy

Cases

Understanding the variable effects of transnational mobilization requires selecting cases with similar external pressures, but with significant differences in the domestic realm. Kenya and Uganda offer important variation with regard to the forms of authoritarian rule and the transition path taken after the initiation of regime change. Transnational human rights mobilization was directed at both countries and its donors, but the interaction of external mobilization and domestic conditions produced different results. Based on Bratton/van de Walle's classification of modal regimes (Bratton and van de Walle 1997: 78), the Kenyan political system moved from a (semi-)competitive *de facto* one-party state under Kenyatta toward a plebiscitary *de jure* one-party system under Daniel arap Moi. Between 1982 and 1989, government repression increased and the regime intensified its control over society. In contrast, Uganda moved from a despotic tyranny under Idi Amin (1971–79) toward a *de facto* one-party system embroiled in a civil war under Milton Obote (1980–85). While Kenya experienced a relatively peaceful form of authoritarian rule, indiscriminate killings and civil war destroyed Ugandan civil society and reflected rule by overt repression.

After the initiation of regime change, both countries took different paths of democratic change. Following Robert Dahl's basic distinction between participatory and competitive dimensions of democracy (Dahl 1971: 3–20), the Ugandan transition after 1986 took a *participatory/ constitutionalist* path, aiming at extending participation and inclusiveness rather than competition and contestation. In contrast, the Kenyan path was decidedly *electoralist*, demonstrated by KANU's grudging acceptance of multipartyism and expanded electoral contestation in 1991. In each case, transnational mobilization remained a significant force after initial reforms, but now had more ambiguous effects on the process of democratic reforms. In Kenya, the Moi regime survived two multiparty elections by manipulating the electoral playing field, instigating 'ethnic violence,' and rhetorically resisting outside interventions. In Uganda, the NRM extended its rule for almost 20 years without facing a single significant electoral challenge from another political force.

Similar transnational mobilization against different forms of authoritarian rule in Kenya and Uganda produced significant variation in the forms of initial regime change and subsequent transition paths. In both cases, the ruling elites prolonged their power not only by agreeing to reforms supported by external actors, but also by effectively restricting either participation (Kenya) or contestation (Uganda) as the complementary to the other aspect of expanding democratic space. The governments did not deceive external actors about their domestic conduct, but pursued and defended a two-pronged strategy of liberalization and repression. The interaction between transnational mobilization and domestic regime change in Kenya and Uganda is reflected in Figure 1.2.

The most significant methodological challenge for the growing literature on transnational activism is to identify and separate the discreet effects of such mobilization. Democracy promotion became a favorite of donor policies during the 1990s. As a result a plethora of external actors, governmental and non-governmental, have become involved in the issue area. This creates the challenge of separating the role of transnational activists from other influences with similar aims. Moreover, principled NGOs rarely promoted democracy as a whole, but emphasized specific aspects of it. Human rights and the rule of law were a specific focus of transnational activists. 'Democracy was most commonly seen as desirable without being a priority of NGO lobbying strategies' (Youngs 2004: 175). Further, the more official donor policies emphasized democracy, the more skeptical NGOs sought to distance themselves from the threat of co-optation. But the results of this study show that a rhetorical distance to democracy and 'good governance' made little difference in the effects of transnational mobilization. NGOs' frequent insistence on being apolitical actually blinded them in many cases to the unintended and often highly political effects of their principled interventions in domestic power struggles.

The book is primarily about the domestic responses to transnational mobilization, rather than the intervening external actors themselves. Those include donor governments, multilateral institutions, businesses,

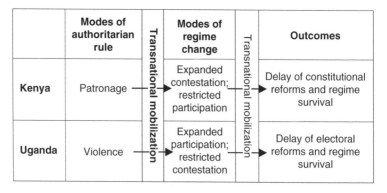

	Modes of authoritarian rule	Transnational mobilization	Modes of regime change	Transnational mobilization	Outcomes
Kenya	Patronage		Expanded contestation; restricted participation		Delay of constitutional reforms and regime survival
Uganda	Violence		Expanded participation; restricted contestation		Delay of electoral reforms and regime survival

Figure 1.2 Transnational mobilization and domestic regime change

and transnational NGOs. Within the transnational civil society sector, specialized human rights and development organizations (e.g. Amnesty International, Article 19, Human Rights Watch, Oxfam) usually did not maintain their own offices in Kenya or Uganda, while foundations (Ford Foundation and the German Hanns Seidel-, Friedrich Ebert-, Friedrich Naumann-, and Konrad Adenauer-*Stiftungen*) had a historical presence in one or both capitals dating as far back as political independence. While the majority of external NGOs are relatively recent entrants to the domestic politics in Kenya and Uganda, the German foundations had long been involved in efforts to strengthen democratic governance. As their initial strategy of aligning themselves with indigenous parties in both countries failed, they shifted their support to the civil society sector more broadly. External NGOs without a domestic presence were more likely to rhetorically separate their human rights activism from the question of democracy as a political system (Youngs 2004: 153), but all groups ultimately had an effect beyond their narrow agendas and on political change in general.

Organization of the book

Chapter 2 builds the theoretical basis for linking transnational mobilization and domestic regime change. I draw primarily on agency-centered explanations of democratization, which highlight the role of elites in negotiated transitions. In this literature, uncertainty plays a crucial role in explaining why democracy becomes a preferred and rational choice for leaders and their opponents. If seriously challenged, leaders choose democratic institutions because they allow both sides to vie for power in future elections. But those models of democratic change fail to explain why powerful authoritarian leaders should feel uncertain about their future in the first place. I argue that transnational mobilization creates such a challenge, which creates conditions conducive to the initiation of a political transition. Transnational mobilization thus creates the link between international norms and domestic practices by weakening authoritarian rule.

Chapter 3 describes the 'base line' of authoritarian rule, which I use to gauge the subsequent impact of transnational mobilization in Kenya and Uganda. Authoritarian rule emerged in both countries within a few years after political independence. The Ugandan governments under Amin and Obote mainly resorted to violence to establish and defend their rule, while the Kenyatta and Moi regimes primarily used patronage and limited repression of dissidents. The variation in authoritarian rule during these periods explains the divergent paths of regime change taken.

The second part of the chapter presents an overview of the democratization process after the onset of outside mobilization in the 1980s. While Uganda primarily followed a participatory model based on constitutional reforms, Kenya's path of regime change expanded electoral contestation by re-establishing multipartyism in 1991. In both cases, rulers emphasized only one aspect of democracy (participation or contestation), while actively undermining the other. The effects of transnational mobilization diminished because governments adapted their power strategies to limit detection and sanctions from abroad. In Kenya, the Moi government severely limited the use of 'detention without trial,' political murder, or systematic torture after 1992. Instead, it now charged dissidents with capital crimes based on fabricated evidence. Most importantly, officials close to the regime used new tactics of 'ethnic violence' prior to the elections to intimidate and displace opposition voters.

The Ugandan government severely restricted party activities and established a system of 'no-party rule' for almost 20 years, lasting from 1986 until 2006. The re-introduction of multipartyism is unlikely to foster democracy. Museveni not only secured a constitutional change allowing him to stand for a third term, but his rule has prevented the emergence of alternative political leaders (Tripp 2004).[5] Kenya under Moi witnessed during the 1990s vigorous party contestation, but without a level playing field and with extra-legal restrictions on individual participation. As transnational human rights mobilization had now increased the costs of open, state-led repression, KANU elites engaged in a 'privatization of state violence' (Roessler 2005) in order to intimidate opposition voters while avoiding donor sanctions. Even when the opposition finally succeeded in removing KANU from power in 2002, the logic of multipartyism turned out to be a liability for democratic reforms. Corruption and abuses of power remain prevalent in the Kibaki government, because the defeat of KANU had been built luring senior KANU leaders into the opposition. Requirements of electoral success under multiparty rule undermine long-term democratic reforms.

Transnational mobilization against government repression in Kenya and Uganda began in the early to mid-1980s. As Chapter 4 explains, the publication of human rights reports created global awareness of human rights abuses and delegitimized the authoritarian leaders in both nations. The mobilization narrowed the range of options for the governments and protected as well as empowered the political opposition.

Initially reluctant donor governments became followers of the sustained NGO mobilization. Human rights served in both nations as a basis for the demands of the domestic opposition. International human rights norms not only protected but also constituted the opposition against a repressive government.

In Chapter 5, I show how transnational and domestic mobilization converged to effect regime change in Uganda and political reforms in Kenya. Donor intervention and domestic mobilization combined with transnational efforts to bring about political change. In Uganda, the NRM prevailed in 1986 and established a new government focused on a transitional path of participatory and constitutionalist reforms. In Kenya, transnational mobilization prompted donors in 1990/91 to cut aid and force the Moi regime to re-introduce multipartyism. But the success story of external interventions ends with the initiation of regime change in both countries.

Chapter 6 offers a comparative assessment of the transition process in both countries. Transnational activism decreased in importance and now had more ambiguous effects on democratic change. This chapter confirms that building sustainable democratic institutions has been much more challenging than mobilizing effectively against authoritarian rule. While donors vacillated between competing goals of strengthening democracy, promoting commercial or strategic interests, and preferences for domestic political stability, transnational mobilization becomes entangled in ethnically driven domestic politics and adversely affects the ability of local groups to build coalitions for political reforms. In Kenya, a lack of consistency in the external interventions allowed entrenched KANU elites to hold onto power in two consecutive elections. Externally imposed multiparty rule undermined rather than advanced democratization (Lindberg 2003). In Uganda, waning international attention after 1986 allowed NRM elites to increase their control of domestic politics. Despite persistent human rights problems and a *de jure* 'no-party system,' transnational activism in Uganda failed during the 1990s to (re)build an effective movement for democratic change. Instead, human rights activists turned their attention to abuses committed by rebel groups operating in the northern and western parts of the country.

Chapter 7 offers a discussion of the most recent political developments in Kenya and Uganda. It provides additional evidence questioning the contributions of multiparty rule to sustainable democratization. While Kenya experienced the first peaceful handover of national power following the third multiparty elections in December 2002, large-scale political corruption remains prevalent and the new Kibaki government reneged on key parts of the constitutional reforms related to the power of the presidential office. In Uganda, the first multiparty elections since 1980 will take place in 2006. While ending, the ban on party activities nominally increases political freedoms, the 'movement' government solidified its control and changed the constitution to allow Museveni to run for a third term as president. After 19 years of 'no-party rule' which impeded the formation of a viable political alternative to Museveni, multipartyism is unlikely to promote sustainable democratic govern-ance. At best, it will remain a fiction; at worst, it will destabilize Ugandan politics.

The concluding chapter summarizes the underlying claims in light of the empirical chapters. The analysis and results point well beyond these two cases and provide a basis for investigating the effects of transna-tional activism more generally. The conclusions make a strong case for integrating transnational influences as well as African experiences into the mainstream of comparative study of democratization. In turn, the literature on principled activism can gain a more complex understanding of transnational processes by paying greater attention to mediating domestic structures and processes.

2
Transnational Dimensions of Democratization

Chapter 2 deals with two concepts.[1] The first two sections define democracy as a political system maximizing popular participation organized in periodic electoral contests. The rest of the chapter adds a transnational dimension to the comparative study of democratization. The transnational mobilization for democratic change is particularly relevant in challenging authoritarian rule. In later stages external influences combine with domestic factors to produce variation in the paths of regime change. Transnational mobilization not only decreases in importance during later stages of regime change, but also produces more ambiguous effects on democratic change. External actors find it easier to join domestic groups in challenges to authoritarian leaders than to contribute positively to the creation and consolidation of democratic practices.

Defining democratic practices

Democratization is a process, which increases popular participation and electoral contestation. Effective participation and competition require a measure of equality among the populace as well as transparency and accountability of the rulers to the ruled. The claim of participation in public affairs is frequently based on the assumption that human beings share intrinsic qualities and are capable of determining their own affairs, both individually and collectively.

Comparing democratic rule across nations entails significant issues of definition and measurement. Should a definition of democracy primarily focus on the selection process of leaders or should it include references to the broader social and cultural structure of a society? The more narrow definition of democracy reflects a pluralist view (Dahl 1971; Schumpeter 1942) and is used here for two primary reasons. First, by separating democratic governance from larger cultural, economic, and social developments, a narrow definition facilitates the investigation of causal relationships between democracy and the forces shaping it. Democracy is defined as a method or procedure of government rather than a specific commitment 'to any particular set of social and economic objectives' (Weiner 1987: 5). Second, a procedural definition of democracy facilitates comparisons across nations.

Ronald Dahl's concept of 'polyarchy' emphasizes the two dimensions of contestation and participation. Contestation focuses on recurring free and fair elections. This entails the availability of alternatives at the time of voting, the uncertainty about outcomes, the irreversibility of voting results, and assurance that elections occur regularly (Przeworski *et al.* 2000: 16). Participation measures the extent of involvement of the citizenry through partisan, associational, and other forms of collective action (Dahl 1971: 3–20). These measures of polyarchy then offer opportunities to correlate degrees of competition and participation with other aspects of the community and compare the results across nations. Does the regular occurrence of elections make leaders more accountable and responsive to the public? Are so defined democracies less likely to engage in aggressive foreign policies? Does democratization increase the likelihood of internal strife? Is a high level of participation positively correlated with economic growth?

Democratization from a pluralist perspective either enhances levels of competition for public offices or increases the inclusiveness of the political system. For Dahl, the key institutions are elected officials, free and fair elections, inclusive suffrage, the right to run for office, freedom of expression, alternative information, and associational autonomy (Dahl 1989: 221). Such a procedural view is not necessarily incompatible with more substantive notions of democracy. Formally democratic decisions can leave sections of the population below certain social and economic standards which enable them to support democratic procedures in the first place (Merkel 1996: 36; Offe 1994). However, the participatory aspect of polyarchy offers opportunities to integrate questions of economic equality into the definition and measurement of democracy. Apart from guaranteeing the formal right to vote or the freedom of speech, a more democratic society enables its citizens to make informed electoral choices. A procedural definition identifies minimal standards of democratic governance upon which broader processes of social and political change can take place. This is particularly important in developing societies such as Kenya and Uganda, where large sections of the populations live near or below the poverty line.

A final note of caution concerning a narrow definition of democracy focuses on recent experiences of failing political reforms and the re-emergence of authoritarian rule in many countries. The proliferation of terms such as 'informal polyarchy' (O'Donnell 1996) or 'illiberal democracy' (Zakaria 1997) has led some scholars to declare the 'end of the transitions paradigm' (Carothers 2002) and highlighted efforts by political leaders that 'are deliberately contrived to satisfy prevailing international norms of "presentability"' (Joseph 1998: 4). The 'fallacy of electoralism' (Karl 1986: 34) serves as a reminder that a procedural definition of democracy is primarily a research tool and not a normative commitment to a certain political system. Narrowly defining democracy facilitates comparisons across nations and enhances the ability of researchers to understand the interactions of political, economic, and social development.

The challenge to authoritarian rule

Scholars of democratization have used the most recent global shift toward democratic governance to develop an agency-driven literature (Karl 1987; Karl and Schmitter 1991; O'Donnell, Schmitter and Whitehead 1986; Przeworski 1991; Remmer 1995; Schmitter 1994) that challenges the traditional modernization perspective. In an agency-focused perspective of social change, social actors are not primarily driven by their economic positions and systemic imperatives, but make autonomous choices based on defined interests and the interactions with other groups or individuals in their community. I argue here that the focus on elites and their choices during democratic transitions has vastly improved our understanding of democratization, but still neglects both ideational and transnational dimensions of regime change.

Modernization describes a process of social mobilization, where democracy follows economic development, wealth accumulation, and functional differentiation. Early proponents claimed that economic growth beyond a certain threshold level instigates social change in the form of urbanization, increased literacy, and media exposure (Deutsch 1961; Lerner 1958; Lipset 1960). As a result of this transformation, new political actors emerge mainly in the form of middle classes with distinct political interests and a desire to shape national political affairs (Hadenius 1992: 77–80). Such middle classes are likely to demand representation in return for taxation and may be less vulnerable to corruption and repressive practices.

Early skeptics of a linear and unidirectional relationship between economic and political development pointed to 'outliers' such as less developed, but democratic India or the wealthy and authoritarian Arab states. Empirical studies testing the modernization claims of the early 1960s found that socioeconomic development beyond a certain level did not promote democracy (Neubauer 1967). Others warned that modernization theorists failed to fully understand the consequences of social transformations such as urbanization and media exposure. In particular, Huntington predicted that imbalances in economic growth patterns will cause political instability instead of democratic change (Huntington 1968). In response to the empirical and theoretical challenges, scholars with a modernization perspective have either sought to improve upon the first generation of modernization theorists without giving up their original claims or moved away from the stronger claim that economic development always precedes and causes political change. Authors following the first variant are mainly concerned with (1) improving the statistical methods, (2) explaining 'outliers,' and (3) identifying those issues within the broad process of modernization which have the strongest impact on democratization. As a result, factors such as urbanization or mass media have lost prominence over time, and education has emerged as the most prominent link between economic and political development (Hadenius 1992; Helliwell 1994). Modernization theorists also argue that the leaders of rich but undemocratic oil-producing countries have successfully decoupled wealth creation from social change and subverted the emergence of a self-sustained and independent middle class (Moore 1996: 59).

More skeptical scholars of the second variant have questioned the validity of broad-ranging conclusions based on Lipset's original claim and the implied causal path. For Hadenius, '60 percent of the variation concerning the level of democracy' in his selected 132 countries can be explained by seven structural factors (literacy, commodity concentration, trade with the United States, capitalism, percentage of Protestants, military expenditure, and average fragmentation), while 'other things too probably have an impact on democracy, and that these factors could be either of a structural or an actor-oriented nature' (Hadenius 1992: 146). Vanhanen argued that socioeconomic development 'is only an intervening variable that correlates positively with democratization because various power resources are usually more widely distributed at higher levels than at lower levels of socio-economic development' (Vanhanen 1990: 191).

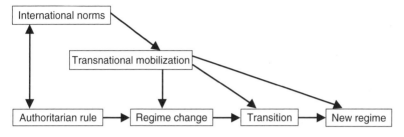

Figure 2.1 A transnational perspective of democratization

Structuralist and agency-based perspectives of regime change offer important answers to the puzzle of domestic regime change, but remain limited in their ability to integrate external and ideational pressures for change into the analysis. A transnational perspective offers opportunities to bridge the gap between structure and agency and draw on the peculiar strengths of International Relations (IR) and comparativist scholarship. International norms and institutions as well as transnational NGOs play an increasingly important role in shaping domestic trajectories of regime change. Human rights norms provide an increasingly dense ideational structure shaping the ideas and interests of transnational and domestic activists. On the agency side, transnational NGOs function as transmission mechanisms for diffusing those international norms into a domestic context. Their peculiar principled character and methods of mobilization are a significant factor shaping regime change. This view expands the study of the structural environment to include norms about what defines acceptable democratic practices. Figure 2.1 shows how international norms and transnational actors influence the domestic process of regime change.

External dimensions of political regime change

Democratization is not just a by-product of economic development or elite struggles for national power, but also a process embedded in an international normative order. Transnational activist networks diffuse democratic principles, support domestic allies, and exert pressure on authoritarian regimes. The constructivist literature in IR explores for some time how international norms shape domestic preferences and policies (Finnemore 1996; Keck and Sikkink 1998; Risse, Ropp and Sikkink 1999; Thomas 2001). This literature has claimed, at least in rhetoric, that agency and structure are mutually constitutive. As a source for social change, it focuses on the emergence of increasingly well-defined guidelines for the domestic conduct of governments and the shape of a democratic polity.

With the creation of the United Nations (UN) in 1945, the international community established universally valid norms of domestic conduct broadly defining ideas of democratic governance. These norms are not merely restrictions. Instead, they are also opportunities to create consensus and direct cooperative relations among actors. 'Norms are therefore not only "guidance devices", but also the means which allow people to pursue goals, share meanings, communicate with each other, criticize assertions, and justify actions' (Kratochwil 1989: 11). The greater the difference between domestic conduct and international norms, the more likely it is that domestic or transnational groups will mount efforts to expose the contradictions. International norms present an opportunity to challenge the status quo with reference to a universally accepted and institutionalized set of principles.

In contrast to the mainstream of the agency-based literature and its focus on self-interested behavior (Colomer 1991; Przeworski 1991), I argue here that the growing relevance and visibility of international norms transforms the domestic competition for national power. This is not simply about self-interested elites negotiating a transition process, but about the ability to use (and adapt to) opportunities offered in the international realm. The reference to universal values represents a necessary condition for the creation of uncertainty and power stalemates in the first place.

The international context

While there is an emerging consensus on the significance of international influences on regime change (Pridham, Herring and Sanford 1994; Schmitter 2001; Whitehead 2001), there is surprisingly little systematic work exploring the exact mechanisms linking international norms and domestic change. The mainstream of scholarship on democratization is still skeptical about the significance of international forces. While IR scholars are increasingly taking an interest in the domestic consequences of international processes (Grugel 2003; Risse, Ropp and Sikkink 1999), their efforts usually underestimates the significance of the domestic realm as the main battleground for social change (Checkel 1998).

Sociological institutionalism as one of the main sources of constructivist thought claims that the international system is primarily social and not material (Finnemore 1996; McNeely 1995; Meyer *et al.* 1997).

Sociological institutionalists typically pursue their claim that '[c]ulture lies at the heart of world development' (Boli and Thomas 1999: 17) by pointing to cases of policy diffusion and homogenization in the absence of similar material conditions. In cases of similar practices and institutional evolution, sociological institutionalists invoke the homogenizing influence of world culture principles, including universalism, individualism, rational voluntaristic authority, rationalizing progress, and world citizenship. Sociological institutionalists assume that those principles 'define the nature and purpose of social action' (Boli and Thomas 1999: 17). 'Culturally and historically contingent beliefs about what constitutes a "civilized" state [...] exert a far greater influence on basic institutional practices than do material structural conditions...' (Reus-Smit 1997: 583). States are not primarily viewed as monadic actors focusing on pre-defined self-interests, but as members of a community they share with other states, international institutions, and increasingly vocal groups of transnational activists. This world culture 'creates and legitimates the social entities that are seen as actors' (Meyer, Boli and Thomas 1987: 12). Social change is not driven by internal functional needs and socioeconomic development but by external norms pressure, institutional isomorphism (DiMaggio and Powell 1983), and mimicry (Klug 2000). Nation-states are understood as 'constructions of a common wider culture, rather than as self-directed actors responding rationally to internal and external contingencies' (Meyer *et al.* 1997: 152).

Many IR scholars and in particular constructivists (Philpott 2001; Wendt 1999) challenge neorealist claims (Waltz 1979) that the logic of the international system has remained unchanged since the emergence of states. With the creation of the UN, principles of domestic governance were universally accepted by the international community of states. Following the Universal Declaration of Human Rights in 1948, states developed and adopted a whole array of human rights and other treaties directly impinging on their domestic conduct. With the significant expansion of such institutions within the last 50 years, state actors face growing formal and informal limits to their domestic policy choices. The number of such agreements has grown, creating a denser network of institutional regulation, while the acceptance measured in numbers of ratification has also increased (Schmitz and Sikkink 2002). Human rights norms have experienced a 'norms cascade' (Finnemore and Sikkink 1998) and are today a common standard for domestic conduct. Although democracy itself is not globally established as a right, the full implementation of all UN human rights agreements would formally create such a state in all nations of the world (Franck 1992). In Europe, membership in the European Union and the Council of Europe is conditional on the establishment of a democratic government. In the early 1990s, the Organization of American States has outlawed the removal of democratically elected governments. Hundreds or even thousands of NGOs promote and diffuse norms of democratic governance on a global scale.

The spread of democratic norms

Although sociological institutionalists acknowledge the role of collective actors in spreading world cultural principles (Meyer *et al.* 1997: 160), their structuralist perspective prevents them from exploring the independent role of those agents (Lynch 2004: 344). In the best sociological tradition, they are reduced to expressing pre-defined social and cultural positions. 'Rapid global changes across dissimilar units suggest structure-level rather than agent-level causes. They do not, however, prove them. One also needs to specify the mechanism of change and show the common source of the new preference and behavior' (Finnemore 1996: 22). In order to trace the process by which international norms enter the domestic realm, I rely on the transnationalist literature and investigate the role of non-state actors in diffusing ideas of democratic governance.

Transnationalism emerges naturally as part of the state system, but traditional theories of IR have largely ignored such interactions or reduced them to the power and interests of states (Charnovitz 1997; Krasner 1995). A brief flurry of the transnationalist literature (Keohane and Nye Jr. 1971; Willetts 1982) in the 1970s did not create a sustained research agenda. After the end of the Cold War, the transnationalist agenda re-emerged aided by the constructivist shift and with a narrower definition of transnational activism. The current scholarship differs in two crucial aspects from the earlier generation. First, it has separated multinational corporations and violent non-state actors from their study of a growing global not-for-profit sector (Price 2003: 580; Risse 2002: 259). Instead of deriving political significance from economic or military might, the new generation focused mainly on organizations promoting norms and ideas such as human rights and environmental protection (Keck and Sikkink 1998: 29). Second, the new generation of scholars did not adopt a zero-sum logic claiming a decline in state power as a direct result of the rising transnational sector. The main research question was no longer *whether* transnational relations really mattered (measured in declining state power), but *how* they mattered.

There is a wide range of terms used to describe the agents using transnational relations to further their goals. Those include references to private citizen networks, NGOs, transnational advocacy networks, or global civil society. In some cases, the transnational network is dominated by state-employed scientists (Evangelista 1999), in others it is a coalition of NGOs (Glasius 2002; Price 1998), and in still others it reflects the bottom–up activism of individual citizens organized in less structured social movements. There is an obvious overlap between the IR literature on transnational activism and the comparative literature on social movements (Khagram, Riker and Sikkink 2002; Tarrow 2001).

Advocacy is used by transnational activists as a form of foreign policy directed at states, IGOs, and other non-state entities. It is no longer primarily aimed from the bottom–up at one single government, but represents a tool of autonomous NGOs challenging their limited formal participation in global affairs (Florini 1999). The most successful NGOs have adopted state-like strategies in order to become significant global actors. Defying the limits of state boundaries, transnational NGOs gather their own information, create and maintain constituencies, raise financial resources, use collective decision-making processes, and develop independent policy goals. Unlike states, transnational NGOs are not limited by diplomatic etiquette or expectations of reciprocity in relation to other state actors.

The research on the effectiveness of transnational mobilization focuses on (1) characteristics of the issues involved, (2) the promotional networks built, and (3) the targets chosen. With regard to issue characteristics, the literature highlights the level of international institutionalization as a reflection of global agreement on a given norm. Keck and Sikkink have claimed that issues of bodily harm and equal opportunity are more likely to succeed than others (Keck and Sikkink 1998: 204), but there is little empirical evidence to support this assertion. Scholars focusing on the network characteristics have emphasized the role of expertise as a crucial aspect legitimizing transnational activism in the absence of significant material resources. This goes back to the idea of 'epistemic communities' (Haas 1992) and is effectively used by Evangelista in claiming that 'transnational networks that have sought to tame the Russian bear by promoting disarmament and respect for human rights were ultimately successful' (Evangelista 1999: 390).

Moral authority is also based on claims of impartiality and refusal to engage in 'politicking.' Human rights NGOs established themselves as actors in global affairs because they collected information about violations across all nations and contrasted it with the rhetorical commitment to human rights expressed by governments. Transnational activists are also effective in linking domestic causes to particular international audiences. The landmines issue became a success after NGOs had collected sufficient information to frame it as a genuine global problem as well as imposed a human rights perspective on a topic previously framed as a national security issue. This source of moral authority based on expertise and appeal to universal principles has been criticized for its alleged lack of democratic accountability and popular representation (Anderson 2000; Price 2003: 590). For the purpose of developing a bridge between the transnationalist and the comparative literature on democratization, the issue of representativeness plays a significant role in the translation of international norms into domestic practice. Authoritarian leaders regularly reject outside interventions promoting democratic principles by asserting sovereignty and challenging the legitimacy of transnational activists. This process shows engagement across the international–domestic divide and shifts attention to the target characteristics of mobilization. Here, the IR literature emphasizes variation in vulnerabilities to network pressures.

In the volume initiating the 'second wave' of transnational scholarship (Risse-Kappen 1995), Risse-Kappen emphasized the central role of the 'domestic structure' understood as the availability of 'access points' and 'winning coalitions' for transnational activism. With little regard to comparative subtleties, a 'weak' and fragmented state was more easily penetrable from the outside, but activists also faced greater difficulties in creating an effective coalition for their goals. Subsequent scholarship has simplified this argument by identifying the degree of 'normative fit' or resonance between international norms and domestic understandings (Hawkins 2002). However, simplified domestic structure or resonance arguments are problematic because they suggest that transnational mobilization is most successful when it is least needed (Price 2003: 593). In the case of democratization and human rights promotion, transnational mobilization typically challenges the domestic structure (authoritarian rule) as such. Here, scholars emphasize the availability of strong ties between transnational activists and domestic allies. In Keck and Sikkink's 'boomerang pattern,' the domestic opposition receives crucial outside protection and support from IGOs and NGOs (Keck and Sikkink 1998). In a subsequent volume (Risse, Ropp and Sikkink 1999), the interactions between domestic activists and international supporters are set against the reactions of authoritarian leaders, who are slowly pushed from a position of denial to tactical concessions and, eventually, significant policy changes. This 'rhetorical entrapment' (Risse 2000) of authoritarian leaders using their own commitment to universal principles contained in the UN Charter depends on the continued activism and pressure of transnational activist collations. 'In this sense, democratization can be seen as both a contributing cause and an effect of the expanding role of transnational civil society' (Price 2003: 595).

This generally positive assessment of transnational activism by the first wave of scholarship has more recently been challenged by a new generation of researchers. Transnational mobilization as a tool of empowering domestic activists is not always available and depends on the ability of domestic groups to 'market' their cause to outside interests (Bob 2005). Even when transnational activists take an interest and turn their attention to a peculiar cause, the effects are not necessarily promoting democratic change. When outside support solidifies, domestic activists may become 'uprooted' and isolated from the local community (Mendelson and Glenn 2002: 23). If domestic groups receive foreign aid and other material support, their agenda is often driven by donor objectives, rather than domestic needs (Henderson 2002). This makes it easier for the opponents of change to frame the interventions as yet another example of 'imperial' imposition (Thompson 2002). By bypassing traditional channels of democratic legitimation, transnational activists may get things done in the short term, but undermine the process of democratization in the long run.

Transnationalists have studied for some time the activism of NGO networks promoting democratic principles on a global scale. Their main goal was to prove to the state-centric IR mainstream that these collective actors matter. Most studies unsurprisingly show that transnational activism does matter and has significant independent influence. The second wave of transnational scholarship builds on those accomplishments and no longer wrestles primarily with the question of relevance. Instead, the study of transnational activism has matured in four important ways. First, social movement scholars have challenged the global bias of the transnational scholarship by engaging it with their more detailed exploration of the domestic sources of contentious politics (Tarrow 2005). Second, scholars have begun to focus on failed campaigns as crucial cases for a more balanced understanding of transnational activism (Bob 2005). Third, transnational scholarship has broadened its focus beyond the study of principled activism to include networks with questionable or outright destructive goals (Price 2003: 601) Fourth, the literature increasingly moves beyond crude assumptions about the principled character of transnational activism and treats their strategies and goals as an open empirical question. Just like states and corporations, transnational NGOs are exposed to competition in a marketplace shaped by desires for organizational survival and growth (Cooley and Ron 2002). Although more recent studies are more critical of transnational activism, this broadening of the research agenda serves as an indicator for the growing significance and mainstreaming of studying activists moving across borders. A synthesis of the transnational literature with comparative scholarship on democratization offers the next step in establishing external non-state actors as significant agents of social and political change.

Modernization: Cause or effect of regime change?

Current debates on the link between socioeconomic and political development are shaped by Przeworski and Limongi's claim that economic wealth *sustains* democracy, but does not necessarily *create* conditions for its emergence (Przeworski and Limongi 1997). Driving this research is the basic empirical observation that a higher percentage of democracies exist among rich rather than among poor nations. Przeworski and Limongi reject the conventional wisdom, which claims that economic growth leads to the emergence of democracy. In their words, the correlation supports only a much less expansive claim: 'Once a democracy is established the more well to do a nation, the more likely that it will survive' (Przeworski and Limongi 1997: 156). In a subsequent study, Przeworski and his collaborators assert that the 'probability that a dictatorship will die and a democracy will be established is pretty much random with regard to per capita incomes, about 2 percent per year. But the probability that, once established, a democracy will survive increases steeply and monotonically as per capita incomes get larger. Indeed, democracy is almost certain to survive in countries with per capita incomes above \$4,000' (Przeworski *et al.* 2000: 273).

In a direct challenge to Przeworski *et al.*'s work, Boix and Stokes maintain that wealthy democracies are not only more likely to survive, but also reassert that economic growth causes democratization (Boix and Stokes 2003). Their crucial variable to explain democratization is not wealth *per se*, but the level of equality in the distribution of income. Additionally, they claim that the role of economic development (measured in per capita income) in democratization was more pronounced before than after World War II. Countries democratized at lower levels of income before 1945, while authoritarian regimes have become less vulnerable to economic growth since the 1950s. Boix and Stokes assert that 'early-industrializing countries achieved income equality at lower levels of per capita income than did later-industrializing ones' (Boix and Stokes 2003: 544).

Przeworski and Limongi challenged the traditional view of democratization within comparative politics, which extrapolates from the West European and North American experience of the 19th century, when rapid economic development coincided with the emergence of democratic governance (Lipset 1960; Neubauer 1967). Modernization scholars have claimed that the 'third wave' of democratization (as well as its ebbing) confirms their claims of an endogenous process. According to Lipset *et al.*, the correlation between socioeconomic development and democracy is 'more pronounced in the early 1980s than in the late 1950s' (Lipset, Kyoung-Ryung and Torres 1993: 157). Democratization is the long-term result of increasing wealth and its effects on levels of urbanization, literacy, education, and availability of information to citizens. Economic development enables the social promotion of individuals and groups within society and allows for the emergence of autonomous political structures. A more educated population will eventually demand greater political participation.

From this perspective, democracy may even be harmful to economic growth. 'Political development must be held down, at least temporarily, in order to promote economic development' (Huntington and Nelson 1976: 23). Conventional wisdom held that authoritarian regimes can generate greater economic growth than democracies (de Schweinitz 1959; Huntington 1968; for a summary of arguments, see Przeworski and Limongi 1993: 52f.), because they are more insulated from popular demands and particularistic interests. Democracies are more likely to waste income for consumption, rather than long-term investments for economic stability and growth. In a more recent version of this logic, Leftwich argues that 'what the West should do is to support only those dedicated and determined developmental elites which are seriously bent on promoting economic growth, *whether democratic or not* (emphasis in the original). For by helping them to raise the level of economic development it will help them also to establish or consolidate the real internal conditions for lasting democracy' (Leftwich 1996: 329).

Reversed causality: Is democracy good for economic growth?

Studies suggesting a possible reversed causality between economic growth and democratic development were taken more seriously when the 'third wave' slowly gathered momentum in the mid-1980s. In 1977,

Arend Lijphart argued that 'to the extent that it (the correlation between economic development and democracy, HPS) indicates a causal relationship, it may well be that democracy rather than economic development is the cause' (Lijphart 1977: 230f.). Przeworski and Limongi argued 20 years later that ideology rather than empirical evidence determined the results of earlier modernization studies (Przeworski and Limongi 1997: 60). As many authoritarian regimes supported the United States in the Cold War, asserting a negative impact of democracy on economic growth made political if not economic sense.

Sirowy/Inkeles identified two additional perspectives to the traditional modernization view (Sirowy and Inkeles 1990). Challengers claim that democracy institutionalizes competition within the political sphere and thus complements a strategy of economic growth based on a free market ideology (Olson 1993). In this view, it is not the (negative) direct effect of increased consumption that makes a difference, but the (positive) indirect effects of institutionalizing complementary structures in the economic and political sphere. Finally, a third perspective argues that evidence shows no significant relationship between the political system and economic development.

The comprehensive study 'Democracy and Development' by Przeworski *et al.* (2000) concludes that the type of political regime has little effect on economic growth. While populations in democracies do experience greater increases in per capita income than their counterparts living under authoritarian rule, this result is due to demographics rather than politics. As wealth grows in both types of regimes, per capita income increases more in democracies because they have systematically lower fertility rates than authoritarian regimes (Przeworski *et al.* 2000: 264). While democracies do not necessarily fare better with regard to economic growth in general, they do a better job in distributing wealth and creating more stable political conditions. Also, particularly vulnerable groups, such as women, experience comparatively higher levels of deprivation under authoritarian rule and are more likely to profit from a combination of democracy and economic growth.

The limits of an endogenous perspective

The limits of a modernization perspective on democratization are linked to both methodological and theoretical issues. The dominance of large-*N* studies in the field creates correlative evidence, but little in terms of process tracing the causal path of complex social change. More recently, scholars have also questioned the validity of the indices used to measure the dependent variable 'democracy.' Many studies face serious measurement and definitional problems (Bollen 1993; Munck and Verkuilen 2002) which affect their explanatory value. 'The central finding of the cross-national statistical research [...] [does] not validate the theoretical accounts that have often been associated with [it], in particularly, modernization theory. Nor do cross-sectional correlations allow us to make adequate inferences about causal sequence' (Huber, Rueschemeyer and Stephens 1993: 72). Qualitative studies have also shown that the underlying theoretical assumptions do not hold across regions and countries. In particular, the Latin American experience since World War II and the persistence of authoritarianism in rich oil-producing states undermine the claim that economic development is a determinant cause of democratic change (Mainwaring and Pérez-Liñán 2003; Ross 2001). Critics also point out that middle classes as the central agents of change do not necessarily promote democracy (Rueschemeyer, Huber Stephens and Stephens 1992).

In addition to these methodological and theoretical challenges from within the comparative field, the results of the modernization research also give credence to the role of external factors. I will focus here on the most recent statement of the theory as presented by Boix and Stokes. There are three distinct international explanations for their results. First, after World War II, the newly established Bretton Woods institutions began to systematically disburse financial resources to developing countries. Especially in the 1960s and 1970s, those aid flows were abused by authoritarian leaders to sustain domestic support through corruption and the acquisition of means of repression. Second, the UN established the principle of national sovereignty and promoted the end to colonial rule. The leaders of newly independent nations used the external recognition and 'negative sovereignty' (Clapham 1996; Jackson 1990) to solidify their domestic power base. Third, during the Cold War, the United States directly supported many authoritarian regimes in Latin America and elsewhere, which actually had relatively high levels of per capita income. These factors offer a competing explanation to Boix and Stokes' domestic focus on economic equality as the main cause for democratization. They account for why authoritarian regimes emerging after World War II survived at relatively higher levels of per capita income.

Socioeconomic explanations artificially insulate domestic economies from the outside world. In many developing nations experimenting with democratization after World War II, economic development was heavily influenced by the global trade system (GATT and, since 1995, World Trade Organization, WTO) and the policies of the World Bank and the International Monetary Fund (IMF). As the interventions of those international financial institutions (IFIs) become more targeted (and contested), the domestic, the international, and the transnational become more intertwined. Bilateral and multilateral donors have redirected large parts of their aid away from governments toward the non-governmental sector both in the North and in the South. In theory, aid can now no longer be used by elites to support corruption and authoritarian practices, but instead reaches the targets with greater precision and effectiveness. The IMF's Structural Adjustment Programs (SAPs) are increasingly intrusive and require specific institutional changes (e.g. independent central bank) and public policies (e.g. privatization).

In the 1990s, the World Bank developed a focus on poverty reduction, which aims to increase equality as a precondition for more sustainable economic growth. While those policies are rhetorically defended in reference to economic growth, they are strongly contested by non-governmental activists (O'Brien *et al.* 2000). Some of the critics reject the work of IFIs altogether, while others call for reforms and more opportunities for developing nations to take advantage of free trade. The WTO can force developing countries to open their markets to foreign products, but it has failed to effectively take on protectionism in the developed world. Large-scale infrastructure programs supported by the World Bank have been criticized for disenfranchising local populations (Khagram 2002). Globalization critics have targeted SAPs for their austerity measures and charged that they increase rather than decrease poverty and foreign debt (Donnelly 2002). What matters in the context of the discussion here is not who is right or wrong concerning the role of IFIs, but that the global context of how development is defined and linked to political change matters to understanding domestic politics.

To conclude, the emergence of democracy is not exclusively linked to socioeconomic prerequisites. While socioeconomic development and political change are closely related, the relationship is neither unidirectional nor necessarily linear. Wealth makes democracies less likely to fall. Moreover, increases in per capita income are positively related to democratization, if the wealth is spread evenly across society. Research also shows that democracy does not create higher (nor lower) rates of economic growth than authoritarian rule, but it does produce greater equality and more protections for vulnerable sections of society. But the most recent research on the modernization paradigm also confirms Rustow's insight that 'the factors that keep a democracy stable may not be the ones that brought it into existence' (Rustow 1970: 346). A shift from a structuralist to an agency-driven perspective offers opportunities to better understand why authoritarian regimes come under pressure and how processes of democratization unfold. Such a perspective also opens the discussion to the influence of transnational actors and international institutions. 'At this stage the problem is less one of identifying ways in which the international system may impinge upon domestic political choice than of integrating international forces within the framework of comparative theory' (Remmer 1995: 108).

The role of agency and contingency

Structural and agency-driven accounts for democratization should not be seen as competing explanations for the same outcome, but as complementary efforts to understand complex social and political change. 'Structural developments may be necessary to create an environment favorable to democratization and eventual consolidation, but unless powerful and determined local actors step up to lead the way, even weakened authoritarian regimes may find themselves with an extended lease on life' (Berman 2001: 459f.). I argue here that understanding the role of domestic actors in leading efforts to democratize is shaped not only by the material context of socioeconomic conditions, but also by the structural environment of international institutions and transnational activism. Before introducing the IR literature on the global promotion of norms related to democratic governance, I will present the agency-driven perspective as the domestic link to this transnational literature.

The more sustained shift from structuralist to agency-oriented approaches builds on a variety of intellectual predecessors. Dankwart Rustow's 'Transitions to Democracy: Toward a Dynamic Model' was the first systematic challenge to the idea of cultural or economic prerequisites (except for national unity) for democracy (Rustow 1970). Also in the early 1970s, Robert Dahl's 'Polyarchy: Participation and Opposition' and Albert O. Hirschman's 'A Bias for Hope: Essays on Development and Latin America' held that successful democratic change should be managed by moderate sections of both the old regime and the opposition (Dahl 1971: 33f.; Hirschman 1972: 37).

Those intellectual predecessors only entered the mainstream of comparative politics in the 1980s when authoritarian regimes in Southern Europe and Latin America began to break down. 'Transitions from Authoritarian Rule' (O'Donnell, Schmitter and Whitehead 1986) supported the earlier claims with in-depth case studies of regime change. Instead of a focus on immutable economic and cultural conditions, the new scholarship emphasized the study of 'possibilism' (Hirschman) and an empirical concern for the role of elite factions in negotiating the so-called 'pacts' of democratic transition (Collier and Norden 1992). Uncertainty, elite actors' concern with future reputation, 'passions'(O'Donnell and Schmitter 1986: 25), or the art of 'crafting democracies' (Di Palma 1990) replaced the prior probabilistic determinism generated through quantitative data processing.

Within the agency-centered school of regime change, several distinct approaches emerged (for overviews see Bos 1994; Desfor Edles 1995). Whereas O'Donnell/Schmitter argued that 'normal science methodology' was not applicable in situations, 'where [...] parameters of political action are in flux' (O'Donnell and Schmitter 1986: 4), Przeworski endeavored to show precisely that this was still a social science project within the grasp of conventional hypothesis testing utilizing a rational choice perspective. Przeworski rejected the more intuitive approach of O'Donnell/Schmitter and others to regime change. 'Yet while this approach focused on strategic analysis, it shied away from adopting a formalistic, ahistorical approach inherent in the abstract theory of games' (Przeworski 1991: 97). In contrast, Przeworski conceptualized transitions as a series of games among changing (elite) actor groups, whose behavior is directed at maximizing their respective utilities.

Przeworski claimed that potential liberalizers (often mistakenly) assume that the controlled inclusion of some sections of the opposition would strengthen their own position within the ruling elites. This leads to a mutually reinforcing process of popular mobilization 'from below' and partial interest in liberalization generated 'from above.' Przeworski explicitly rejects the functionalist idea that authoritarian regimes break down as a result of a legitimacy crisis. 'What matters for the stability of any regime is not the legitimacy of this particular system of domination but the presence or absence of preferable alternatives' (see Przeworski 1986: 52). Individual discontent will remain meaningless as long as avenues for collective action are missing. If such projects of counter-hegemony are available and credible, the perceptions, strategies, and actions of relevant actors determine the process and the outcome of change. These strategies are dictated by cost–benefit calculations of the collective actors 'opposition' and 'regime elites.' If the expected results for the opposition (more freedoms, material well-being, and political participation) are higher than the risks (threats to life, imprisonment, etc.) then the opposition will continue to press for change.

In turn, the regime elite is likely to split into hard- and soft-liners over the question of liberalization. Successful transition is most likely when soft-liners continue to ally themselves with the opposition and become reformers in this process. With growing societal mobilization, the incentives increase for potential liberalizers to separate themselves from the rest of the ruling elite and resist further repression. In turn, the threshold for individual participation in societal mobilization lowers with the growing visibility of splits within the regime (Collier and Norden 1992: 234; Przeworski 1992: 108). As challenges to leaders become more pronounced, uncertainty increases and a moderating spiral produces ideas about viable alternatives to authoritarian rule. 'This is why they (authoritarian leaders, HPS) are so afraid of words, even if these words convey what everyone knows anyway, for it is the fact of uttering them, not their content, that has the mobilizing potential' (Przeworski 1992: 107).

This uncertainty creates incentives for all parties to choose democracy as a common institutional framework. Democracy is the only governing system which establishes minimal protection against arbitrary rule and guarantees for all parties involved the chance of (re-)gaining power in the future. Democracy is attractive for outgoing authoritarians because it allows them to compete for political power in the future. The opposition does not primarily gain, but abstract institutions such as the parliament and the judiciary do. 'Political forces comply with present defeats because they believe that the institutional framework that organizes the democratic competition will permit them to advance their interests in the future' (Przeworski 1991: 19). Hence, it is not the substantive but the procedural and representative side of democracy, highlighted by Robert Dahl, that makes democracy a likely choice in situations of fundamental political struggle. In this intriguing scenario, democracy emerges in the absence of any positive material or cultural developments and reflects merely the interest maximization strategies of powerful actors. From this rationalist perspective, democratic transition is not an end in itself but a means to a seemingly universal strife for maintaining and maximizing one's economic or power position vis-à-vis other societal groups.

The move toward an agency-centered view is limited neither to the initiation of regime change nor to the outcome of democratization. After initial steps toward more democratic governance, elites are repeatedly faced with choices to restrict or expand participation and contestation. Even when a new and democratically elected government takes power, it is faced with such choices and the logic of maximizing their interests in the face of uncertainty. Moreover, recent scholarship has also emphasized the central role of elites in the breakdown of democracy

(Bermeo 2003; Bunce 2000). While understanding regime change requires paying attention to the choices of elites and leaders, it also points beyond the domestic to the international realm.

Limits of an elite perspective

An agency-centered perspective puts emphasis on the choices of leaders and elites. The emergence of democracy is explained on a 'shoestring,' since it does not require any normative commitments and altruistic behavior. Elites simply maximize their interests under uncertainty, and democratization happens to be the most compatible course of action. Only democratic institutions guarantee all parties that they do not permanently lose power to their enemies. This explanation of democratization demands little and is appealing because it can account for changes in behavior of authoritarian leaders without having to assume their sudden conversion to democratic values.

There are two main challenges to this view. First, the perspective creates insufficient room for the role of normative considerations often promoted by external actors and institutions representing democratic values. Second, the agency-level explanation of democratization neglects to account for the source of initial uncertainty. Why should we assume that decision-makers have confidence in the power of newly created and untested democratic institutions? If authoritarian leaders are in control, why would they choose democratic change as their first preference? What precisely is the source of uncertainty, which moves them to choose this and not another course of action?

While an agency-level view of democratization represents an important shift away from faceless structuralist explanations, it remains biased toward a domestic account and neglects two important dimensions of social interactions during processes of regime change. First, democratization is shaped by international and transnational forces outside of the domestic realm. These actors actively intervene in transition processes and influence the outcome by mobilizing material and normative resources. Second, democratization cannot be reduced to a mere exchange of strategic information among elite groups, but requires parties to make normative choices and expose themselves to shifts in their self-identification and changes of fundamental preferences.[2] The structure in which elites are embedded can be reduced neither to a rational pay-off matrix, nor to the underlying socioeconomic conditions. Instead, the structural context contains not only non-material factors, such as human rights and other norms established in international society, but also social relations with other groups and, in particular, connections between elites and their followers (Haggard and Kaufman 1995). Sustained popular protests are frequently a condition for the initiation of regime change (Bratton and van de Walle 1997), and elites' relations with the general public influence the power they yield during negotiated transitions.

A more embedded view of elites and their interactions shifts attention away from the preferences of agents to a fuller understanding of the interactions among them. While conventional views portray actors as mere 'incumbents of social positions or systemic imperatives' (Macy and Flache 1995: 74), a relational perspective gives agents more autonomy in seeking opportunities and rejecting constraints. The social position of an actor does not in itself determine the choice of preferences and actions taken to further one's interests (Emirbayer and Goodwin 1994: 1416). Preferences form as a result of interactions with other actors and the social environment, which provides actors with models of self-definition and appropriate behavior. In this essay, the focus of discussion is mainly on the social relations across borders, rather than the domestic relations among different groups.

The case of democratization is an example for the growing significance of transnational linkages across state borders. Transnational mobilization diffuses norms of democratic governance across the globe and affects domestic political change. Those interventions become part of a domestic struggle among elites and the populace seeking to influence the direction of political regime change. Global norms of democracy do not simply obliterate domestic practices, but create unique patterns of political development in concert with domestic conditions. Political regime change is a domestic process exposed to international and transnational interventions. These continuous and often principled interventions are not just 'shifting winds of change that blow in intermittently from abroad' (Bratton and van de Walle 1997: 32), but sustained efforts of shaping regime change by strengthening principles of democratic governance.

Conclusion

Understanding the effects of outside influences on domestic change is a joint task for comparative and IR scholars. The modernization perspective is particularly helpful in understanding the long-term viability of democracy. Research over the past decades confirms that economic development is positively related with democratic governance. A complementary agency perspective of regime change offers opportunities to trace the process of change and to inquire into the motives of individual and collective actors. It also opens the analysis to the integration of influences generated on the transnational and international levels. The mobilization of transnational activists explains why and how authoritarian leaders face political uncertainty and pressures to democratize. The focus on 'pacted transitions' elaborates the choices of elites once the first step is taken, but it does not explain where this initial uncertainty comes from. International institutions and transnational actors shape a social environment for domestic actors as well as the distribution of opportunities and constraints for mobilization and activism.

The integration of transnational mobilization into the analysis of democratization is not a one-way street. Transnational scholarship has yet to fully embrace the existing comparative literature on domestic regime change in order to develop more nuanced versions of how external mobilization interacts with domestic forces. The transnational literature contributes to our understanding of regime change and diverging paths of political transition by emphasizing the external institutional and social context of decision-makers. Elites negotiating democratic change are embedded not only in a domestic context, but also in a transnational context of international institutions, allies, and global norms.

3
From Repression to Democratic Reforms in Kenya and Uganda

This chapter is divided into two main sections. The first section of this chapter provides a description of the political developments in Kenya and Uganda prior to the onset of transnational mobilization against authoritarian rule. Differences in the initiation of regime change are the result of variation of authoritarian rule emerging after political independence. Transnational mobilization against authoritarian rule targeted both countries with similar strength, but produced a fundamental regime change in Uganda in 1986 and more limited political reforms in Kenya in 1991. Transnational mobilization and domestic conditions create distinct paths of political change.

The second section summarizes the trajectories of regime change in Kenya and Uganda since the emergence of transnational mobilization for human rights and democracy in the 1980s. It presents a comparative evaluation of constitutional safeguards for basic rights and electoral democracy as they evolved in Kenya and Uganda during the main periods of transnational activism since the mid-1980s. The subsequent chapters will then illuminate how a combination of transnational activism and domestic conditions produced those paths of regime change.

Variations of authoritarian rule

Patrimonial political systems are ruled by an individual who treats the state as his or her personal possession. Personal relationships expressed in patronage, clientelism, and corruption rather than rational efficiency are the main features of neopatrimonial rule. Neopatrimonialism 'is internalized in the formal institutions [...] and provides essential operating codes for politics that are valued, recurring, and reproduced over time' (Bratton and van de Walle 1997: 63). Shortly after political independence, the paternalism present in many African societies combined with a perceived necessity to consolidate the newly independent entities in a process of 'nation-building' formed the basis for strengthening the executive over other formally independent democratic institutions such as the judiciary or the parliament. The distribution of state resources became a major tool in establishing the clientelist networks which underlay or substituted formal bureaucracies.

Neopatrimonialism integrates elites into the political system by the strategic allocation of resources from the top–down. This material co-optation was frequently supplemented by overt repression of political dissent. The specific combination of both mechanisms reveals significant differences between political developments in Kenya and Uganda. While the Kenyan political system remained primarily integrated by means of corruption combined with limited repression against political dissidents, Ugandan society disintegrated during the 1970s and first half of the 1980s. In Uganda, neopatrimonialism as a form of societal integration was largely destroyed by a brutal dictatorship and civil war, and the logic of patronage was replaced by a logic of violence.

At independence

Kenya

Political independence in Kenya followed a decade of widespread rebellion and repression by British authorities. The indigenous resistance against colonial rule turned violent after the end of World War II as a result of population pressures and increasing tensions between white settlers and mainly Kikuyu squatters living in the agrarian heartland of the Rift Valley (Anderson 2005; Throup 1987). In 1947, Jomo Kenyatta returned from Great Britain and became the leader of the Kenya African Union (KAU), a nationalist movement defending the rights of the disenfranchised African population. From 1952 to 1956, the *Mau Mau* rebellion not only challenged colonial rule by violent means, but also divided the Kikuyu community and threatened to kill moderate leaders such as Kenyatta.

In October 1952, the British authorities declared a state of emergency as a reaction to the growing rebellion (Edgerton 1989). Subsequently, many of the repressive laws surviving political independence were enacted and the British authorities committed extensive gross human rights violations primarily against the Kikuyu population (Elkins 2005). Although the British authorities were successful in brutally repressing *Mau Mau* by 1957, the scandals around the detention camps combined with the Suez crisis of 1956, and international pressures for decolonization brought a quick end to British rule in East Africa (Darwin 1988). In 1957, the first African members of the legislative council were elected and about 60 percent of the African population was able to participate in the electoral exercise. Subsequently, the colonial administration dismantled the detention camps and revoked the state of emergency in January 1960. It followed a constitutional conference in London, which ended with the legalization of political parties and the recognition of universal franchise. Upon returning to Kenya, the nationalist leaders formed the KANU, led by Tom Mboya and Oginga Odinga.

In the wake of political independence, KANU was supported by the larger ethnicities led by the Kikuyu and Luo. Kenyatta was released from prison in August 1961 and joined KANU after assurances that it would not be dominated by former *Mau Mau* rebels and remain a conservative national movement (Anderson 2005: 334). The competing Kenya African Democratic Union (KADU), led by Daniel arap Moi and Ronald Ngala, united smaller ethnicities such as the Maasai and the Kalenjin, which feared the domination of larger groups and sought to regain control over their homelands frequently occupied by members of larger ethnic groups (Adar 1999).[1] The white settlers staying in Kenya lent their support to KADU, but found themselves largely abandoned by their home government. KANU won the national elections of May 1963 which brought Kenyatta to the presidency. Kenya attained internal sovereignty in June and official independence on 12 December 1963. Final constitutional negotiations led to the establishment of distinct federal features such as a second chamber (Senate) and extensive local autonomy (*majimbo*).

Uganda

British colonial rule integrated several kingdoms and tribal communities in a protectorate, which would later become independent Uganda. Leaders of the kingdom of Buganda in the southern part of the territory played a dominant role during the colonial period, and their desires for independence created increasing tensions with colonial authorities. In the 1950s, Buganda separatism intensified as the new British colonial governor Andrew Cohen made efforts to democratize the kingdom and the protectorate at large. Cohen sought to strengthen the *lukiiko*, the Buganda parliament, against the ruling *kabaka*. In 1953, the Buganda leadership demanded a timetable for Buganda's independence and a transfer of its affairs from the Colonial to the Foreign Office (Ofcansky 1996: 35). After negotiations failed to resolve the issue, the colonial authorities deported *kabaka* Mutesa II to England. Further negotiations led to the creation of a constitutional monarchy in Buganda, while Mutesa II returned triumphantly to his kingdom in 1955 (Tumusiime 1992: 25). Buganda emerged with a strengthened domestic and international position and served as a major source for local identity in the ongoing struggle for independence.

Encouraged by the British authorities, a number of non-Bugandan intellectuals challenged Buganda separatism and began to embrace an alternative vision of a united and independent Uganda (Low 1962). The emerging party system split along religious and ethnic lines as well as the basic North–South division (Tumusiime 1992: 26). Whereas the Democratic Party (DP), established in 1956, represented predominantly Catholic and conservative Baganda, the Uganda People's Congress (UPC) created in 1960 a reservoir for mainly Protestant voters as well as an emerging progressive intellectual elite (Ward 1995).

Uganda People's Congress and Democratic Party contested the 1961 elections to the Legislative Council, which were held by British authorities as a prelude to political independence. The Buganda *lukiiko* had called for a boycott and unilaterally declared independence on 31 December 1960. The DP emerged as the winner with 43 seats (about half came from Buganda), followed by the UPC with 35, and two smaller parties with a total of three seats. Benedicto Kiwanuka, the DP leader, was subsequently named head of the Legislative Council. In September 1961, a Constitution Conference in London negotiated the final steps of political independence. During the deliberations, Buganda's delegates continued to demand an autonomous federal status for their kingdom (Ssekandi and Gitta 1994: 195).

On 1 March 1962, the Legislative Council was transformed into a unicameral National Assembly, Kiwanuka became Prime Minister, and Uganda attained internal independence. While the DP and the colonial authorities favored continued direct elections to the new National Assembly, the Buganda elites insisted on a preservation of autonomy and only indirect elections of Buganda's representatives to the national parliament. This disagreement became the basis for a strategic alliance between the traditional Buganda elite and the nationalist UPC. The Buganda elite created the *Kabaka Yekka* (King Alone, KY) party and won 65 out of 68 seats in the February 1962 *lukiiko* elections. Hence, KY was able to capture all 21 Buganda seats, which had previously been filled by DP representatives. Outside of Buganda, UPC won 37 and DP 24 seats. UPC and KY agreed on forming a coalition government and the UPC leader Milton Obote, a Langi from Northern Uganda, became the first post-independence Prime Minister. The *kabaka* was named non-executive President of the country as well as Commander-in-Chief of the Uganda Armed Forces. The political system was semi-federal and united eleven districts and four kingdoms. Buganda retained a special status, collected its own taxes, passed separate laws, and maintained local courts.

After political independence

Human rights conditions deteriorated in Kenya and Uganda after independence as a result of intensified domestic competition over the control of state power. Democratic and federal conflict-mediating mechanisms which had been put into place at the eve of independence failed to take sufficient root in the domestic arena and gave way to centralization and executive preponderance in the name of nation-building. In both cases, deteriorating human rights conditions were preceded by a process of excluding formerly politically as well as economically dominant sections of society from national politics. In Uganda, the main victims were the Baganda, while in Kenya a similar fate was experienced by the Kikuyu after 1982. As a result of intensified domestic conflict, the executive branch of government in both countries dominated other democratic institutions and increasingly defied limits set by the existing constitutional framework and the rule of law.

Kenya, 1963–1982: Establishing neopatrimonial rule

The KADU dissolved shortly after losing the first post-independence elections in 1964 and its leadership, including Daniel arap Moi, joined KANU in return for public or parastatal positions. In 1967, Moi was appointed to the post of the Vice President. During the next two years federalist provisions (*majimbo*) and other safeguards against executive dominance in the independence constitution were abolished. Executive control over other governmental and societal actors slowly increased, although limited political competition within KANU was possible. Until the early 1980s the ruling party was weak and mainly served as a tool to organize individual electoral competition within a one-party system. Consequently, Joel Barkan generally qualified the Kenyan political system during the Kenyatta years as 'accountable authoritarianism' (Barkan 1993: 87). However, challenges to the all-dominant position of Kenyatta from both within and outside of KANU were repressed with violent means.

In 1966, the original Kikuyu–Luo coalition began to disintegrate when Vice President Oginga Odinga left KANU with his fellow Luo, Tom Mboya. Odinga and Mboya established the Kenya People's Union

(KPU) and distanced themselves from Kenyatta's Western-leaning economic and social policies. Kenyatta's tolerance of political dissent on the national level ended abruptly in 1969 when KPU was banned. Tom Mboya was murdered under mysterious circumstances the same year, while Odinga intensified his leftist policies from his constituency in Central Nyanza.

In the early 1970s *de facto* single-party rule and increasing powers in the President's office marked the Kenyan political system. Kenyatta reacted to decreasing support from the original KANU independence alliance with a strategy of elite rotation which also allowed leaders from smaller ethnicities to benefit from the system of personal favoritism. At the third general elections in October 1974 close to 90 out of the 158 parliamentary incumbents were defeated. Many prominent former KPU members succeeded now on KANU tickets. However, political reforms were inhibited by Kenyatta's growing inability to rule the country. In 1975, an outspoken critic of corruption and the most popular political leader after Kenyatta, Josiah M. Kariuki, was found murdered. Following public pressure, the government agreed to an official investigation of the murder but no one was ultimately charged for the crime.

During the last years of Kenyatta's rule, his cronies opened a debate about his possible successor and sought to delete from the constitution the automatic succession of the Vice President in case of the President's death (Karimi and Ochieng 1980). The succession question led to deep divisions within the dominant Kikuyu elite. Constitutional efforts by one section to prevent the Kalenjin Moi from taking over the presidency were thwarted by competing elites within their own community, including the prominent leaders Charles Njonjo and Mwai Kibaki (see Widner 1992b: 110–118). In order to silence any further discussion on the issue, Njonjo declared in front of the parliament that 'it is a treasonable offence punishable by mandatory death sentence for anyone to encompass or even mention the possible death of the head of state' (wa Wamwere 1992: 24).

The stalemate was finally resolved when Kenyatta died at the age of 82 on 22 August 1978. Vice President Daniel arap Moi became his successor for the three-month period specified in the constitution. He immediately rewarded his Kikuyu supporters and appointed Charles Njonjo as Attorney General, and Mwai Kibaki as Vice President. Moi also released all political prisoners and pledged to address issues of corruption. At the same time, Moi engaged in a more open pro-Western foreign policy by allowing the United States to establish military facilities in the strategically significant coastal region of Mombasa. Moi skillfully consolidated his position by wooing both domestic and international support crucial for his political survival. At home, he primarily relied on Charles Njonjo, who he appointed as Minister of Home and Constitutional Affairs.

Below the surface of liberalization, however, Moi began consolidating his power position by slowly removing potential threats to his presidency. While he claimed to continue in the footsteps of Kenyatta (*'Nyayo'*) he promoted members of his own Kalenjin tribe or other smaller ethnicities as more reliable allies into public offices. Potential critics of the new regime were offered a choice of either accepting their inclusion under Moi's terms or being repressed. The Luo Oginga Odinga and other former KPU politicians were barred from running in the 1979 general elections unless they joined KANU. The efforts to integrate Odinga into the system of patronage ended in April 1980 when it became clear that he was unwilling to end his outspoken criticism of US military presence without parliamentary consent (ACR, Vol. XIV, B 187).[2]

In July 1980, all societal organizations promoting only the interests of one ethnicity were banned. This measure was mainly directed against the Kikuyu-dominated Gikuyu Embu Meru Association (GEMA), which refused to subject itself to the control of the Moi government. Prior to the decision, the Minister for Information and Broadcasting, Peter Oloo-Aringo had accused GEMA of having set itself up as an alternative government. The organization was also linked to efforts to prevent Moi from succeeding Kenyatta after his death. During the following two years, Moi's position remained fragile as Odinga was expelled from KANU on 20 May 1982 and wrangles between the Vice President Mwai Kibaki and Charles Njonjo about who was 'more *Nyayo*' (ACR, Vol. XIV, B 191) threatened their unequivocal support for Moi.

On 9 June 1982, parliament turned Kenya into a *de jure* one-party state after less than an hour of debate and amid earlier rumors that Odinga was about to announce the creation of a new opposition party. Student unrest at Nairobi University and other colleges had increased steadily during the year, and security forces made sweeping arrests of student leaders and lecturers (ACR, Vol. XV, B 177). After three years of consolidating his control over national affairs, Moi reintroduced the practice of detention without trial. On 20 July, the editor-in-chief of the weekly *The Standard*, George Githii, published an editorial titled 'Detention without Trial' and was promptly removed from his position. Consequently, the International Press Institute (IPI) declared that Kenya 'is now becoming one of the worst offenders against free speech' (cited in ACR, Vol. XV, B 179).

On 1 August 1982, Kenyan Air Force officers staged a coup attempt and for several hours controlled vital parts of Nairobi, the airport and the radio station. As the news of the revolt spread, hundreds of students filled Nairobi streets in celebration. Other parts of the Kenyan army loyal to Moi ended the coup violently. While student organizations claimed a much higher death toll, the government put the official number at 159. Moi disbanded the Air Force, closed the universities, and ordered the arrest of several thousand army officers and civilians suspected of supporting the coup. The President and his aides specifically targeted the Luo community by dropping the information minister Oloo-Aringo from the Cabinet and putting its leader Odinga under house arrest. The independence of the parliament was also significantly curtailed (Widner 1992b: 146).

As the evidence of growing repression mounted, prominent exiles such as the writer Ngugi wa Thiong'o sought to draw attention to the situation at home by demonstrating outside of Kenyan embassies in Europe and the United States. The government denounced the activities in an official statement: 'The attempt to portray the government of Kenya as undemocratic and blood-thirsty will no doubt fail. Those who have nothing to say against the way the Government handled the disturbances and the subsequent treatment of those found to have been involved should face the truth and desist from backing the few cowardly, unpatriotic elements now bent on discrediting their motherland' (cited in ACR, Vol. XV, B 183). The Nairobi offices of the *Associated Press* were briefly closed by Special Branch officers, and the representative for the Ford Foundation was harassed for producing a report on the coup. Domestically, ongoing conflicts between the government and a still largely independent press led KANU to announce on 5 April 1983 the publication of its own newspaper. In the first edition of the *Kenya Times*, Moi promised that the paper would not be 'a mouthpiece or propaganda machine for KANU and the government, but will be guided by press freedom, which has been recognized in the Kenya system' (cited in ACR, Vol. XV, B 194).

Moi also used the coup attempt to depose of the Kikuyu faction, which had been instrumental for his ascendancy to the presidency. On 9 May 1983, during a speech in Kisii, Moi ominously referred to an alleged *Msaliti*[3] within the government who was supported by an unspecified foreign power. One week later he announced general elections for September, one year earlier than constitutionally required. Within days backbenchers in parliament, led by Martin Shikuku and Elijah Mwangale, openly accused Njonjo of cooperating with the South

African apartheid regime in order to take over the presidency in Kenya. Njonjo denied the unsubstantiated allegations, but was removed from the Cabinet until an official inquiry was complete.

In September 1983, an unopposed Moi and KANU were returned by voters to the presidency and the parliament. Moi further tightened his control over parliament by appointing more than 40 percent of its members to his expanded cabinet. All members of the new government were forced to sign a letter declaring that they would not criticize government policy in public.[4] The formerly powerful Njonjo announced his withdrawal from public life. As Moi completed the consolidation of his power, he announced the release of several dissidents arrested after the 1982 coup, including Willy Mutunga, Vincent Otieno, Koigi wa Wamwere, and Edward Oyugi. Moi was careful to declare that dissidents were not released because of demands from AI but because they had qualified by promisings to change their political viewpoints (cited in ACR, Vol. XVI, B 168).

By 1984/85, the Moi regime had almost total control over domestic society. Moi had skillfully used divisions within the dominant Kikuyu elites to consolidate his power and exploited the failed coup attempt to further repress his critics. Political dissent was largely driven underground and found refuge in church organizations or the academic environment. Nairobi University was repeatedly closed by the government, which suspected students and lecturers to be a major recruiting source for an alleged underground conspiracy referred to as *MwaKenya*. International human rights organizations began in the mid-1980s to publish increasingly alarming reports about deteriorating human rights conditions in Kenya. The mounting repression reported by domestic dissidents caught the attention of the Western public and led to a period of transnational mobilization against an increasingly entrenched authoritarian regime.

Uganda, 1962–1974: The destruction of societal integration

At independence, an alliance of Buganda monarchists (KY) and northern nationalists (UPC) effectively shut out the DP as the strongest single political power representing the Catholic and more Western-oriented population in the South. The Baganda elite feared the modernizing DP as a competitor for the control of Buganda, while the UPC contested DP over national power. Beyond these short-term interests, the coalition had no common agenda. Worse, their basic interests (separatism vs national control) were incompatible. The *kabaka* Mutesa II had little respect for Obote[5] and was sure that the main profiteer of the alliance was Buganda. Initial signs of a deteriorating relationship became apparent when UPC began to establish political branches in Buganda. By November 1964, the tensions between KY and UPC intensified, when defections by KY and DP representatives gave the UPC an absolute majority in parliament.

Within less than a year, UPC and Baganda leadership were accusing each other of plotting assassinations and coups. On 4 February 1966, a Buganda-friendly Member of Parliament (MP) introduced a motion in parliament that called for the suspension of second-in-command of the army Idi Amin Dada for alleged gold smuggling and an investigation of Obote's role in the affair. Obote countered the attack with a coup from above; on 24 February he suspended the constitution and abolished the Office of the President and Vice President. A new interim constitution made Obote Executive President and removed all federal privileges of Buganda. Subsequently, the Baganda representatives demanded the withdrawal of the central government from Buganda and civil unrest broke out in the Buganda region. Obote ordered the Ugandan Army to take control of the *kabaka's* residence, sending Mutesa II into exile (Ofcansky 1996: 40) for the second time. 'The victory over Mutesa II institutionalized violence as the main instrument of political control' (Kasozi 1994: 88). In September 1967, Obote abolished all kingdoms.

Obote banned all political parties, except for the UPC, after another attempt to assassinate him in October 1969 (Nsibambi 1994). Military expenditure rapidly grew from 4.4 percent of the budget in 1964 to 12.3 percent in 1967. New paramilitary organizations such as the Special Force and the General Service Unit (GSU) as an internal secret service increasingly used violence against the opposition, in particular in their attempts to remove the Buganda elite as a political force from national politics. Outside of the army, Obote relied on the support of the 70,000 members of the Asian community originally brought in by the British colonial authorities. Those communities primarily located in the capital region of Kampala competed with Baganda elites in the industrial and trade sector as well as government services. While Obote's resort to violence and the army strengthened his position in the short term, this strategy ultimately backfired and led to his political demise (Khadiagala 1995: 36).

With conservative Buganda effectively shut out of national politics, UPC embarked on a program called 'move to the left' by announcing in May 1970 the nationalization of major firms and a ban on strikes. The Ugandan Army had gained control of domestic politics and its increasingly independent commander Idi Amin openly recruited a private army from his home region, the West Nile. In January 1971, Obote gave Amin an ultimatum to disband any private units until his return from a Commonwealth Summit in Singapore.

On 25 January 1971, Amin used his forces to depose Obote and take control of the government. Apart from the military, Amin relied on support from the previously disenfranchised Baganda as well as the benign neglect or thinly veiled support by Western governments. Donor governments welcomed the coup primarily because it promised an end to Obote's increasingly socialist-leaning economic policies (Clapham 1996: 188). Obote had also openly attacked the British government for selling arms to South Africa, and 'it was a certainty that Obote would be a sharp thorn in the flesh of Britain. While Obote was at the conference, the coup took place, and there have been many suggestions that it took place with the connivance not only of Israel but of Britain also' (Furley 1989: 276). Both Britain and Israel immediately recognized the new regime. Although colonial attitudes of superiority toward the African continent were no longer 'politically correct' they remained deep-seated and informed the British public's perception of Uganda in 1971/72.[6] 'Amin's obvious lack of education, his love of showmanship, his self-awarded decorations and his claim to be the "conqueror of the British Empire" caused the British public to see him in amiable light as a clown and figure of fun: hence the long-running series about him in *Punch* and the many cartoons in British newspapers' (Furley 1989: 277).

Domestically, the coup was initially greeted by many Ugandans in spontaneous street demonstrations. The Baganda hoped for a restoration of their kingdom and its autonomy. Indeed, Amin initially freed about 100 political prisoners, most of them Baganda adopted by AI, and arranged for the return of the body of the late *kabaka* Mutesa II to Uganda. However, a systematic campaign of killing former supporters and tribal kinsmen of Obote (Acholi and Langi) began as early as July 1971 while Amin himself was soliciting arms and cash in London (Kyemba 1977: 46; Seftel 1994: 105–135). Within months after Amin took power, gross violations of human rights spread across Uganda (Kasozi 1994: 4). Even minimal formal protections of human rights disappeared, as Idi Amin assumed dictatorial powers and ruled by decree. The whole country was brought under the jurisdiction of military tribunals, while the National Assembly was dissolved. Spending on 'state security' skyrocketed with the creation of new agencies such as the infamous State Research Bureau which had 3,000 employees alone. Alarming reports of repression and violence quickly dampened the international and domestic support for Amin and his regime. As Amin lost support at home and abroad, he reacted with increasing repression on the domestic level and sought new allies in the Arab and the Communist world.

In early 1972, Israeli military advisers in Uganda were replaced by instructors from the German Democratic Republic (GDR) and the Palestine Liberation Organization (PLO). In August 1972, Amin ordered the expulsion of the entire Asian community and gave their assets to his cronies (Amor 2003). Many expelled members of the Asian community took refuge in Great Britain, where the government temporarily severed diplomatic relations and imposed a trade embargo. Amin retaliated by seizing British assets in Uganda and recalling the High Commissioner in London. In September 1972, pro-Obote guerrillas under the command of Yoweri Museveni sought to take advantage of the situation and launched an attack from neighboring Tanzania. The invasion failed in large part due to the military support Amin had received from Arab leaders such as Muammar el Qadhafi.

By 1974 press reports about massacres and public executions in Uganda began to dominate the Western press. Prominent victims of the targeted and indiscriminate killings were the Chief Justice and former DP leader Benedicto Kiwanuka and the Vice Chancellor of Makerere University Frank Kalimozo. By 1975, virtually all foreign aid came from either the Soviet Union (about $50 million) or Arab countries, which rewarded Amin for his break with Israel. In June 1976, PLO terrorists hijacked an Air France plane and redirected it to Entebbe, where Amin welcomed the terrorists. An Israeli commando eventually freed all but three hostages, killing all terrorists and many Ugandan soldiers.

It would take another three years and an open military provocation against Tanzania to bring an end to one of the worst dictatorships in Africa. International human rights organizations alerted the Western public since 1974/75 to the widespread atrocities committed in Uganda and David Martin's 'General Amin' detailed already in 1974 the deadly rule of Amin (Martin 1974). Despite this transnational mobilization, there was no concerted international effort to remove Amin from power.

Conclusions

Democratic institutions established at the eve of political independence did not survive in Kenya and Uganda. Instead, they gave way to auto-cratic rule by a dominating executive branch and a powerful president. Differences in the institutional strength of main opposition groups and early failure of conflict-mediating mechanisms in Uganda account for the variation in the use of violence to settle domestic conflicts. While the Buganda kingdom as the main opposition within Uganda was eliminated by force, the main opposition force in Kenya was peacefully co-opted by the emerging patronage system under Jomo Kenyatta.

In Uganda, all domestic actors vying for national power at independence were included in a fragile arrangement of formally democratic institutions. In contrast, the more violent anti-colonial struggle in Kenya decidedly tipped the balance for Kenyatta and KANU. This weakness of the opposition in Kenya enabled the establishment of a prevalent mode of patronage, whereas the strength of the Baganda and Obote's reaction to their resistance set Uganda on the path to violence. In Kenya, state violence slowly increased under Kenyatta, but was generally directed at prominent individual members of the opposition. When Daniel arap Moi led parts of the original KADU coalition of smaller ethnicities to power, the levels of repression increased and eventually caught the attention of transnational human rights activists.

Transnational mobilization took much longer to gather support for the Ugandan situation than it took to have an effect in Kenya. Why did transnational activism mobilize less effectively around the atrocities committed in Uganda, while it emerged rather quickly and effectively in the Kenyan case with much more limited human rights violations? There are primarily two issues responsible for the difference. First, the extent of violent repression in Uganda and its comparatively greater isolation from the outside world undermined the ability of transnational networks to gather and distribute information about atrocities. Uganda's capital Kampala was much less visible compared to Nairobi, which not only hosted various UN bodies but also served as the regional base of many foreign journalists. Second, the international human rights movement led by AI was much more powerful in the 1980s during the Kenya campaign than 10 years earlier. Campaigns against the Amin dictatorship created the groundwork for later campaigns of transnational mobilization. Amnesty International was awarded the Nobel Prize for Peace in 1977, only a few months before the end of Amin's rule.

In the following second section of this chapter, I will present a more detailed account of regime change for the period from the onset of transnational mobilization until today. Kenya and Uganda have taken different paths of political development after political independence. As authoritarian rule was increasingly challenged by transnational human rights mobilization, the two countries also embarked on different patterns of regime change and democratic reforms. While the Kenyan government implemented in the early 1990s multiparty electoral reforms, Ugandan leaders preferred a constitutionalist path and refused to introduce multiparty politics until 2005.

Regime change in Kenya and Uganda

Shortly after political independence, Kenya developed into a relatively stable one-party state with strong clientelist networks, while Ugandan politics degenerated into military dictatorship and civil war. After regime change, the Ugandan process was characterized by an emphasis on the extension of participation and constitutional reforms. In contrast, Kenya expanded party competition on the national level. In the first part of this section, I will compare indicators of *participation* by reviewing human rights conditions and constitutional safeguards in Kenya and Uganda since 1986. In the second part, the section will shift attention to the *competition* expressed in the evolution of electoral democracy in both countries.

Constitutional safeguards and human rights record

Establishing constitutional safeguards is not the same as effectively protecting human rights. Laws to protect human rights are significant indicators for a government's willingness to honor international norms, but only independent human rights reports make it possible to match the rhetoric with the actual practice (Risse and Sikkink 1999). To illustrate the general development of human rights, the focus here is on torture, detention without trial, and extra-judicial killings. The state of basic rights, in particular during election periods, offers an important indicator for the progress and sustainability of democratization. The information presented here is based on human rights reports published by domestic groups in both countries, reports by AI and Human Rights Watch (HRW), and the annual human rights reports published by the US State Department.

Human rights conditions

The general human rights record in Uganda since 1986 shows strong improvements right after the end of the civil war and up until the early 1990s. During the 1990s, human rights conditions deteriorated as a result of the entrenchment of NRM rule as well as significant violent insurgencies in the northern and western part of the country. Throughout the reporting period there is a persistent gap between the generally improved situation in the south and frequent reports of gross violations committed by rebels and the Ugandan army in the war regions. The US State Department calls the Ugandan human rights record 'poor' during the 1990s. In reports up to 2000, this conclusion was qualified by noting 'improvements in several areas,' but after 2000 the reports have become more critical.

In Kenya, repression levels increased until the introduction of multi-partyism in 1991. Afterwards, certain violations such as torture and disappearances of dissidents decreased, while extra-judicial killings as a result of electoral violence increased. After the second multiparty elections in 1997, repression by the government generally decreased. The end of KANU rule in 2002 brought many former human rights activists to power and led to the formal establishment of stronger protection mechanisms. The effects on the actual human rights situation are positive, but it would be too early to diagnose the sustainability of those improvements.

Freedom House rankings provide a rough approximation for the development of democracy in both countries.[7] Kenya was classified as 'not free' from 1987 to 2002, except for the year of the first multiparty elections in 1992 ('partly free'). The ranking improves dramatically after Moi lost the 2002 elections and Kenya received again a 'partly free' ranking.[8] Uganda was ranked 'partly free' from 1986 until 1991 and as 'not free' from 1991 to 1993. The country returned to 'partly free' in 1994, but the record deteriorates again after 1999.[9]

Uganda

Incidences of torture, extra-judicial killings, and detention without trial dramatically dropped immediately after the end of the civil war in early 1986. The repressive practices survived at a less aggravated level during the rule of the NRM. Ugandan police and army regularly use torture and extended detention in their criminal investigations as well as in the battle against rebel groups in the northern and western part of the country. Ugandans in those areas are also victims of non-state violence. The Lord's Resistance Army (LRA) has killed, maimed, and abducted thousands of civilians in the border region. While the south of Uganda has enjoyed relatively peaceful and much improved human rights conditions since 1986, the north continues to face conditions of civil war and gross abuses from both sides of the conflict.

Right after the NRM came to power, AI maintained that 'the incidences of torture of civilians by soldiers have diminished' (Amnesty International 1987a: 169). In 1988, the Ugandan army reported to AI that it currently held about 4,000 civilians as part of its military operations in the north, most of them in preventive detention (Amnesty International 1992b: 44). AI estimated that from 1987 to 1989 several thousand people were temporarily detained. AI also called on the Ugandan army to investigate persistent patterns of extra-judicial killings in the conduct of military operations (Amnesty International 1991: 15–21). Reports of abuses ebbed with decreasing rebel activities in the early 1990s. When the LRA again stepped up its operations in 1994, the rebels began to systematically target the Acholi civilian population, which had earlier supported the struggle of the rebels against the government. The LRA began its practice of randomly maiming adults, abducting children, and recruiting the latter as sex slaves and soldiers (Amnesty International 1996). With the increasing rebel activities, the Ugandan army again became notorious for gross violations, including the practice of summary detentions euphemistically called 'protected villages.'

While the State Department asserted in 1993 that there was 'no evidence for government-sanctioned torture' or 'government-sanctioned political killings' (U.S. Department of State 1994b), human rights conditions in Uganda were already deteriorating again. The insurgencies negatively affected human rights conditions in the rest of the nation and created conditions of greater insecurity for civilians. The government now specifically targeted political dissent and sought to identify its critics with 'terrorism' and the violence in the north. The most serious case of political arrests occurred in 1993 when more than a dozen politicians from northern Uganda were arrested and charged with treason (Amnesty International 1994). Following the August 1998 bomb attacks on US embassies in Nairobi and Dar es Salaam, dozens of suspects were detained and some of them tortured in the so-called 'safe houses' (*New Vision*, 27 October 1998). Currently in Uganda, the police regularly detain suspects beyond the constitutional limit of 48 hours before a court appearance or release.

During recent years, the State Department report continues to deny the existence of systematic patterns of torture by security forces. In contrast, HRW alleged such practices as recently as in the 2004 report 'State of Pain. Torture in Uganda.' It claims that torture has become more prevalent again since the NRM rule and the party ban has come under increasing political criticism from a strengthening opposition (Human Rights Watch 2004). During the 2001 presidential campaign, several supporters of Museveni's main opponent, Kizza Besigye, were killed by police or supporters of the NRM. Dozens of opposition supporters were detained, harassed and intimidated during the electoral campaign. Besigye and many of his followers fled Uganda in the summer of 2001, at least partially as a result of government harassment. The Ugandan police regularly conducted several operations across the country called 'panda gari' where hundreds of alleged suspects are arbitrarily arrested. For the year 2002, the State Department report acknowledged for the first time in several years 'unconfirmed reports of politically motivated killings by government forces' (U.S. Department of State 2002b). Since the adoption of an anti-terrorism law after 11 September 2001, several individuals were charged and convicted of terrorism. The government regularly uses the 'war against terrorism' in justifying its military campaign in the north as well as the need for limiting political and civil freedoms in the country (International Crisis Group 2004).

Kenya

Reports of systematic and targeted government repression, including torture, detention without trial, and extra-judicial killings, increased for Kenya during the 1980s and slowly abated only in the 1990s. After the re-introduction of multipartyism the pattern of abuses shifted away from open to more subtle forms of repression. As electoral contestation increased, human rights violations were less targeted at individual dissidents but were the result of politically motivated 'ethnic violence' and the general intimidation tactics of KANU politicians threatened by the multiparty era (Aidoo 1993).[10] Hundreds of Kenyans were killed and thousands displaced during those episodes of violence during electoral campaigns (Africa Watch/Human Rights Watch 1993; Young 1996: 61). Despite official denial, these acts of extra-judicial killings and internal displacement were backed by high-ranking KANU members. '*Leurs actions commandos s'effectuent à partir des fermes gouvernementales d'où ils sont transportés par de camions sur les lieux de leurs exactions.*' Moreover, '*les assaillants kalenjin [. . .] sont souvent en réalité des forces paramilitaires déguisées.*' An initial parliamentary investigation into the 1992 clashes named prominent KANU politicians in connection with the violence (Republic of Kenya 1992), but was never accepted by the KANU majority. In 1998, after similar electoral violence during and after the second multiparty elections in December 1997 (Brown 2003; Kenya Human Rights Commission 1997), a new parliamentary commission was created against Moi's resistance and confirmed again the responsibility of KANU operatives for many of the 'ethnic clashes.' The Akiwumi Commission held extensive hearings and accumulated more compelling evidence for the involvement of KANU members in the creation of the violence. The final report was handed over to the government in 1999, suppressed again, and finally released to the public on 18 October 2002. Within days after the release, police stormed several NGO offices searching for evidence cited in the report. NGO representatives were questioned whether they had plans to take legal actions against the government and Moi (U.S. Department of State 2003). The government's own Standing Committee on Human Rights concluded in 2002 that 'incitement has played and continues to play a very significant role in the genesis, escalation, and recurrence of ethnic conflicts' (cited in U.S. Department of State 2004).

Human rights organizations and the U.S. Department of State also documented frequent torture by police forces in the late 1980s[11] and well into the 1990s (Africa Watch/Human Rights Watch 1991: Ch. 17; Kenya Human Rights Commission 1995; U.S. Department of State 1994a). Although torture of dissidents was much less prevalent during the 1990s than in the previous decade, human rights groups alleged that a special torture unit within the police force continued to operate until Moi was ousted in 2002. Moi himself frequently declared in public that torture was not a part of the government's policy (Africa Watch/ Human Rights Watch 1991: 99; Andreassen 1993: 215). But the UN Special Rapporteur on Torture, Nigel S. Rodley, 'advised the Government (on 18 September 1995, HPS) that he had received information indicating that the use of torture by police to obtain confessions was almost systematic' (UN Commission on Human Rights 1996: 77). This information was confirmed again two years later when AI accused the Kenyan government of not taking any measures against the widespread use of torture.[12] Human rights groups suggest that the situation began to improve after the 1997 elections and dramatically changed with the electoral victory of the opposition in 2002. In February 2003, the new government under Mwai Kibaki opened the infamous torture chambers in the basement of the *Nyayo House* as a symbol of his government's intentions to respect basic human rights.

The practice of deliberate killings of prominent critics of the government has also only slowly abated during the 1990s. Many of these violent deaths remain unsolved today. The most prominent victims included the Foreign Minister Robert Ouko in February 1990, Anglican Bishop Alexander Muge in August 1990 (*Nairobi Law Monthly* 1990), a member of the Kenya Human Rights Commission (KHRC) in 1994, and the General Secretary of Release Political Prisoners (RPP), Karimi Nduthu, on 24 March 1996. Many other, less prominent human rights activists have also been killed under mysterious circumstances. Again, there have been no high-profile political murders since the second multiparty elections in 1997.

The practice of detention as a form of political repression also underwent significant changes during the 1990s. The practice of detention without trial was widely used in Kenya, both by Kenyatta and Moi. When transnational human rights groups began in the late 1980s to mobilize against these practices, the Kenyan government shifted its strategy from detention without charges or trial to misusing criminal charges against government opponents (Amnesty International 1995a; Article 19 1995: 13–27). Some prominent opposition members, such as Koigi wa Wamwere, were charged with capital offences and held in prison using questionable evidence. 'From a political perspective, activists charged with capital criminal offences are therefore effectively held under detention *with* trial' (African Rights 1996: 131). After the first multiparty elections in 1992, about half of the opposition members of parliament (36 in 1993, 15 in 1994) were detained and released after various periods of incarceration. The Attorney General, Amos Wako, responsible for most of the charges filed against political dissidents defended his actions in private as responses to pressures from the executive. Most of the charges were quickly dropped and reflected an uneasy balance between increasing limits on harsher forms of repression and the continued efforts of the Moi regime to stay in control of the domestic arena.

A decisive change occurred in late 1997 when the government and the opposition reached agreement on minimal constitutional reforms weeks before the second multiparty elections. As a result, levels of repression decreased markedly. After the elections, the Kenyan parliament became also more assertive in investigating human rights abuses. In 1998, parliament created a new commission to investigate the ethnic violence of 1992 and 1997, which held regular hearings exposing the responsibilities of KANU operatives. In 2000, almost 100 members of parliament released a report titled 'The Politicization and Misuse of the Kenyan Police,' while the government's own Standing Committee on Human Rights asserted the same year that the 'majority of cases have involved torture and brutality meted out to individuals mainly by law enforcement agencies' (cited in U.S. Department of State 2002a). While the government was progressively losing its tools of repression against a more assertive civil society, dissidents remained a target of attacks until the end of Moi's rule. Prominent human rights activists, such as Wangari Maathai and Kivutha Kibwana, were still arrested as late as

2001 and an April 2002 report by the Standing Committee noted the 'widespread use of lethal, excessive, and unnecessary use of force on civilians by police.' The KHRC summarized a decade of its work by documenting over a thousand cases of extra-judicial killings for the 1990s.

After NARC and Mwai Kibaki came to power in December 2002, human rights NGOs demanded the creation of a 'truth commission' to investigate the abuses under the Moi and Kenyatta presidencies. In a 'report card' written in April 2003 on the first 100 days of the new administration, KHRC applauded the appointment of many former civil society leaders to the Cabinet and noticed important improvements in the administration of justice and the cooperation between the government and the NGOs.

Domestic monitoring and complaint procedures

Effective human rights protection requires not only the domestic incorporation of international human rights law as well as independent monitoring by civil society actors, but also the functioning of an independent government agency investigating and adjudicating human rights complaints. Since the mid-1990s, both countries created formally independent domestic human rights bodies with quasi-legal powers. After Museveni and the NRM came to power, Uganda welcomed numerous delegations of AI, while the Kenyan government lifted a ban on visits by transnational human rights representatives in 1992.

Uganda

After 1986, the government took several steps to institutionalize individual complaint procedures, both for past abuses and for current human rights problems. These included the establishment of (1) a Commission of Inquiry into Violations of Human Rights before 1986, (2) the Office of the Inspector General of Government (IGG), (3) a Human Rights Desk in the Ministry of Justice, and (4) the Uganda Human Rights Commission (UHRC) under the new Constitution of 1995. The Commission of Inquiry, led by Justice Arthur Oder, selected exemplary cases of severe human rights abuses and toured the country to obtain testimonies from hundreds of witnesses. For the first time in post-independence history, this gave the Ugandan population the opportunity to openly debate the past gross violations of human rights committed under Idi Amin and Milton Obote (Republic of Uganda 1994). The commission relied heavily on donor funding, and the NRM largely ignored its work once it had scored politically from the creation of the investigative body. The final 700-page report did not address any human rights issues after 1986 and led to only a small number of less significant criminal investigations. Idi Amin and Milton Obote were never charged with any crimes in Uganda or their respective exiles.

In 1987, the NRM government established the Office of the IGG with significant donor help by Scandinavian countries. The IGG was charged with fighting corruption and human rights abuses under the present government. The office received human rights complaints from the public and also served as a gateway for foreign human rights education programs by organizing seminars for local administrators and politicians together with the Raoul Wallenberg Institute (Lund, Sweden). However, the IGG generally shied away from going beyond isolated cases and did not have a clearly defined human rights mandate (Andreassen 1993: 323; Oloka-Onyango 1993) with strong enforcement powers. In 1992, the Deputy Inspector General, Waswa Lule, was removed from his post, when he sought to expand the human rights mandate of his office and became more outspoken against human rights violations committed by government agencies. Under the 1995 constitution, the mandate of the IGG in the human rights area was then transferred to the newly established UHRC.

The Human Rights Desk within the Ministry of Justice was created in 1998. As a government the office was not independent, but still investigated several hundred complaints annually. The creation of the Desk was ordered by Museveni after he was dissatisfied with the Justice Department's handling of human rights inquiries from UN bodies. For domestic purposes, the UHRC became in the late 1990s the main official agency to receive individual human rights complaints. The UHRC began its work with a two-year delay after the adoption of the 1995 constitution and shortly after Margaret Sekaggya was appointed chairperson in November 1996.

The UHRC can access all detention facilities in the country and can order the release of a detained person and the payment of compensation. It makes recommendations to the government about implementing international obligations and has a mandate to raise human rights awareness in the general public. Government funding for the Commission is generally inadequate and supplemented by donor aid. The chairperson and six commissioners are appointed by the president with parliamentary approval for six years and have security of tenure equivalent to a High Court judge. Initially, they were trained at the Wallenberg Institute in Sweden, which had already cooperated with the IGG before the human rights mandate shifted to the UHRC. One of the initial commissioners was Aliro Omara, a former rebel leader fighting against Museveni, who had returned from exile only in 1995. None of the commissioners were appointed in consultation with domestic or international human rights NGOs.

On 18 August 1998, UHRC published a 68-page report covering its first year of operation. During that year, UHRC officials visited prison and military facilities and received a total of 352 complaints, mostly relating to unlawful arrests, detention, and torture.[13] The report detailed many cases of torture and some of the remedial measures taken by UHRC. It criticized the Ugandan People's Defense Forces (UPDF) and the Internal Security Organ (ISO) for detaining civilians, although only the police were allowed to do so. On several occasions during the year, Sekaggya openly criticized the government on human rights issues (*The Monitor*, 25 August 1998). The total number of received human rights complaints increased to a high of 1,543 in 2000 and dropped again to 1,306 in 2001 and to 1,186 in 2002. An average of 50 percent of the cases was resolved within 12 months.

In 2001, HRW called the UHRC in a comparative study of commissions across Africa a 'strong example' of success but also warned that the success may not last beyond the term and 'progressive vision' of the chairperson (Human Rights Watch 2001b). Since its creation, the commission has regularly awarded compensation to human rights victims of government repression, but the government frequently refuses to comply pointing to budgetary constraints. A 2005 HRW report submitted to the UN Committee against Torture confirms the continued endemic use of torture by Ugandan security forces (Human Rights Watch 2005). While the UHRC was largely free to investigate such cases, its work is ineffective in addressing the root causes of torture.

One of the early major successes of the UHRC was raising awareness about prison conditions and bringing together donors as well as government officials to address those issues. But beyond the individual cases and donor-supported projects, the UHRC had little effect on repressive governmental practices and army operations in northern Uganda. By the end of 2003, the government introduced constitutional changes, which included the abolition of the UHRC. Domestic and international NGOs have since successfully mobilized against weakening the only independent monitoring body within Uganda.

Kenya

President Moi announced the creation of a Standing Committee on Human Rights in July 1995, a few days before a Donor Consultative

Meeting in Paris and weeks after AI and HRW had released reports on (once again) deteriorating human rights conditions in the country. The move by Moi was clearly aimed at appeasing donors and external activists without actually having to cede any political power. It would take a full year for the appointment of members to the committee as well as the release of an official announcement of its launch. Moi personally appointed 10 commissioners in May 1996, who were reporting directly and only to the president himself (African Rights 1996: 236).

The rules of the committee's work were drawn up by its first chair, Onesmus Mutungi. All members were prohibited from talking publicly about their work and the reports were not released to the public. After submitting several reports to the president and following pressure from the civil society sector, the committee released its first 170-page report in 1998 to the public. In this report, the committee asked the government for an act of parliament to establish its independence. It also noted receiving technical assistance from the Office of the United Nations High Commissioner for Human Rights (OHCHR). The first report of the commission counted 394 complaints received between July 1996 and February 1998. Due to lack of resources, only 87 of those cases were investigated. The committee made direct recommendations to the president, but there is no further record of action. In the report, the committee addresses the ethnic clashes of the 1990s, but generally absolves the government from any responsibility. In its first years of operation, the committee also failed to work with the thriving NGO sector and largely operated in secrecy. In its interactions with international human rights groups, the committee took a defensive position and rejected any criticism of Kenya's human rights record. In 2000, a bill was introduced in parliament, which included security of tenure for the commissioners, financial autonomy, and subpoena powers. By July 2003, the newly elected government replaced the Standing Committee with an independent Kenya National Commission on Human Rights (KNCHR). The nine commissioners are now drawn from the civil society sector and operate with greater financial and political independence.

In creating domestic complaint procedures, the Ugandan government was initially more committed to their success and independence than the Moi regime. These reforms have been pushed from both the bottom–up and from external sources in Kenya, while they were implemented top–down in Uganda. The parliamentary investigations of human rights abuses during the 1990s indicate for Kenya a growing emancipation and effectiveness of such mechanisms. While the UHRC had greater financial and political independence and more powers to investigate individual abuses and force redress, it could hardly rely on civil society support and remained unable to address the root causes of human rights abuses within the Ugandan army and government. The recent threats to the survival of the UHRC contrast strongly with the increasing commitment to domestic monitoring in Kenya. Table 3.1 offers a summary of the constitutional measures designed to limit arbitrary rule.

The table reveals that Uganda experienced strong human rights improvements after 1986 and until the early 1990s. Those improvements were not just the result of the civil war ending, but reflected sincere reform efforts by the NRM government in the areas of expanding participation and constitutionalism. But as the NRM continued to hold onto power, the reform process slowed and human rights conditions began to deteriorate again. For Kenya, the record shows a period of consistent growing repression until 1989/90, a mixed record between 1990 and 1997, and finally some signs of sustainable improvement in late 1997 and 1998. While the Kenyan reform process after 1991 focused on electoral competition, constitutional changes lagged behind and the violence against potential opposition voters severely limited meaningful political participation. In Uganda, the emphasis on participation contrasted with extensive limits to part competition in the electoral realm.

Electoral democracy

Whereas the Ugandan government implemented constitutional reforms and an expansion of popular participation from the top–down, the Kenyan reform process focused on the national arena of electoral competition. The selection of indicators in this section reflects an understanding of democracy as defined in Chapter 2. Kenya experienced its first peaceful handover of executive power in 2002. The Ugandan government has been in power since 1986 and has only slowly increased the room for multiparty activities. In 2005, the Museveni government finally agreed to multiparty competition in exchange for a constitutional amendment allowing Museveni to stand for a third term.

Kenya

The dissolution of the KADU in 1964 created a *de facto* one-party system shortly after political independence. Occasional efforts to create new parties rivaling KANU were thwarted by Kenyatta and his successor Moi. Still, there was significant electoral competition within KANU,

Table 3.1 Constitutional safeguards and human rights development, 1986–2005

	Kenya				Uganda		
	1986–1990	1991–1997	1998–2005	1986–1990	1991–1995	1996–2005
Protection against torture	low	medium	high	high	medium	medium
Protection against detention without trial	low	medium	high	medium	medium	low
Protection against extra-judicial killings	low	medium	high	medium	medium	low
Domestic complaint procedures	weak	weak	weak	weak	weak	medium
Judicial independence	low	low	medium	medium	medium	medium

where candidates competed in primaries for securing parliamentary seats. Regular elections on the national level held every four years led external observers to qualify the Kenyan political system of the 1970s and early 1980s as 'semi-competitive' (Barkan 1992: 162). In the mid-1990s, President Moi increased his executive control over all parts of the government and society by using KANU as a vehicle of strengthening personal rule (Widner 1992b). By 1988, KANU replaced the secret ballot in its primaries with a queue voting procedure, where voters line up behind pictures of their candidates. Parliament also voted to declare a *de jure* one-party system.

The policy of repression and decreasing electoral choices abruptly ended in late 1991, when donors forced the government to re-introduce multipartyism. While the first multiparty contest in December 1992 was neither free nor fair, the subsequent elections in 1997 and 2002 created an increasingly level playing field between KANU and its competitors. The manipulation of voter registration and district sizes as well as the violent intimidation of opposition voters (Africa Watch/Human Rights Watch 1993) allowed KANU and Moi to hold onto power in 1992 and 1997. In addition, a KANU majority in parliament passed legislation in 1992, which prohibited coalition governments, extended the terms of office for the president to five years, and required a successful presidential candidate to gain at least 25 percent of the votes in five out of the eight provinces of Kenya.

Although the 1992 elections were seriously flawed, international observers gave their vote of approval calling the contest a reflection of the popular will of the people. 'Despite the fact that the whole electoral process cannot be given an unqualified rating as free and fair, the evolution of the process to polling day and the subsequent count was increasingly positive to a degree that we believe that the results in many instances directly reflected, however imperfectly, the expression of the will of the people' (Commonwealth Observer Group 1993: 40). While this was hardly true for the 1992 contest, electoral fairness improved as a result of domestic pressure prior to the 1997 elections.

Minimal constitutional reforms adopted before the December 1997 elections abolished the requirement for opposition parties to register their meetings with local authorities. The opposition was also empowered to appoint 10 out of the 21 members of the Electoral Commission, giving it a crucial hold in the most significant body charged with organizing national elections. There was also a significant decrease in instances of 'ethnic violence' instigated by politicians primarily against opposition voters. The gradual loss of KANU control over the electoral process became first visible on election day in December 1997 and finally led to a change of government in 2002. The KANU majority in parliament dwindled to four seats in the 1997 contest, thus forcing Moi to enter into political alliances with the opposition parties FORD-Kenya and the National Development Party of Kenya (NDP) led by Raila Odinga. While the 1992 contest was won by KANU using electoral fraud, the 1997 elections were primarily lost by an ethnically divided opposition unable to agree on a single challenger to Moi. In 1997, 21 parties and 15 presidential candidates contrasted with a field of 8 parties and presidential hopefuls in 1992.

By 2001, the majority of the opposition succeeded in uniting behind Mwai Kibaki as the challenger to Moi's handpicked successor and son of Jomo Kenyatta, Uhuru. Major opposition parties such as the DP and FORD-Kenya created the NARC as a serious challenge to KANU in all parts of the nation. The end of almost 40 years of uninterrupted KANU rule came when Odinaga took the NDP in 2002 from the coalition with KANU to the opposition camp. The election results of the multiparty era are summarized in Table 3.2.

Uganda

Multipartyism ended in Uganda four years after independence with a coup d'état by Prime Minister Milton Obote on 24 February 1966. In October 1969, political parties except for Obote's UPC were banned and the whole country was put under a state of emergency. During the Amin dictatorship from 1971 to 1979 no elections were held. The multiparty elections in 1980 brought Obote and UPC back to power, but were hardly free and fair (Bwengye 1985). Yoweri Museveni, a loser in these elections, justified his violent rebellion with reference to the electoral fraud committed by Obote supporters. After Museveni and the NRM prevailed militarily in the subsequent civil war, the new government declared party politics as one of the main evils responsible for the past chaos. While parties were not banned, their activities remained sharply restricted. Parties were prohibited from opening offices outside of Kampala, supporting candidates in elections, and holding public rallies. All candidates running for office had to do so in their individual capacities and not as representatives of parties.

The NRM extended this ban on party activities twice until it called a popular referendum on the issue in 2000. Opposition parties called for a boycott of the exercise, but failed to prevent the government from winning enough support for the measure. A low turnout of less than 50 percent of the registered voters produced a 90 percent support for

Table 3.2 Presidential and parliamentary elections in Kenya, 1992–2002[14]

	1992		1997		2002	
	Presidential votes in percent	Parliamentary seats	Presidential votes in percent	Parliamentary seats	Presidential votes in percent	Parliamentary seats
KANU	40	100	41	107	31	64
NARC	–	–	–	–	61	125
Democratic Party	20	23	31	39	–	–
FORD-Kenya	17	31	8	17	–	–
FORD-Asili	27	31	–	–	–	–
FORD-People	–	–	<1	3	6	14
Social Democratic Party (SDP)	–	–	8	15	<1	0
National Development Party (NDP)	–	–	11	21	–	–

the continuation of the party ban. What looked initially like another victory for the 'movement system' soon turned into the first sign of an end to 'no-party rule.' The opposition continued to demand the basic respect for political freedoms and successfully used the court system to challenge the ban on party activities. By 2003, the Ugandan Supreme Court declared the referendum invalid and the majority of restrictions on party activities unconstitutional. While Museveni rejected those rulings as 'undemocratic,' the advent of multiparty rule was inevitable. By 2005, parliament agreed to hold the upcoming 2006 elections under multiparty rules. The NRM agreed to this only after a constitutional change giving Museveni a chance to run for a third term in office.

The return to multipartyism followed a long period of delayed political reforms and a failure of the NRM to establish an alternative form of grassroots democracy throughout the nation. After 1986, the NRM created Resistance Councils (RCs), which established electoral processes on the village level and challenged existing hierarchies dominated by a Chief system. Two positions in the nine-person village level RC (I) were reserved for women and youth representatives. The primary village level council elected a representative for the parish level (RC II). This process of delegation continued upward to the sub-county (RC III), the county (RC IV), and the district level (RC V). The National Resistance Conference (NRC) topped the pyramid of RC institutions. In practice, the RC system did not transform Ugandan politics in fundamental ways. Issues such as peace and security as well as economic growth created more immediate benefits for individual Ugandans, while RCs were more likely to reproduce the existing social order on the local level.[15] Moreover, the government never intended to take the idea of grassroots democracy to the national level and began with the first presidential and parliamentary elections in 1996 to create a parallel system of traditional representative democracy.

The entrenchment of NRM elites during the 1990s was facilitated by the party ban and the intentional insulation of national politics from the local level (Mamdani 1996: 209). During the entire NRM rule, regular elections created at least an impression of accountability and legitimacy. The first elections held in February 1989 took more than one month to determine representatives for all RC levels. The NRC was expanded from 98 to 278 seats, representing now 38 unelected NRA veterans of the civil war period, 20 presidential nominees, 10 army representatives, women and youth representatives, and elected members from the RC II and III level. In March 1994, the population directly elected 214 delegates for the Constituent Assembly (CA), which was charged with writing a new constitution for Uganda. With close to 90 percent voter turnout, about two-thirds of the seats went to NRM supporters. International observers commended the first elections for a national body as generally free and fair. The CA not only proposed a new constitution, but also supported an extension of no-party rule until 2000 and proposed a referendum on multipartyism at the end of that period. The NRC was to be transformed into a representative body of directly elected parliamentarians.

In 1996, the members of parliament (MPs) and the president were for the first time directly elected by the Ugandan people. On 9 May, Museveni won the presidential elections with more than 74 percent of the vote. Two weeks later, NRM candidates also clearly dominated parliamentary elections. The trajectory from 1989 to 1994 and 1996 not only was marked by increased electoral competition within the 'movement system,' but also indicated a growing shift away from the alternative grassroots to a more conventional representative democracy. While the NRM insisted on the party ban, the establishment of more representative forms of democracy favored the eventual reintroduction of multipartyism.

After heavy domestic and international criticism of the 2000 referendum and another extension of 'no-party rule,' Museveni appointed a Constitutional Review Commission (CRC) charged with developing recommendations about the future of the Ugandan political system. No measures were taken prior to the 2001 presidential and parliamentary elections, which ended again with a victory of Museveni and the NRM. Museveni gained 69.3 percent of the vote, while his main challenger, Kizza Besigye, received 27.3 percent. In April 2001, Besigye called on the Supreme Court to nullify the elections as flawed and unfair. The judges decided three to two against the application, and Besigye was subsequently repeatedly interrogated by security forces and left the country for South Africa in August 2001.

Table 3.3 summarizes the major differences in the expansion of electoral democracy in Kenya and Uganda from the mid-1980s until today. While Uganda took the lead on constitutional reforms and expanding local participation, Kenya's transition path focused on contestation in a multiparty era. During the 1990s, the electoral playing field in Kenya became increasingly level and ultimately yielded the first peaceful elite turnover in 2002. Limits to the participatory aspects of democracy allowed the Moi regime to survive two multiparty elections in 1992 and 1997. In Uganda, the NRM government failed to establish an alternative form of grassroots democracy and returned in the mid-1990s to a

Table 3.3 Electoral democracy in Kenya and Uganda, 1986–2005

	Kenya			Uganda		
	1986–1990	1991–1997	1998–2005	1986–1990	1991–1995	1996–2005
Elected officials	yes	yes	yes	no	no	yes, but party activities limited
Transparent voter registration	low	low	medium	medium	medium	low
Protection against electoral fraud	low	medium	high	medium	medium	medium
Access to alternative information	low	medium	high	medium	medium	medium
Protection against electoral violence	medium	low	medium	medium	medium	medium
Freedom of assembly	low	medium	medium	medium	medium	medium
Freedom of speech	low	medium	high	medium	medium	medium

representative model without lifting its ban on party activities. Since then, it has faced significant domestic pressures and accepted the holding of multiparty elections in 2006.

Comparison

Kenya and Uganda took distinct paths of regime change after effective domestic and external challenges to authoritarian rule emerged. While the Kenyan government reluctantly accepted multipartyism in 1991 and resisted substantive constitutional reforms until the late 1990s, the Ugandan government under Yoweri Museveni emphasized participation and constitutional reforms, but rejected party competition as means of democratization. Within a decade of the initial reforms, both countries have begun to implement measures designed to strengthen the previously neglected dimension of democratization. In Kenya, minimal constitutional reforms were adopted in late 1997, and individual participation in national politics has markedly improved due to decreasing electoral violence and fraud. In Uganda, the participatory model of democracy had some successes, but was ultimately replaced with a representative model of directly electing the president and the members of parliament. The ban on party activities became increasingly anachronistic and the country is today on the verge of its first multiparty elections since 1980.

4
Successful Challenges to Authoritarian Rule

In the previous chapter, I argued that variation in the strength of opposition forces in Kenya and Uganda at the time of independence explains differences in the modes of authoritarian rule. In Uganda, Milton Obote planted the seeds of violence and his own removal from power shortly after political independence in the mid-1960s. After Obote was deposed from power by Idi Amin, the military dictatorship removed all constitutional limits to executive dominance and spread violence across the country. In contrast, Kenya emerged from political independence as a textbook version of patronage, with the establishment of strong clientelist networks radiating from the presidential center. While Kenyatta's rule contained elements of overt repression, it mainly relied on co-opting dissent. After Kenyatta's death in 1978, Daniel arap Moi continued to rule by positive integration, but increasingly resorted to repression against a strengthening political opposition.

Transnational human rights groups represented the early warning systems reporting the increasing repression in Uganda during the early 1970s and in Kenya about 10 years later. This chapter will show how transnational activists created highly visible campaigns against authoritarian governments and affected international perceptions and policies. It also reveals that international norms of human rights and state sovereignty shaped international perceptions of domestic affairs in Kenya and Uganda. While the norm of state sovereignty insulates authoritarian leaders from international pressure (Clapham 1996; Jackson 1990), transnational human rights mobilization challenges this weakening protective shield.

Uganda, 1974–1985: The killing fields

In their efforts to raise international awareness about human rights violations in Uganda, AI and the International Commission of Jurists (ICJ) were initially keen on using mechanisms provided by the UN system. On 27 May 1974, the ICJ sent the first letter concerning the human rights situation in Uganda to the Secretary General of the UN (International Commission of Jurists 1977: 3). The submission was based on ECOSOC resolution 1503[1] and was initially forwarded to the Sub-Commission on the Protection of Minorities and the Prevention of Discrimination.

One week later, the ICJ released the report to the international media and Idi Amin responded by threatening to expel all British nationals if the British Broadcasting Corporation (BBC) continued to report on human rights issues in Uganda (Tolley Jr. 1994: 207). Amin also announced the appointment of his own Commission of Inquiry to investigate the allegations, while the practice of public executions and gross violations against Ugandans continued largely unabated.[2] Consequently, the ICJ added three additional communications to the UN on 16 June, 26 July, and 23 August 1974.

The failure of UN human rights mechanisms

Despite the urgency of the situation, the UNCHR refused to take immediate action and postponed the matter for one year until its next meeting in 1976. The Commission had only looked at the first ICJ communication because the three others were not received within six weeks prior to meetings of the Sub-Commission. There was also considerable irritation among state delegates because the ICJ had informed the international media about the information provided under the confidential 1503 procedure. In Uganda, the Commission of Inquiry appointed by Amin acknowledged in June 1975 that human rights violations existed. However, the Commission failed to take any further actions and maintained that the president was not responsible for any of the acts. During the same month, Amin threatened in a letter to Queen Elizabeth II the execution of the British national and writer Dennis Hills unless the British Foreign Minister, James Callaghan, would come to Kampala within ten days time and ask for a pardon (Furley 1989: 278; Hills 1992).

On 1 October 1975, Amin told the UN General Assembly that AI was 'fed on rumors and concoctions from discredited criminals and exiles,' while also accusing the organization of having 'taken no trouble to investigate or send a team to Uganda to see for themselves' (Amnesty International's 1976: 104). The reference was a direct reaction to AI's 1974/75 human rights report, which repeated earlier accusations of gross violations of human rights. In a subsequent press conference in New York, Amin invited an Amnesty delegation to Uganda. One month later, the Secretary General of AI, Martin Ennals, followed up on Amin's speech and requested a meeting with the Ugandan ambassador at the UN. The ambassador confirmed Amin's invitation to AI, but would not agree on a specific time period for the mission. Subsequently, the Ugandan government stopped responding to further inquiries by Amnesty representatives.

During the 1976 meeting of the UNCHR, a larger than usual Ugandan delegation participated in the deliberations. No information about their responses to the human rights reports was made public or communicated to the ICJ or other NGOs. The Commission decided to end its investigation and took no further action. Idi Amin immediately claimed that his government had been cleared by the UN. The ICJ reacted by preparing a new report and submitted it to the United Nations on 2 June 1976. Diplomatic relations with Western countries remained largely unchanged, despite the reports about increasing violence and random gross human rights violations against civilians committed by Ugandan security forces. This situation only changed in mid-1976 when an Israeli commando freed airline passengers held by Palestinian hijackers at Uganda's main Entebbe airport. In the operation, all but three hostages were rescued and the entire Ugandan airforce was destroyed. In retaliation, Amin's soldiers killed one of the hostages, Dora Bloch, who had been treated at a hospital in Kampala at the time of the rescue operation (Kyemba 1977: 166–178). In the aftermath of the hostage crisis, Britain broke off diplomatic relations with Uganda on 28 July 1976.

Based on the second ICJ report on Uganda, the Sub-Commission decided on 25 August 1976 to recommend to the UNCHR the resumption of an inquiry into the Ugandan human rights situation. The Sub-Commission requested the Commission to 'make a thorough study of the human rights situation in Uganda, based on objective and reliably attested information.' In the history of the UNCHR similar studies had only been approved for South Africa, the Occupied Territories in the Middle East, and Chile. On 7 February 1977, AI supplemented the ICJ communication on Uganda under the 1503 procedure. However, the UNCHR was already in session (7 February–12 March) and refused to take the new materials into consideration. Amnesty International published its first comprehensive human rights report on Uganda in June 1978 (Amnesty International 1978).

On 17 February 1977, Ugandan Archbishop Janani Luwum and two ministers were killed, probably at the hands of Amin himself (Kyemba 1977: 179–192). During the same week, the Ugandan Attorney General Godfrey Lule attended the annual meeting of the Human Rights Commission to defend Uganda's human rights record. Uganda had just been elected for a two-year term to represent the African region on the UNCHR.[3] According to Lule's own account, Amin called him twice during that time. On one occasion he informed Lule about the death of the Archbishop and added 'God has punished them.' With regard to the UN investigation, Amin told Lule to decline all knowledge about the accusations. Lule himself knew that he could not simply deny the burgeoning evidence, because 'I would not have been taken seriously.' Instead he tried to further delay the procedures and told the Commission that more time should be given for the investigation of the allegations. Knowing that he was now in danger for his life, Lule fled into exile to London immediately after the Geneva sessions (Lule 1977). There was no follow-up by the UN bodies on Lule's departure to London or the human rights situation in Uganda. The UNCHR decided to rest the case and return to it again in the following year.

The end of Amin's tyranny

It took until June 1977 for the Commonwealth of former British colonies to issue a warning of possible action against the Ugandan government. The Head of States declared in a resolution that 'cognizant of the accumulated evidence of sustained disregard for the sanctity of life and of massive violation of basic human rights in Uganda, it was the overwhelming view of Commonwealth leaders that these excesses were so gross as to warrant the world's concern and to evoke condemnation by the heads of governments in the strong and unequivocal terms' (Kyemba 1977: 237). However, no immediate action was taken. The same month, the US ambassador to the UN, Andrew Young, broke diplomatic decorum, comparing the violence in Uganda to the Holocaust of the 1930s and 1940s.

In August 1977, Ugandan exile groups in Kenya, Tanzania, Great Britain, and the United States formed an umbrella coalition and met in Lusaka (Omara-Otunnu 1987: 139). At the same time, exiles in London formed the Uganda Group for Human Rights (UGHR), began to intensify networking with organizations such as AI, and raised their voices for government sanctions against the Amin regime. Amnesty International continued to plan missions to the country, but such requests were not answered by Ugandan authorities. Despite the additional evidence provided, the UNCHR decided in March 1978 to take no action, but merely to continue its observation of the Ugandan situation (Tolley Jr. 1994: 208). The Commission had previously rejected a British proposal to further investigate the human rights situation and, in particular, the death of Archbishop Luwum. On 3 April 1978, Amin announced the creation of a national human rights committee composed of members of the security forces and other government agencies. It was charged with overseeing all contacts between the UNCHR and the people of Uganda (Amnesty International 1979: 166) and had no other *raison d'être* than to deflect further criticism without changing repressive policies.[4]

At the very end of Amin's rule, there were only a few significant official responses to the human rights reports, which had little or no effect on the domestic situation. Following a hearing on the situation in Uganda in June 1978 (Committee on Foreign Relations 1978), the US Congress demanded a trade embargo against the country. However, a majority of votes was only secured after three Communist countries (Cambodia, Cuba, and Vietnam) had also been added to the list (Forsythe 1988: 78). The embargo only went into effect after Amin was already removed from power. While Members of Congress demanded from their government actions against the Amin regime, the US Administration continued friendly relations with the Ugandan regime.

After the break of diplomatic relations between Great Britain and Uganda, the United States was the single largest purchaser of Ugandan coffee and all the airplanes used by Amin for his travels and imports of luxury goods continued to be serviced in the United States. British politicians became increasingly concerned that they would loose their influence in their former colony, while the US government sought to keep Amin from forging even closer ties with Communist regimes. '[The] British press in 1977–79 was full of accounts of atrocities – but various types of trade were allowed to continue, along with the activities of British banks' (Furley 1989: 279). In particular, British companies continued to supply the infamous State Research Bureau up until 1979 with radio equipment and the army with night vision cameras and telephone tapping devices. After heated debates in the press and parliament, the British government agreed to ban Amin from attending the Commonwealth Summit in London in June 1979 (Omara-Otunnu 1987: 138). However, the Minister of State for Foreign and Commonwealth Affairs, Lord Goronwy-Roberts, refused to consider a suspension of Uganda from the Commonwealth, arguing that Britain had to consider 'how best to sustain and help the people of Uganda as a whole' (cited in Furley 1989: 279).

The October 1978 release of AI's *Human Rights Violations in Uganda* increased pressures to cut off all trade in order 'to create the conditions in which Ugandans themselves can remove the government' (*The Guardian*, 20 October 1978). The British government remained reluctant, arguing that it had appropriately condemned the Amin regime, while avoiding 'punish[ing] the Ugandan people.' Despite growing demands for sanctions from Ugandans themselves, Britain remained a major trading partner of Amin and allowed the dictator to maintain enough loyalty within his own army (Kyemba 1977: 254). Particularly infamous were the so-called 'whiskey runs,' which allowed Amin to supply his cronies with alcohol, a practice defended by Baroness Stedman in the House of Lords by claiming 'that we need to keep trade lines open for other things' (cited in Furley 1989: 280). Trade stopped only temporarily after Tanzanian troops invaded Uganda in March 1979.

The norm of state sovereignty as well as competition among potential allies played a crucial role in preventing an effective and coordinated international response to the atrocities committed in Uganda from 1971 to 1979. Nonetheless, the transnational human rights movement succeeded in identifying the Amin government as one of the worst human rights violating regimes. Human rights norms were now established competitors of the sovereignty norm when it came to international debates on Uganda. While no foreign government and international organizations took decisive steps against Amin solely based on his human rights record, debates in the media and among policy makers indicate a significant influence of human rights activism.

The end to Amin's rule was a result of internal divisions within his regime and the dictator's efforts to divert attention by launching a military attack on neighboring Tanzania. In order to defuse the mounting tensions within the military (Ofcansky 1996: 47), Amin ordered the annexation of Tanzanian border territory. The Ugandan army briefly occupied the region, but was quickly repelled by Tanzanian forces in November 1978. In January 1979, Tanzanian troops and about 1,000 pro-Obote exiles invaded Uganda. Airlifted troops from Libya and several hundred Palestinian fighters could not prevent the downfall of the Amin regime on 11 April 1979 (Sathyamurthy 1986: 513). Amin fled with his family into exile to Libya and eventually to Saudi Arabia, where he died in August 2003 without ever facing justice for the atrocities he committed.

The return of Milton Obote

One of the significant newcomers on the Ugandan political scene was Yoweri Museveni, who had started his political career as a member of UPC, but left the party during the Amin period. Museveni came from Ankole which historically tended to side with the UPC against the perceived Baganda dominance in Ugandan politics. However, the first Obote government discredited the party for many intellectuals, who called for reforms from within or sought new platforms of political activism. During the first Obote regime in the late 1960s, Museveni studied Political Science and Economics at the University of Dar es Salaam. After finishing his studies, Museveni worked in the Ugandan Foreign Ministry and later in the President's Office just before Amin took power.

Between 1971 and 1979, Museveni became the leader of a small guerilla group called *Front for the National Salvation* (FRONASA) and spent some time in guerilla training camps in Mozambique. In an interview in 1972, Museveni declared that FRONASA fought 'to remove Amin's tyranny and when that is done questions such as leadership and ideology can be settled through a democratic process by the people of Uganda. In Africa we continuously talk about Sharpeville where 67 people were killed, but in terms of human waste that does not compare to Uganda. Life is so cheap in Uganda now, that it is useless to try to keep accounts' (cited in ACR, Vol. XVIII, B 474). After his return to Uganda in 1979, Museveni briefly became Defense Minister under the transitional government but lacked a domestic power base outside of the private army he had built (Sathyamurthy 1986: 663).

Political differences within the anti-Amin coalition of exiles surfaced as soon as the end of Amin's rule was in sight. Although the Tanzanian government made strong efforts to facilitate an inclusive exile government, internal divisions prevented the emergence of a truly stable political consensus. The negotiations in Moshi/Tanzania led in April 1979 to the appointment of Yusuf Lule as president and the creation of a National Consultative Council (NCC) to fulfill legislative functions. The Uganda National Liberation Front (UNLF) was created to unite the diverse movements aimed at removing Amin from power. The Moshi negotiations and results were strongly supported by Great Britain, which quickly recognized the new government and reopened its High Commission in Kampala. But the internal divisions between Buganda and the rest of the country, only temporarily repressed by Amin's tyranny, resurfaced with the new government. The Baganda Lule clashed with the NCC as he tried to increase Buganda's influence on national affairs and reshuffled the Cabinet without consulting the NCC. In retaliation, the NCC replaced Lule[5] after only 68 days and appointed Godfrey Binaisa, a former Attorney General under Obote (Tumusiime 1992: 53). The British government refused to recognize the new government, fearing that Binaisa was a transitory figure soon making room for the return of Obote himself.

Binaisa made significant efforts to increase his power and avoid the fate of his predecessor. In August 1979, Binaisa declared a two-year ban on all party activities and began preparations for national elections. Two months later he restored the Public Order and Security Act, which had established the practice of detention without trial in 1967 (Ofcansky 1996: 50). In November, Binaisa removed Yoweri Museveni from the post of Defense Minister (Omara-Otunnu 1987: 147) after Museveni and other political leaders refused to disband their private armies (and political ambitions) in favor of a truly national force. Binaisa lost both international and domestic support after proposing that all candidates for the upcoming general elections should run under a common UNLF umbrella. Tanzanian President Julius Nyerere threatened to withdraw his troops from Ugandan territory and the fragile domestic coalition sustaining the transitional government fell apart (ACR, Vol. XIII, B 359). On 10 May 1980, the Army Chief of Staff David Oyite-Ojok ordered the army out of the barracks and took control of Kampala.

In the next few hours, a Military Commission consisting of Paulo Muwanga (chairman), Yoweri Museveni (vice chairman), Tito Okello, David Oyite-Ojok, William Omaria, and Zeddi Maruru took control, placed Binaisa under house arrest, and scheduled multiparty elections for December. The commission declared in a statement 'whereas Ugandans and their Tanzanian allies who took up arms against Amin did so because they wanted and still want peace, stability and freedom re-established in Uganda, Godfrey Binaisa and most of his close colleagues made the politics of intrigue, greed for power and wealth and rampant corruption, their central concern and preoccupation. [. . .] Binaisa has made no attempt to build a clean government' (cited in ACR, Vol. XIII, B 360). The commission appointed a civilian cabinet and sent envoys to win the support of Tanzanian President Nyerere.

On 27 May 1980, Milton Obote returned from exile. In his first public statements he revived his anti-Western rhetoric of the late 1960s and attacked Great Britain for having supported Amin. Western diplomats put their hopes on the upcoming elections and the DP, which seemed to re-emerge as the main challenger to the UPC. In June 1980, a party conference elected Paul Ssemogerere as temporary DP leader. Despite early signs of pre-election manipulations, Western donor governments stuck with their initial decision to support and finance the election process. This position was driven again by the fear that any kind of engagement was better than leaving Uganda open to a takeover by Communist forces. 'It now seems clear that if the West does not take some action to ensure a fair Ugandan election, yet another portion of former British Africa will be lost to the influences of the Eastern Bloc. Kenya will stand alone as last bastion of Western influence' (*Daily Telegraph*, 7 October 1980).

A few months before the elections, Yoweri Museveni launched his own party, the Uganda Patriotic Movement (UPM). Along with other intellectuals and former UPC members, Museveni argued that Uganda needed an entirely new political structure, ending the rule of hopelessly discredited parties. The Conservative Party (CP) completed the four-party elections as a more liberal successor of the KY party. The pre-election period continued with strong disagreements about election procedures between the UPC and the other three parties' representatives. Although all parties had delegates in the Military Commission and the NCC, 'the effective leadership was in the hands of UPC supporters' (ACR, Vol. XIII, B 369). On 27 November, 14 candidates of the DP and UPM were disqualified, meaning UPC could count on 14 unopposed seats two weeks prior to the elections. DP and UPM also protested without avail the creation of additional constituencies in the UPC-dominated Northern part of Uganda. Despite these controversies, which were openly discussed in the Ugandan press, all parties ultimately agreed to participate in the elections.

On 10 December, voting commenced in 5,000 polling stations. In some areas, including the capital Kampala, the ballot papers arrived late. When initial results showed a DP lead, its supporters took to the streets in celebration. In the midst of the counting procedure, UPC leader Muwanga declared that the Electoral Commission was no longer in charge of the process. Instead, all results would have to be reported to him personally. The Commonwealth Observer Group protested the change of procedure in vain. After this intervention, UPC was declared a winner with an absolute majority with 74 out of 126 parliamentary seats, leaving DP with 51, UPM with only one, and CP with no seat.[6] After a few days of deliberation, the Commonwealth observers held that 'despite the imperfections and deficiencies to which we have drawn attention, and subject to the concern expressed on the question of nominations and unopposed returns, we believe this has been a valid electoral exercise which should broadly reflect the freely expressed choice of the people of Uganda' (ACR, Vol. XIII, B 370).

On 15 December, Obote was sworn in as President for the second time in Ugandan post-independence history, while Paulo Muwanga was rewarded with the vice presidency and the defense portfolio. DP representatives agreed in January 1981 to acknowledge the results and form a parliamentary opposition. Within a few months seven MPs crossed the floor from DP to UPC, while other DP leaders left the country to join Yusuf Lule and Godfrey Binaisa. The British government accepted the victory of UPC, and Obote successfully courted the British government by publicly distancing himself from socialist ideas and appointing Shafiq Arain, a Ugandan of Asian origin, as High Commissioner in London. In light of the nightmare Amin brought to Great Britain in 1972 with the expulsion of Asian citizens, this highly symbolic decision insured goodwill for years to come. Arain became a crucial force in selling a 'new' Obote (Furley 1989: 284) and isolating the inter-governmental relations between Uganda and Great Britain from a generally hostile British press and re-emerging human rights concerns soon to be expressed by the AI.

The deterioration of human rights conditions

The domestic situation, however, did not justify the initial optimism of external observers. After losing the elections, Yoweri Museveni abandoned his party and went underground to create a guerrilla movement soon known as the NRM/A. In August 1981, the NRM declared that 'after toppling the Obote regime, the NRM, in consultation with the other fighting and political groups working against the Obote dictatorship, will ask for a broad-based Interim Administration.' In its effort to bring back a democratic government, 'the Interim Administration shall see to it that a new Constitution, based on the popular will, is drafted and promulgated by a Constituent Assembly elected by the peoples themselves' (cited in Waliggo 1995: 22). Within one year after the elections, the NRA controlled significant parts of the country and enjoyed considerable popular support. In contrast, the challenged Obote government began to resort to increasingly violent tactics in its efforts to uproot the NRM and end the popular support in rural areas.[7]

Following the Amin tyranny, the transnational human rights mobilization quickly returned when the first reports about new atrocities appeared in the international press. But the official response by the British government indicated a continued belief that constructive engagement was preferable to punitive sanctions. 'The British press was [again] full of atrocity stories, it was now that the government responded to Uganda's request for a Commonwealth military training team to try to remedy the situation' (Furley 1989: 285). Hence, the Obote regime received support, although the *Observer* claimed on 15 November 1981 that 'Britain and other Commonwealth countries would certainly hesitate to send troops to train an army set to crush a popular rebellion sparked by its own brutality.'

In an effort to root out the rebels, the Obote government recruited new army and police personnel, who were poorly trained by the Tanzanian occupational force, the Commonwealth military training force, and a few North Korean advisers. The idea of the Commonwealth group 'to train those who would train the rest' (Furley 1989: 286) failed to have much positive effects on the conduct of the army in fighting the rebel insurgency.[8] At the same time, the counter insurgency operations only strengthened Museveni's rebels, which now controlled three Buganda districts (Luwero, Mpigi, and Mukono) and were able to launch attacks on the capital Kampala. The guerillas systematically attacked police stations and military installations where they captured large quantities of arms and met with little or untrained resistance. Afterwards they retreated to the countryside to avoid any large-scale confrontations with government troops.

On 24 September 1981, leaders from the Anglican, Roman Catholic, and Orthodox churches as well as the Muslim community claimed in an open letter that 'within three weeks, a total of over 100 innocent citizens have been murdered, mainly by the gun and by people who are there to protect and defend the people of Uganda. [...] Road-blocks around the country have become places of torture' (ACR, Vol. XIV, B 307/310). The church leaders demanded that the government should restore the rule of law, discipline the army, and initiate round-table talks with the opposition. Obote countered the allegations and blamed the 'incidents' on 'bandits wearing army uniforms' (ACR, Vol. XIV, B 307).

By January 1982, the NRM had established itself as the main political body bringing together various anti-Obote forces, including Museveni's guerrillas, Binaisa, Lule, Kayiira, and even some former Amin supporters under the leadership of Amin's former Finance Minister, Moses Ali. London became the center of the growing exile community, while the NRA became the official military wing of the NRM inside Uganda. The same month, Obote invited an AI delegation to visit the country. Government officials denied allegations of 'systematic human rights abuses' and answered allegations about 361 individual abuse cases high-lighted by Amnesty (Amnesty International 1983: 124). Amnesty remained unsatisfied, and in April published an updated report, which included another 100 cases of torture and extra-judicial killings. Amnesty asked the government to create an independent commission for the thorough investigation of the incidences (*International Herald Tribune*, 16 April 1982).

The government refused to follow this suggestion and Obote criticized AI for not discussing the content of the follow-up report with his government. Later, the Ugandan High Commissioner in London, Shafiq Arain, presented a 26-page rebuttal and claimed, 'my government has nothing to hide on human rights in Uganda.' The Information Minister, David Anyoti, claimed that his country's reputation was being damaged by 'irresponsible reporting' and by 'second-rate yellow journalists' to whom 'sensationalism and subjectivity become the rule of their operations' (ACR, Vol. XIV, B 312). He added that only the Tanzanian (Shihata), the Sudanese (SUNA), the Soviet (TASS), and the Chinese news agencies were properly accredited and that new rules would make access for freelance journalists impossible (implemented in February 1982).

The Amnesty report of 'widespread tortures and killings' sparked renewed debates about the British engagement in Uganda. While liberal and conservative papers more or less agreed on the dismal state of human rights in Uganda, they drew very different conclusions from that analysis. *The Times* described human rights conditions today as even worse than under Amin, but concluded that 'the task of the Commonwealth training mission – disciplining the army – is all the more pressing and urgent.' A standard argument repeated in this article also held that Obote had proven to be incapable of unifying the country, but 'yet it is not at all certain that anyone else could do it better' (*The Times*, 8 July 1982).

A November 1982 report by Sir Peter Archer for the Human Rights Group of the British House of Commons commended the Ugandan government for being 'cooperative to a degree far in excess of what I have experienced from many governments in similar situations.' The report identified the army as the main problem and recommended to Western observers to 'temper their criticisms with a measure of under-standing, to recognize and encourage real attempts at improvements, and to attempt to lower the emotional temperature and diminish the feeling of insecurity.' Other independent observers invited by Obote in 1982 were the Roman Catholic Cardinal Emmanuel Nsubugu and the

British Scholar Colin Legum. Both were allowed to visit Luzira Maximum Security Prison where they found conditions to be generally tolerable.

Obete skillfully used these restricted visits by international observers to counter the increasingly negative reporting on human rights conditions in Uganda. All military barracks were off limits although AI had for some time identified those installations as the main torture centers. Moreover, the ongoing massacres by Uganda National Liberation Army (UNLA) soldiers in villages surrounding Kampala were completely ignored. When Colin Legum confronted Obote in an interview using his own experience from visits in Kenya, Cyprus, and Algeria on the differences between civilian and military prisons, the President admitted that 'since liberation in 1979, something similar to what you have described has happened, but not on the scale you may have experienced elsewhere, or anything like that which was portrayed by our opponents or by the media abroad. The important point to note is that these happenings are now under control, and this is the great difference between the past and the present' (cited in ACR, Vol. XV, B 312).

Despite Obote's efforts to uplift his government's international image, international reporting became more and more critical. In May 1982, the *Guardian* and the *Los Angeles Times* simultaneously published stories by Charles Powers titled 'Horror Story from Africa's True Heart of Darkness' and 'The Capitalist Lifeline that Skirts Uganda's Graveside.'[9] On 16 June, the *International Herald Tribune* titled 'Ugandans call conditions worse than under Amin.' Three weeks later *The Times* posited in an editorial that, despite some economic strides, 'very little progress has been made in the observance of human rights in Uganda' (cited in ACR, Vol. XV, B 313). On 29 August, the *Sunday Times* headline across eight columns held that 'Obote's Uganda Plunges Back into Bloodbath.' Hence, activities by human rights organizations such as AI had put Uganda back on the international agenda very shortly after Obote took power for the second time.

Although reports on the deteriorating human rights situation were already abundant in late 1981 and early 1982, the May 1982 donor meeting in Paris still voted to give $557 million aid to the Obote government. Under a series of standby agreements the IMF lent Uganda a total of $305 million until 1984 (Henstridge 1994: 53). In return, the Ugandan government agreed to follow fiscal measures proposed by the IMF. Only West German, Danish, and Dutch representatives expressed some concern about human rights issues by citing information provided by the AI. There were two major reasons why the donor community largely ignored NGO input and failed to recognize the permanent instability emanating from the 1980 elections. First, donors felt that there was no alternative to the 'elder statesman' Obote, who was now supporting economic austerity programs developed by the IMF, including a sharp devaluation of the Ugandan shilling and a privatization program of state-run companies. Second, Western donors became increasingly concerned about regional stability in East Africa after the aborted coup attempt against Daniel arap Moi in neighboring Kenya in 1982. As one observer concluded, 'the international community is lending support to Uganda because of its strategic significance, but it is ignoring a state of internal chaos that amounts to disaster for most of its citizens' (Anonymous 1984a: 220). Gross human rights violations had again reached alarming levels in Uganda, but Western governments once again failed to intervene because they had no alternatives and were driven by strategic rather than principled concerns.

A lack of response: The international community

At the end of 1982, the contract of the Commonwealth Military Training group was extended for another year and its strength doubled to 70 officers. At the same time, the Ugandan government hired the private British training group Falconstar to build a 5,000-men Special Force. Great Britain remained the largest provider of foreign aid, followed by the Soviet Union, Italy, West Germany, and France (ACR, Vol. XV, B 323). The year 1983 was marked by a continued worsening of human rights conditions, especially in the now infamous Luwero Triangle. Kampala remained insecure with reports of at least 16 people shot dead within 1 week in April.

From June to August 1983, government troops killed thousands of peasants and filled detention camps with more than 100,000 people (Ofcansky 1996: 55). The army unit charged with the intensive sweep was specially trained by former British Special Air Service (SAS) officers (ACR, Vol. XVI, B 295). In many cases, the attacks were also ethnically motivated, because the army was again dominated by soldiers coming from Obote's home region in the northern part of Uganda (Langi and Acholi). These soldiers now killed and looted in the South, but also in Idi Amin's West Nile region. Videos taken by the NRA documented the atrocities committed by the Ugandan army and were sent abroad to intensify international mobilization against the Obote government (Kasozi 1994: 172). Obote refused to open talks with the opposition and argued that 'parliamentary democracy will never be established in

Uganda and unity will be illusory if after every dispute, be it on elections or something else, Ugandans decide to take to the gun and are appeased by the so-called round-table conference' (ACR, Vol. XVI, B 292/3).

The transnational human rights mobilization had shifted from focusing on the slow and ineffective UNCHR to a more direct and media-oriented campaign. But donor governments remained largely unimpressed and failed to develop a comprehensive policy to deal with the situation in Uganda. In August 1983, Obote invited the Australian, British, and Canadian High Commissioners to a tour of the newly established detention camps in the Luwero triangle. During the visit he declared that 'the people who had got displaced due to bandit activities were voluntarily returning to certain centers such as police stations, army posts, administrative headquarters and schools' (Kasozi 1994: 184).

Despite the horrendous violations of human rights committed by the army in early and mid-1983, the outgoing British High Commissioner Hillier-Frye commended the economic progress in the country and held that 'Uganda's security position had improved considerably' (ACR, Vol. XVI, B 307). Quite the opposite assessment was given by non-governmental sources also based in London. In response to Amnesty's continued criticism, the Ugandan government accused the organization in September 1983 of 'hostile criticism' and 'rude behavior.' In an interview with the *Financial Times*, Obote accused Amnesty of not being able to distinguish between political prisoners and common criminals (quoted in Sathyamurthy 1986: 673).

The ongoing civil war ended any efforts of cross-party reconciliation after the disputed 1980 elections. Since the elections, UPC's majority in parliament had grown from 74 to 90 seats, while several opposition MPs were imprisoned, one shot dead by an army soldier and another listed as disappeared. The remaining opposition press, largely controlled by DP supporters, came under growing pressure. Vice President Muwanga accused the press in July 1983 of 'lies' and deliberate efforts to breed 'antagonism among Ugandans.' Despite the hard evidence presented in human rights reports, he refuted claims by the DP paper *Munnansi* that several thousand Ugandans had been killed in the Luwero Triangle. In his counterattack, Muwanga alleged that *Munnansi* was financed by a 'foreign source.' He continued to warn the press that the government would not 'sit and watch the country go to the dogs' (ACR, Vol. XVI, B 304). Opposition papers continued to be published, and *Munnansi* remained the most widely read paper in the country.

Military success of the National Resistance Movement (NRM)

By 1984, Museveni's rebels had begun to surround Kampala and organize the occupied territories under their own system of government. The NRM/A became known for harsh disciplinary measures taken against its own members in case of human rights violations committed against civilians. The NRM also replaced the traditional chief's system with more elected 'resistance councils.' In its so-called 'Ten Point Program,' the NRM/A guaranteed basic human rights and democratic governance (Tumusiime 1991: 5). In 1985, this program was officially adopted during a meeting of the NRM leadership in Austria. 'The NRM believes that it is the inalienable right of all peoples to freely choose their government and determine the manner of that government. Rigged or manipulated elections are an insult to the people, and a sure recipe for instability, conflict and upheavals. Constitutions imposed on the people by guise, wile or force cannot be the basis of stable and peaceful governance of men. It will be one of the primary duties of the NRM government to affect a swift but systematic return to democratic government after toppling the Obote regime' (National Resistance Movement 1985: 4).

While the Obote government further lost domestic and international legitimacy in 1984 and 1985, the rebels extended their domestic power base and international recognition. The downfall of Obote was further accelerated when the Army Chief of Staff David Oyite-Ojok died in a helicopter crash while visiting the Luwero war zone on 12 December 1983. The fellow Langi Oyite-Ojok had earlier followed Obote into exile and had established firm control over the military (ACR, Vol. XVIII, B 465). After Oyite-Ojok's death, factions within the army re-emerged and began to clash with one another, in particular along the lines of the two dominant Northern tribes Acholi and Langi.

The Uganda Consultative Group meeting of donor governments in Paris on 25–26 January 1984 passed without much criticism of the human rights situation. As was the practice in previous years, donors pledged a total of $430 million in aid money. The only contentious issue arose when the donors refused to cover a debt of approximately $120 million incurred by Uganda in military contracts with Israel in the early 1970s. The debt was still open after Amin had abruptly ended diplomatic relations with Israel and turned for support to Arab nations instead. The transnational human rights mobilization had changed perceptions about the domestic situation in Uganda, but provided no definite answers on how to end the cycle of violence. By March 1984, all Commonwealth countries except for Britain pulled out of the military training program, following a massacre of several dozen civilians in Muduuma. While Commonwealth governments cited the massacre and other human rights concerns as their reason to end military cooperation with Obote, the British Minister for Overseas Development, Timothy Raison, announced that Great Britain would continue its aid after being 'satisfied that the Muduuma massacre had been carried out by gangs with an aim of discrediting Obote's government' (Furley 1989: 287).

United States government officials were also slow to discuss the human rights situation in Uganda. In May 1984, Assistant Secretary of State for Human Rights, Elliott Abrams, and the ambassador to Uganda, Allen Davis, began to openly accuse the Obote government of systematic killings and torture. The diplomatic attacks followed a massacre of students, teachers, and priests committed by the Ugandan army at Namugongo Anglican Theological College close to Kampala. In August, a Congressional hearing on the human rights situation in Uganda provided a platform for NGO activists to describe the atrocities committed by the Ugandan forces against their own population. In his report to Congress, Abrams described the human rights situation as 'horrendous' and 'one of the worst in the world.' Without naming its sources, the report claimed more than 100,000 deaths due to direct army action and subsequent starvation mainly in the Luwero Triangle (Anonymous 1984b: 529). The Ugandan government reacted by expelling a US military attaché and canceling a training program for army officers in the United States. In its rejoinder, Kampala dismissed the numbers circulating in Western capitals and claimed that only about 15,000 Ugandans had been killed by both sides in the civil war since 1981.

While West Germany, Denmark, and the Netherlands also began to distance themselves from Obote, the British government continued its military and financial support. The British High Commission in Kampala declared that it had not found sufficient evidence for the allegations contained in the Abrams report (Furley 1989: 288). The private British firm Falconstar was encouraged to complete its training of a 3,000-men Special Force in 1984 (ACR, Vol. XVI, B 298). Representatives from the World Bank and the IMF preferred to emphasize the economic progress Uganda experienced since Obote had agreed to follow a fiscal stabilization program in 1981. Those economic advisers cited indicators of progress such as a drop of the inflation rate from 100 percent in April 1982 to 16 percent in June 1984.

By late 1984, the human rights mobilization finally had some effect on the British government. In September, the British Minister of State for African Affairs in the Foreign and Commonwealth Office, Malcolm Rifkind, slowly retracted from the initial rejection of the Abrams report. 'This was quite a switch, and he was responding to strong criticism from the Cambridge group of Amnesty International, which had accused the Foreign Office of being "craven" and "pussy footing" in its response to the Abrams claims' (Furley 1989: 290). Reacting to Amnesty International's report *Six Years after Amin: Torture, Killings, Disappearances*, published in June 1985, the British government finally 'cautioned the Ugandan High Commissioner that if the human rights situation in Uganda did not improve, Britain might terminate its [...] assistance program to Uganda' (Furley 1989: 291).[10] However, the British government still did not take any immediate action against the Ugandan government and continued to keep its military advisers in the country. On 20 June 1985, Obote defended his human rights record in a budget speech before parliament. He claimed that 'no one here or abroad' should 'entertain the false belief that this government is not interested in the rule of law, human rights, the unity of the people of Uganda, or in the promotion of democracy and democratic institutions' (ACR, Vol. XVII, B 396).

In his official response to the Amnesty report, Obote invited an Amnesty delegation to visit the country and also asked the British government as well as the European Community to send parliamentary delegations for on-the-spot investigations. He claimed that virtually all 12 demands for human rights improvements listed by Amnesty were already government policy. Obote admitted that he was not sure if Uganda had already accepted international instruments against torture, but would be anxious to do so: 'This government is fully committed to the observance of human rights in all parts of Uganda. Members of this government led the struggle against the regime of Idi Amin and it is most painful and disheartening that this government should be equated, either here or abroad, with the atrocious regime of Idi Amin. To do so cannot be supported by the facts of the situation and borders on a deliberate campaign to undermine the image and the authority of the government. Even in the report of Amnesty International it is acknowledged, though indirectly, that peace has returned to the whole country, except in areas where we have had armed dissident activities. Members of this government cannot negate the very objective – the enjoyment of human rights by all Ugandans – for which they fought and many of their colleagues lost their lives, by resorting to and condoning massive violations of human rights in Uganda.' Obote sought to explain existing human rights violations in reference to the problems created by the Amin tyranny: 'We inherited a most difficult security and economic situation. We inherited a very young army and a demoralized and depleted police force. [...] We have not banned or proscribed any political party, organization or institution' (cited in ACR, Vol. XVII, B 396/405). Before AI and other international observers could react to the invitations and defenses, Obote had been removed from power by his own army for the second time.

Transition: The military government

The Acholi Brigadier Basilio Okello led his troops from Gulu to Kampala and seized the capital on 27 July 1985. Another Acholi army general, Tito Lutwa Okello, was appointed Head of State and declared in his first radio message the 'total end to Obote's tribalistic rule.' He accused Obote of having brought to Uganda 'heinous murders, arsons, kidnappings, looting, robbery, destruction of property, rape, corruption, arbitrary arrests, detention without trial, flagrant abuse of human rights, contempt, disregard of the rule of law *as testified by Amnesty International* (emphasis added), all based on ethnic, tribal, religious, political and regional considerations and groupings. [...] Our only aim is to put an end to Obote's despotic rule' (cited in ACR, Vol. XVII, B 392). The new leadership dissolved parliament, suspended the 1967 constitution and dismissed all ministers. Obote fled into exile to Kenya and later to Zambia.

The new Military Council identified the formation of a national coalition government and negotiations with the rebels as its two most important tasks. The DP leader Ssemogerere was appointed Interior Minister, while several close associates of Obote were also included in the new Cabinet. Yoweri Museveni demanded half of the seats in the Military Council in return for ending his military campaign. But instead of an end to the violence, a new cycle of revengeful killings now targeted Obote's Langi provincial capital Lira. The NRM/A consolidated its position in the Southwestern part of Uganda and took advantage of the further weakening of the central government. The RCs set up in the 'liberated areas' existed now for several years and provided a sense of stability and protection to the population. 'The RCs were first organized to enlist sympathetic civilians in the acquisition of food, recruits, and intelligence for the NRA war effort...' (Kasfir 1998: 55). Later the RCs became elected local bodies governing the affairs of villages in a democratic fashion. The NRA/M was first to bring the idea of a 'citizen' to the countryside (Mamdani 1996: 200–203). This resulted in an 'unprecedented degree of village level participation in decision-making' (de Waal 1997: 631), and also reinforced growing international recognition of Museveni. Over time the rebel leadership was positively integrated into the transnational human rights network, or as Mamdani chose to put it, 'bathed as it was in global ideological influences' (Mamdani 1996: 207). Yoweri Museveni and his comrades frequently traveled to European capitals, where increasingly prominent hosts such as political parties and parliamentarians were eager to engage with Museveni as a promising new leader in a war-ravaged region.

During 1984–85, Museveni and other NRM leaders made several semi-official visits to European countries and had continuous contacts with international human rights groups (Weyel 1995: 555). In August 1985, Museveni wrote in the *Guardian* about his movement that 'we have been labeled "Marxist radicals", but of course such labels do not matter. I would very much like to be a "conservative" if I am shown something worth conserving. What should I conserve in the present situation? Intestinal worms, malnutrition, a high infant mortality rate, a low average life expectancy, a low calorie and protein intake etc. in the population? Or the complete denial of basic human rights by the present regimes, including the security of human life?' (*The Guardian*, 23 August 1985).

Kenyan President Daniel arap Moi brokered and chaired peace talks between the Military Council and Museveni's rebels between 26 August and 17 December 1985.[11] Museveni initially agreed to participate but stated that he considered the others at the table to be 'part of an endless system which has been responsible for the massacre of 1 million Ugandans since independence in 1962' (ACR, Vol. XVIII, B 469). The NRA used the negotiations to extend its control to important areas such as Mbarara, Masaka, Kasese, or Fort Portal. By the end of November, the NRA camped some 20 miles from Kampala. Its leadership continued the negotiations until mid-December and even agreed on a peace accord, but never had intentions to share power with the existing regime. The peace accord was never implemented and the NRA seized Kampala on 26 January 1986. Three days later, Museveni was sworn in as new President.

The transnational human rights mobilization targeting the second Obote government played a powerful role in shaping a domestic resistance committed to human rights and democracy. While donor governments failed once again to take decisive actions against a repressive regime, there was more significant trans-societal support for the NRA/M. The failure of official diplomacy to strongly support human rights norms was not a result of competing norms of state sovereignty, but indicated a lack of policy alternatives and tools in dealing with gross human rights violations in situations of civil war. Obote's agreement to structural adjustment programs contrasted strongly with Amin's flirtations with anti-Western governments and additionally divided donors by placating those primarily focused on economic indicators. Human rights mobilization effectively de-legitimized the Amin and Obote regimes, but a relatively principled ally only emerged with the NRM/A during the 1980s.

Kenya, 1983–1988: Executive outcomes

By 1983/84, Daniel arap Moi had been in power for almost six years and was in the process of establishing a suffocating executive control over the judiciary, parliament, and society at large. Governance issues that Moi deemed vital for his political survival were formally moved from ministries, parliament, or the judiciary to a expanding Office of the President. Using a system of directly controlled Provincial and District Commissioners, the President's Office reached directly to the regional and local levels. In 1985, the government required the members of the civil service to become members of KANU. A new KANU youth organization provided security services to senior officials and was soon accused of intimidating dissidents and the political opposition (Widner 1992b: 153). KANU experienced a calculated revival for the purpose of serving as a 'vehicle for transmitting the views of the president to the grass roots and for controlling the expression of interests within the country and their influence over policy. [. . .] And in that sense Kenya had become what some have called a "no-party state". The use of the party structures by the Office of the President had distinct consequences for patterns of political behavior . . .' (Widner 1992b: 158 and 161).

Establishing one-party rule

In the following years, executive tolerance for dissenting voices decreased sharply and the human rights situation deteriorated (Africa Watch/Human Rights Watch 1991; Howard 1991). In 1985 and 1986, several hundred people were arrested, mistreated, and temporarily disappeared as part of the clamp down of student protests in Nairobi (Anonymous 1987). In March 1986 six university members, including a close friend of Oginga Odinga, were arrested under the Preservation of Public Security Act and received sentences between 18 months and five years in prison. Moi claimed that they were part of the *MwaKenya* conspiracy, which allegedly involved persons supporting the 1982 coup.

International human rights organizations now began to raise alarm about the human rights conditions in the country (Amnesty International 1987b). They also reported hundreds of killings and detentions in the Northeastern part of Kenya where security forces tried to control feuds between various Somali clans (Africa Watch/Human Rights Watch 1991: xi; Amnesty International 1985: 66). In one such incident, in February 1984, government forces rounded up hundreds of members from the Degodia clan, which they blamed for a recent outbreak of violence. Many Degodia held for days on the Wagalla airstrip died of thirst, while others were killed when they tried to escape. A month after the massacre, the issue was raised in the Kenyan parliament and the government admitted that 57 people were killed as part of an effort to disarm the Degodia. These numbers were widely disputed and local observers claimed that up to 1,000 were left dead by the security forces (*Daily Nation*, 30 October 1998).

The incident was also noticed outside of Kenya. Similar to the Ugandan story, the first to take up the issue were individuals and NGOs whose perceptions were not framed by norms of state sovereignty. Instead, they interpreted the incident in reference to universal human rights standards and soon came into conflict with their own government's diverging norms hierarchy. For example, 'Three Norwegian volunteers stationed in the area had witnessed the aftermath of a massacre of ethnic Somalis on the airstrip at Wagalla near the provincial capital of Wajir. Very upset about what they had seen, they reported the incident to the Norwegian ambassador to Kenya. His muted reaction, which they interpreted as hushing the matter up, disgusted them' (Baehr, Selbervik and Tostensen 1995: 64). At the same time, AI demanded the creation of an independent commission to investigate the massacre. After returning back to Norway, the volunteers contacted the foreign ministry and the issue was raised in the Norwegian parliament. The issue was then established within the Norwegian domestic political discourse.

In September 1986, Norway granted political asylum to the former Kenyan MP and Cornell University student Koigi wa Wamwere, who had been jailed during the *MwaKenya* purges. With his charisma, wa Wamwere became a crucial figure in the process of moral consciousness-raising and redefinition of Kenya's image abroad: 'Arguably, he was the most important opinion leader in Kenyan affairs in Norway in the late 1980s' (Baehr, Selbervik and Tostensen 1995: 68). However, the bilateral relations between Norway and Kenya slowly deteriorated as sections of the Norwegian public began to criticize the foreign ministry and the

Norwegian embassy in Nairobi for allegedly suppressing information about human rights abuses in Kenya. Thus, Norway became the first Western donor country which was profoundly affected by the activities of the human rights network on Kenya. From there, long-held perceptions of Kenya changed in concentric circles starting in neighboring Scandinavian countries and moving to Continental Europe and the United States.

In November 1986, Moi declared the revival of KANU a success and claimed that the party was now 'supreme over Parliament and the High Court' (ACR, Vol. XIX, B 324). On 2 December 1986, the Kenyan parliament further strengthened executive powers by curtailing the right to bail (24th amendment) and by abolishing constitutionally guaranteed tenure for the Attorney and Auditor General (23rd amendment). The amendments passed parliament with 131 votes in favor and 38 abstentions. KANU's Governing Council was also empowered to discipline or even expel KANU members, including ministers and civil servants. Finally, KANU substituted the secret ballot in its primaries with a public queue-voting system, which also increased party control over the election process.[12] Voters were now asked to line up in front of the preferred candidate's poster. Two MPs who dared to criticize the measures in public were briefly detained in January 1987.

The formation of domestic dissent

The expansion of executive powers and some initial international criticism of Moi's rule provided the backdrop for the emergence of a more outspoken domestic opposition. Progressive church organizations as one of the last remaining independent societal actors provided the crucial space for dissidents to meet and voice their concerns. The *National Council of Churches of Kenya* (NCCK) and the *Law Society of Kenya* (LSK) sharply protested Moi's increasingly authoritarian style. In September 1986, the NCCK released an open letter in which 1200 clergy threatened to boycott elections unless the secret ballot in KANU primaries was reintroduced (Sabar-Friedmann 1997: 33). Moi retorted in October 1986 by demanding that dissidents should 'stop hiding behind a certain church' which now produced 'subversive pamphlets' (cited in ACR, Vol. XIX, B 328). In December, other ministers openly linked leading clergy to *MwaKenya*, while one of the NCCK employees, Dr. Walter Osewe, was arrested and charged with being a member of the alleged underground organization (Throup 1995: 155).

In the following years, the NCCK became the largest domestic organization, which could preserve its institutional independence and consistently challenge government repression. During the 1950s and the early 1960s, the NCCK had emerged as an ecumenical organization supported by significant amounts of overseas church donations to 'meet the Christian challenge of the post-*Mau Mau* reconstruction [...]. New missionaries were recruited, employed directly by the NCCK rather than its member churches. Their theology was liberal, their gospel as much social as individual. [...] The NCCK staff had no organic or historical connection with the local environment. [...] [It] was free to be "alongside" the new African politics [...] in a way in which the local churches would have found difficult even if their leaders had thought it desirable' (Lonsdale, Booth-Clibborn and Hake 1978: 269–270). Consequently, in the period right after independence the NCCK became the major 'focus of cooperation between Church and State,' while the organization continued to develop its international contacts. Lonsdale *et al.* point out that during that period 'the presence of its expatriate staff bears witness to the fact that Nairobi is a suburb of Ecumenopolis, World City' (Lonsdale, Booth-Clibborn and Hake 1978: 272–273). During the 1960s and 1970s the NCCK worked closely with government agencies mainly in areas of education and health.

The brief history of NCCK activism shows that the organization was an early transnational actor, which transported liberal values into Kenyan society prior and after political independence. In the immediate post-independence period, the NCCK aligned with the government to improve the living conditions of the local population. Once Moi successfully replaced the Kikuyu elite with his alliance of smaller ethnicities dominated by Kalenjin leaders, the close relationship between the NCCK and the state broke down. Church representatives now became major government critics framing their grievances as principled human rights values. Based on its reputation as a representative umbrella organization as well as the international contacts (Throup 1995: 160), the NCCK was able to defend its independence and even mobilize domestic and international resistance. Other representatives of societal modernization such as lawyers and university lecturers joined the dissident movement. A majority of the dissidents were members of the now disenfranchised ethnicities, mainly the Kikuyu and Luo.

The internationalization of the domestic struggle

When Daniel arap Moi announced two state visits to Europe and the United States for 1987, transnational human rights groups transformed the picture of domestic dissent, repression, and initial international mobilization into a powerful human rights campaign. The Kenyan government contributed to this campaign by arresting prominent opposition members shortly before Moi's departure to the United States. One of them, Gibson Kamau Kuria, an Oxford-educated defense lawyer in the *MwaKenya* trials, filed a lawsuit against Kenyan security officials accusing them of torturing the suspects. In anticipation of the likely consequences, Kuria provided Blaine Harden, the *Washington Post* correspondent in Nairobi, with the compiled evidence. On 26 February 1987, Kuria disappeared.

On 12 March, one day before Moi met with President Reagan in Washington D.C., the government announced Kuria's arrest under the Preservation of Public Security Act and accused him of 'disrespect of the President.' At the same time, Congressman Howard E. Wolpe, chairman of the US Foreign Affairs Subcommittee on Africa diagnosed during a press conference in Nairobi an 'emasculation of the Kenyan parliament' and a 'concentration of executive power.' The US State Department took the Kuria case and other allegations seriously and its spokesman, Charles Redman, declared that human rights would be on the agenda for the talks between Moi and Reagan. 'The allegations of torture, apparently supported by signed affidavits from those in Kenya who claim to have been tortured, raise serious questions of human rights abuses' (cited in ACR, Vol. XIX, B 334).

The day after the talks between Moi and Reagan, the *Washington Post* subtitled a picture of both politicians on the front page with 'Police Torture is Charged in Kenya.' The Kenyan government had clearly underestimated the international interest in the disappearance of Kuria whose fate immediately turned into a *cause célèbre* (ACR, Vol. XX, B 324). The same day, State Department officials and members of Congress demanded full explanation and an impartial investigation of the allegations (Africa Watch/Human Rights Watch 1991: 374). Moi cancelled his planned visit to New York and a meeting with the Secretary General of the UN and flew directly to less hostile Great Britain.

Upon his return to Nairobi,[13] Moi declared that all torture allegations against his government were false. Moi dismissed allegations by the foreign press that torture existed in Kenya. He made specific reference to allegations that detainees were held in flooded cells. 'Who could survive in water for two weeks? No one could survive 10 hours, let alone two weeks. The passengers trapped when a British ferry sank did not survive more than 30 minutes. [...] We know about a few detainees, 10 or 11, and their records from 1965 show that they have been in and out of jail. In 1978, I personally released all of them in the belief that they harbored good intentions toward this country. When they came out, they behaved like pigs who soil themselves even after you have washed them' (FBIS-MEA, Vol. 5, No. 051, P. R1, 17 March 1987).[14] Moi also denied that he was trying to solicit support from the United States and claimed that only the people of Kenya could be addressed for that. He accused Wolpe of supporting 'dissidents, crooks, and swindlers' and claimed 'Kenya was the freest country in Africa.'

While Moi was abroad defending his human rights records, his government's actions at home spoke a different language. Throughout 1987 a number of journalists were briefly detained and four Western journalists were beaten at police stations after they reported about student riots at the University of Nairobi and the city. The Minister for Information, Noah Ngala, alleged 'a deliberate move by Nairobi-based foreign correspondents to disinform the world about events in Kenya.' Moi himself threatened to ban the *Daily Nation*, the main independent newspaper. A dozen US missionaries were rounded up and ordered to leave Kenya after a forged letter surfaced alleging that they were part of a 'Klu [*sic*] Klux Klan operation' to topple the Kenyan and other African governments. One missionary died of a heart attack in police custody. After it became clear that the Ku Klux Klan (KKK) story was untrue, the Kenyan government withdrew the expulsion orders without explanation or apology. It also refused a request by the US government to explain its wrongdoing to the general public.

As a result of the growing domestic and international tensions, British dailies began to report more critically on the situation in Kenya. In an editorial, *The Times* held that 'suppressing student protesters, while treating Western correspondents and American missionaries as subversive elements, will do nothing to [...] strengthen the President's position' (cited in ACR, Vol. XX, B 322). In April 1987, the Bishop of Nairobi (*Anglican Church of the Province of Kenya*, CPK), Rev. Alexander Muge,[15] told a congregation in Eldoret that 'human rights abuses in Kenya were worse than those in South Africa.' In May, the Catholic Bishops of Kenya openly joined the critical voices in the country. In a letter to the President they accused KANU of 'assuming a totalitarian role. [...] Officials of KANU were now unable to distinguish between constructive criticism and subversive conspiracy' (cited in ACR, Vol. XIX, B 328).

In July, the AI followed up on the Kuria affair and published the report *Kenya: Torture, Political Detention, and Unfair Trials* (Amnesty International 1987b). The Kenyan government immediately denied all allegations contained in the report. Moreover, the Assistant Minister

John Michuki demanded in parliament that AI should be brought before the ICJ because it allegedly financed a coup of London dissidents against the Kenyan government. Pressure by human rights groups continued throughout the rest of the year and peaked again in the fall when Moi planned to travel to a number of European countries. Contrary to his original plans, Moi only visited Finland and Romania, but decided to skip Sweden and Norway because of the negative press coverage prior to his visit (Baehr, Selbervik and Tostensen 1995: 69). In Finland, members of his delegation met with representatives from AI. Upon his arrival back to Nairobi, he called the press reports 'malicious and baseless' emanating from 'a few criminal fugitives.' He argued that South Africa was a much better target than Kenya for criticism from the Norwegian and Swedish press and that the existence of 150 foreign correspondents in Nairobi was a clear indication of peace and stability. He said this situation 'had probably made envious outsiders become hostile to Kenya' (FBIS-WEU-87-172, 4 September 1987, p. 8). In his Independence Day speech on 12 December 1987, Moi called AI a 'South-African agent,' promised to 'arrest all members of Amnesty International found in Kenya' and advised them 'to go to hell' (Amnesty International 1988: 86).

The strong denial of international criticism shows that the Kenyan government was acutely sensitive to the human rights issue. International norms and their supporters were not ignored, even as Western governments were still slow in taking the human rights information on Kenya seriously. Early on, government officials in Kenya took notice of the issue and consciously devised strategies to counteract human rights reports. In their reactions, government officials made explicit reference to the competing norm of state sovereignty. The emerging human rights discourse pitted mainly Western supporters of universal values against Moi, whose reaction was influenced not only by the international norm of non-intervention but also by domestic values he himself regarded as constitutive to his rule. Moi's interpretation of human rights criticism was strongly influenced by the struggle for national independence as well as cultural factors sustaining the patronage system. Moi's behavior was not limited to a narrow strategy guided by the desire to stay in power, but was driven by underlying values which came in direct conflict with the external values advocated by transnational activists.

Protecting domestic activists

While the international mobilization still had few effects on major donor governments, it protected individual members of the opposition and consistently challenged the Kenyan government and its allies on principled grounds. Occasionally, domestic dissent even became institutionalized, although government repression remained a constant threat. In September 1987, the first issue of the journal *Nairobi Law Monthly* was published, soon to be one of the most important and influential independent journals devoted to human rights and the administration of justice. Until 1991, the journal was banned several times and government lawyers kept charging its editor, the lawyer Gitobu Imanyara, with sedition (FBIS-AFR-90–147, 31 July 1990, p. 6). In the absence of independent societal organizations, individual lawyers and church officials from both Catholic and Protestant denominations remained the main human rights critics of the regime (Peters 1996: 20–23).

Despite the increasingly successful efforts of human rights groups to deconstruct Kenya's international image as a stable Western ally, domestic repression levels tended to increase for the time being. In late 1987, the University of Nairobi was again closed. One student leader, Robert Wafula Buke, was sentenced to five years in prison for allegedly 'spearheading a Libyan-backed plot that had led to the closure of the university' (ACR, Vol. XX, B 329). At the same time, the Office of the President increased its control over the judiciary. In October 1987, High Court Justice Derek Schofield resigned after the Chief Justice had removed him from a 'sensitive case.' After he left Kenya, Schofield exposed and harshly criticized the executive interference in judicial affairs (Schofield 1992).

Outside relations with Western governments now became more strained, but decisive steps were only taken by the Scandinavian nations. Norway and Sweden temporarily halted their bilateral aid in 1987. During state visits of West German Chancellor Kohl in November 1987 and British Prime Minister Margaret Thatcher in January 1988, the human rights issue was not raised. A British parliamentary delegation visiting the country in December 1987 also avoided any criticism and explicitly commended the state of the Kenyan political system. In January 1988, several visiting members of foreign NGOs, including the Lawyers Committee on Human Rights and the American Association for the Advancement of Science (AAAS) were temporarily detained in Nairobi. The government-critical journal *Beyond*, published by the NCCK was banned in March, because it had continued to criticize the abolishment of the secret ballot for KANU primary elections (Widner 1992b: 191). In the following months, several church officials and government representatives openly clashed on the issue of queue voting. The *Kenya Times* declared that Alexander Muge was not 'as you would like to be the country's answer to Archbishop Tutu' (ACR, Vol. XX, B 321).

At the height of his personal rule and after the general elections in early 1988, Moi removed the moderate Kikuyu Mwai Kibaki from the post of the Vice President and demoted him to the position of the Health Minister. Moi replaced Kibaki with another Kikuyu, Josephat Karanja, who had no substantial following in his own community. Only one month later, Karanja was also removed and replaced by George Saitoti. Robert Ouko returned to his post as Minister for Foreign Affairs. Such frequent reshuffles of the cabinet and the subsequent distribution of material benefits remained an important means to secure loyalties from local communities. After his reelection, Moi announced the release of 10 political prisoners. AI welcomed the releases, but demanded a thorough review of all sentences given to political dissidents still in prison. In August 1988, new amendments to the constitution removed tenure for all judges in Kenya,[16] while the period a suspect of a capital offence could be detained before being brought to a courtroom was extended from 24 hours to 14 days (25th amendment).

Moi continued his attacks on the independent media and claimed that his critics were 'disgruntled enemies with foreign masters.' In another interview he demanded that KANU should set up branches in every hotel, because this is 'where gossip is at its most open' (cited in ACR, Vol. XXI, B 317). He also claimed that the Kenyan laws 'had been inherited from Britain and, as such, were based on British traditions and customs.' Hence, 'our law is clear on the question of human rights, the dignity of men, and the sanctity of life. This was indeed the main objective of our struggle for independence.' However, the continued attacks also led to occasional rhetorical missteps such as admitting the use of torture on a visit in London in March 1989: 'Of course we torture people. But we don't torture everybody. We torture the ringleaders of *MwaKenya*; otherwise, how do we find out information from them?' (quoted in ACR, Vol. XXI, B 317).

Mounting pressure

Members of the human rights network answered the continued executive dominance by intensifying their transnational activities. The Robert F. Kennedy Memorial Center for Human Rights honored Gibson Kamau Kuria in March 1989 with its Human Rights Award during a ceremony held in Nairobi. The ceremony had to be moved from the Washington D.C. to Nairobi, because the Kenyan government refused to issue a passport to Kuria.[17] The Memorial Center delegation traveling to Kenya included the wife of the late Robert F. Kennedy and their daughter, whose request for a meeting with President Moi was accepted (*Nairobi Law Monthly* 1989). While Moi made no concessions in the meeting and denied the existence of human rights problems, the meeting at State House significantly contributed to the continued transnational mobilization. On the international level, the general awareness of the political situation in Kenya further increased, while on the domestic level, international norms and the extent of their respect remained an important political topic.

The day following the delegation's departure, Moi flatly rejected the ideas expressed by the visitors during the talks. 'A young person born not long ago, born after independence. She comes here, why? There are people in other parts of the world who are harassed, why don't they go there? They even say Kenya should not hold people for 14 days for interrogation. We do not keep ordinary people for 14 days; it is the troublemaker who wants to kill, who wants to overthrow the government. [...] People should respect us, so that we can respect them. *We are not children, to be told you have made a mistake here. You must do this, you must do that. We are no longer under colonialism. What we demand is equality, equality, and it is our right. It is not a demand, it is our right. We are equal with anyone, regardless.* The thing I want to tell you is respect yourself. When you meet a person do not open your mouth wide telling everything. Such a person will despise you' (FBIS-AFR-89-063, 4 April 1989, p. 8).

In June 1989, Moi announced a general amnesty during a public rally in Nakuru and declared that 'problems affecting Africa were subtle and only Africans could understand them better, but not foreigners' (FBIS-AFR-89-107, 7 June 1989, p. 6). Two weeks later he addressed a KANU delegates' conference at Nyayo Stadium on the issue of human rights. 'All the propaganda being spread about Kenya is completely baseless, because outsiders do not understand the Kenyan people. They do not know that Kenya is *number one in propaganda*. [...] Even this morning I received a strange letter from Amnesty International. It said: *I am very concerned about the fact that Mr Noah arap Too has been detained without charge [laughter] or trial under the republic security regulations of the Preservation of Public Security Act....* [Moi reads the whole letter in English]. Do you hear this filth? I do not know whether Too himself is here. The head of CID is here. And this comes from West Germany, the Amnesty International People. This shows that all those people with all their lies write filthy and non-existing stories. [...] When people are released from detention, they run to the BBC. Why don't they run to the NATION or the KENYA TIMES and tell them "the mistakes I saw are such and such". Instead you run to the BBC. Is the BBC mother? (applause). It is not mother. Is it not an imperialist? And if it is an imperialist, then it is the mother of an imperialist. You are afraid, but the settler was nothing but a settler. What I believe is equality (applause). If you believe you are *number two*, it is your own affair' (FBIS-AFR-89-116, 19 June 1989, pp. 4–5).

By mid-1989, the continuous efforts of the human rights groups to reframe the domestic and international image of the Kenyan government showed considerable effects. Targets of these efforts, such as other state actors and the general public in and outside of Kenya were increasingly willing to filter information coming from Kenya through the interpretative framework provided by transnational human rights organizations. However, until 1989 only the Scandinavian countries openly criticized the Kenyan government for its human rights violations. Denmark was the first country to commission a study on Kenya's past use of foreign aid and the possible effects of human rights abuses on the proper use of aid. Kenya lost its image of a relatively stable and reliable partner not as a result of the impending changes in Eastern Europe, but following the continued activities of non-governmental organizations since the mid-1980s.

Mobilization against the Kenyan government occurred now almost instantaneously whenever security organs were accused of committing human rights abuses. Moreover, the new interpretative framework provided by international human rights groups did not only cover the most apparent abuses, but even extended to cases where the responsibility remained initially unclear. Most prominently, in this respect, the violent deaths of Foreign Minister Robert Ouko in February 1990 and government-critical Bishop Alexander Muge in mid-August 1990 outraged the Kenyan public and many donors (*Nairobi Law Monthly* 1990). Although there was no immediate evidence that the government was directly involved in the deaths, dominant interpretations of the events focused almost exclusively on the alleged responsibility of government officials. The gap between the outside perceptions of Kenya and the Western-leaning self-image promoted by Kenyan government officials widened considerably.

Comparison

Transnational activists played a crucial role in disseminating information about systematic human rights abuses in Uganda and Kenya. Although the atrocities committed in Uganda were much more extensive than in Kenya, it took the transnational movement much longer to expose the responsibilities of the Amin dictatorship as well as the second Obote government. The three primary reasons for this difference are related to the level of domestic repression, the time gap of 10 years between the two cases of mobilization, and the relatively greater prominence of Nairobi and Kenya as a tourist destination and as a hub for international journalists and aid workers. Ironically, the Moi regime also became a preferred target for transnational mobilization because it was a staunch ally of the West. Transnational activism especially thrives on exposing significant gaps between a rhetoric of liberalism and authoritarian repression. A regime seeking to be part of the Western world was more likely to become an object of intense mobilization than a government consistently denying the validity of those norms.

Within a few years, human rights issues played a major role in the external relations of both countries. Transnational activists had changed the international image of both countries and undermined the legitimacy of the repressive regimes. Without the work of organizations such as the ICJ or AI, neither the UN nor the general Western public would have learned the full details of human rights abuses. In both cases, individuals and non-governmental groups successfully challenged a dominant norm of state sovereignty, which earlier dominated the perceptions of the international public and Western governments.

The effects of human rights mobilization in Kenya and Uganda differed considerably not only because of the variation in the kind of authoritarian rule but also because Uganda came into the international spotlight about 10 years earlier than Kenya. During the Amin era, non-governmental human rights reporting had little effect on the behavior of other states toward Uganda. Only shortly before Amin was violently removed from power, did the international community consider serious actions. The widely available information and considerable mobilization, however, did have effects on the Western public, UN experts, and individuals working in donor and foreign affairs offices.

While the mobilization failed to elicit adequate responses from the UNCHR and major donor governments, it profoundly changed the international discourse on Uganda. The Amin and Obote regimes were sustained by outside material aid, but they were simultaneously delegitimized by transnational human rights mobilization. Over a period of time, transnational activists succeeded in reframing international perceptions and interests and replaced a predominant respect for sovereignty with a concern for atrocities.

Following the establishment of human rights in the international discourse on Uganda, the period after 1980 witnessed the diffusion of this issue into the domestic realm. The main rebel leader, Yoweri Museveni, regularly traveled to Europe and met with the various government officials, media, and NGO representatives. The NRM's 10-point program was written during a retreat in Austria. By 1985, he was the only Ugandan leader recognized by non-governmental activists abroad. Museveni skillfully utilized the opportunities offered by such international support. Even without clear condemnation from UN human rights bodies and donors, the second Obote government quickly lost domestic and international credibility. Efforts by Obote to get outside support from the IMF and World Bank did nothing to change the international perception in favor of his critics.

In contrast to the Ugandan experience between 1974 and 1985, non-governmental human rights criticism with respect to Kenya diffused much faster and had more visible effects in a shorter period of time. It took the global human rights movement less than three years from 1984 to 1987 to completely change the global perceptions of domestic affairs in Kenya. When Daniel arap Moi visited the United States in 1987, the US State Department voiced deep concerns on human rights issues. The same year, Moi cancelled official visits to Norway and Sweden in the face of even more pronounced criticism mounted by transnational activists in Europe.

As a result of the transnational mobilization, domestic human rights activists enjoyed greater personal protection and opportunities to criticize the Kenyan government. Within a short period of time, they became internationally known representatives of the Kenyan human rights movement. The NCCK and the LSK became in the 1980s the main organizations for the expression of dissent. In contrast to other societal organizations, which were forced to become a part of KANU, these two groups had strong relations to the international arena and mobilized these connections to defend their domestic autonomy. This outside support supplemented an existing domestic base of support. Especially the ecumenical NCCK enjoyed more independence and domestic credibility than other church organizations, because it had not emerged out of missionary societies and was not co-opted by the post-independence political leadership.

Transnational mobilization on human rights issues in Kenya found several favorable conditions absent from the situation in neighboring Uganda. First, relative political stability insured that a reservoir of politically active and Western-trained intellectuals remained intact and contributed to the sharp increase of domestic mobilization. In contrast, Idi Amin's rule and the subsequent civil war destroyed the intellectual elite in Uganda and drove the remaining individuals into exile. Second, tourism and strategic Western interests kept Kenya on the international agenda. Charismatic exiles such as Koigi wa Wamwere found it relatively easy to find audiences in Europe and North America to spread their message of human rights abuses. The very fact that Kenya was always portrayed as a reliable Western ally and stable country created more interest in information contradicting the conventional wisdom. Finally, transnational human rights organizations were particularly interested in pointing their fingers at authoritarian regimes at the fringes of the Western alliance. Here, the tension between the rhetorical claim to be part of a liberal community of states and ongoing violations is particularly vivid and can be exposed more easily by outside activists. Being allied to the United States or its friends also helps transnational activists to create a natural link to the Western public opinion. This mechanism worked well for human rights organizations targeting authoritarian rulers in South America during the 1970s. In the 1980s, Kenya became another case fitting this logic.

5
Diverging Paths of Regime Change: Electoralist and Participatory Reforms

Transnational human rights groups reframed the international image of East African governments during the 1970s and 1980s. Uganda's Amin and Obote in his second term as well as Kenya's Moi after 1985 all faced significant principled international challenges to their domestic rule. The mobilization created, empowered, and protected domestic allies in support of human rights. Although responses by the UN and donor governments were slow and ineffective, the targeted governments did not simply ignore the challenge but were vulnerable to the published information and sought to counteract the efforts to de-legitimize their rule. This pressure played a crucial role in bringing about democratic reforms in both nations.

This chapter describes how the interaction between outside mobilization and domestic conditions produced unique patterns of regime change. While the Ugandan reform process was tightly controlled by the government and highlighted the expansion of popular and local participation in public affairs, the Kenyan path began with electoralist reforms establishing party competition on the national level. In Uganda, the NRM under the leadership of Yoweri Museveni took over power in early 1986, ending a civil war of six years. Museveni was the only Ugandan leader with significant international recognition and a proven record of human rights enforcement in areas the NRM had occupied prior to its march on Kampala. After 1986, human rights conditions as a prerequisite for meaningful democratic participation of the population improved in most but not all areas of the country. The external mobilization significantly declined and began to shift its focus on gross violations committed by rebel groups active in Northern and Western Uganda.

99

In Kenya, the external and domestic pressure further increased from 1989 to 1991. Outside pressures forced the government to make tactical concessions and loosen its control of the press and civil society. However, intimidation and harassment of the strengthening opposition continued well beyond initial reforms. In contrast to Uganda's complete turnover of power in 1986, the Moi government was not removed by a revolution from below, but was able to hold onto nominal power for another 10 years. In Kenya, allowing increased electoral contestation was accompanied by a refusal to complete constitutional reforms and deliberate efforts to restrict popular participation by potential opposition voters. The reverse strategy was used by the Ugandan government after 1986. The expansion of local participation and constitutional reforms were accompanied by severe restrictions on electoral contestation. In both cases, leaders secured their political survival by promoting only one aspect of expanded democratic governance, participation, or contestation.

Uganda, 1986–1992: Revolution from above

In his swearing-in address on 29 January 1986, the new President of Uganda, Yoweri Museveni, announced that 'no one should think what is happening today is a mere change of guard: it is a fundamental change in the politics of our country.' He continued with the first three points of the NRM program and declared, 'the people of Africa – the people of Uganda – are entitled to democratic government. [...] In our liberated zones, the first thing we started with was the election of village Resistance Committees. [...] Later we shall set up a national parliament directly elected by the people. This way we shall have both committee and parliamentary democracy. We don't want to elect people who will change sides once they are in parliament. If you want to change sides, you must go back and seek the mandate of the people who elected you. [...] Past regimes have used sectarianism to divide people along religious and tribal lines. [...] We want people to have different individualities, tribes, religions, but this must not be used in politics' (Museveni 1992: 21–23). With this program, the NRM focused on a participatory path of democratization, which focused primarily on constitutional reforms while limiting party competition.

On 1 February 1986, Yoweri Museveni appointed 21 members to the National Resistance Council (NRC), which would take over interim legislative functions. He also announced that elections planned for 1985 were postponed by four years. Political parties were not banned, but new laws restricted them from holding public gatherings and rallies. Instead, the NRM invited all Ugandans to participate in a broad-based and non-partisan government. In his inaugural speech, Museveni also emphasized the discipline of the NRA and the Code of Conduct now applicable to all national army units (Amnesty International 1989: 15). The code explicitly prohibited the killing of a civilian or prisoner, drinking of alcohol during service, and taking anything from civilians without cash payment. All political detainees at the infamous Luzira prison in the outskirts of Kampala were released by August 1986 and the government appointed new judges to the High Court. Several former members of the Obote and Amin regimes were arrested and charged with human rights violations. The new government also sent a clear message to the international community by acceding to the UN Convention against Torture and Other Cruel, Inhuman or Degrading Treatment or Punishment on 3 November 1986.

Museveni's double-edged strategy to create a broad-based government while excluding or punishing some of the worst human rights offenders of the previous regimes had a divisive effect on the political opposition. While some UPC, DP, and even original Amin supporters were integrated into the NRM, many prominent representatives of those regimes who refused to support the new government chose to go into exile. These individuals gradually regrouped in 1986/87 and formed either exile organizations in London or rebel groups, including the Uganda People's Democratic Movement/Army (UPDM/A, mainly Acholi), the Holy Spirit Movement (HSM, mainly Acholi), and the Ugandan Freedom Movement (UFM, mainly Baganda). Over time, only the rebel groups forming in the northern part of the country (Obote's home area) survived and were able to find some indigenous support against an allegedly southern- and Banyarwanda-dominated new government. All other rebel groups over time fell apart or joined the NRA after various offers of amnesty.

Political reconstruction

As the next step in breaking with the violent past, the NRM government created a 'truth commission,' which was charged with the investigation of the human rights abuses committed between 1962 and 1986. The commission was initially supposed to complete its work within two years, but the report was delayed and only published with additional donor money after almost eight years in 1994 (Republic of Uganda 1994). At the same time, an IGG was appointed and his office charged with investigating current cases of human rights abuses and corruption. The first NRM cabinet included the DP leader Paul Ssemogerere as Interior Minister and consisted of representatives from all major political bodies, including the NRM, DP, UPM, UPC, and CP. Immediate efforts of the Baganda to re-establish their kingdom failed and Museveni declared that kingdoms could only be reintroduced as cultural, not political, entities.

One of the first major political initiatives by the new government was a proposal to draft a new constitution. The NRM had begun to establish its form of grassroots democracy throughout the country and created about 40,000 RCs on the village, parish, sub-county, county, and district level (Tumusiime 1991: 15). The NRC was on top of this pyramid, although its members were not elected by representatives from lower levels of the council system. In 1987, the membership in the NRC was expanded to 96 members to also include district council representatives (RC V) and all government ministers.

The British government formally recognized the new regime and declared that its 'principal concern was to help Uganda establish security and to assist in its economic recovery' (cited in ACR, Vol. XVIII, B 481). Little more than a month earlier the same government had announced that its further aid to Uganda was dependent on strict adherence of all parties of the December 1985 Nairobi peace accord. The small British Military Training Unit continued its work. US–Ugandan relations also improved dramatically in early 1986. The US ambassador in Kampala commended 'the dramatic improvement in the security situation' (ACR, Vol. XVIII, B 481) and President Reagan claimed that Museveni had 'ended the terrible human rights abuses of an earlier era' (ACR, Vol. XIX, B 484). US aid to Uganda was restored.

The first Amnesty delegation to officially visit Uganda arrived in Kampala in April 1987. A member of the delegation, Richard Carver, declared that Amnesty commended the appointment of a truth commission. He went on to say that the current problems identified by Amnesty should be seen 'in the context of a massive qualitative improvement in the human rights situation [. . .].' The past patterns of mass killings by the army and of torture had ended. The delegation found no indication of 'widespread use of torture' but alerted the authorities to the fate of more than 1,000 detainees without trial, mainly soldiers of Obote's UNLA (*The Guardian*, 1 May 1987). Critics of the NRM government soon sought to use the transnational human rights mobilization for their own political purposes. On 15 April 1987, the government-owned *Kenya Times* published a summary of a 17-page report by the Ugandan Human Rights Activists, a group of mainly

Obote supporters. It claimed that 'human torturers in Uganda are said to have invented a host of other savage methods, quite a good deal have been tried by neo-fascists elsewhere in the world' (cited in ACR, Vol. XIX, B 474). Apparently, the article reflected more accurately the indignation of Kenya's President Daniel arap Moi over the failed peace talks and Museveni's military victory than the human rights situation in Uganda at that time. Relations with Kenya remained uneasy for the following years.

While the majority of the country experienced unprecedented peace and security after the NRM victory, the civil war retreated to the northern and northwestern part of the country. Gross human rights violations were committed by both sides and led to legitimate criticism of the military campaign conducted by the NRA (*The Independent*, 11 September 1987). The exile opposition sought to capitalize on the situation in the north and copied the earlier NRM strategy of involving transnational activists in the domestic battle for power. A document titled 'Memorandum to the International Community,' published on 9 October 1987, contained information about alleged atrocities committed by the NRA in 1986–87 (cited in ACR, Vol. XX, B 448). However, these attempts largely failed in raising international concern because organizations such as AI refused to accept information provided by former members of the Amin and Obote governments. In contrast to the early 1980s, the new Ugandan exile community in Great Britain and the United States was viewed as illegitimate and closely tied to the atrocities committed during the early 1970s and 1980s.

The international community maintained its positive attitude toward the NRM as Museveni attended his first Commonwealth Summit in October 1987 and was invited to the United States by President Ronald Reagan the same month. In his first speech in front of the UN General Assembly, Museveni declared in October that 'the Ugandan government under the NRM begins in the first place with an immutable commitment to guarantee human rights and the inviolability of human life' (cited in Amnesty International 1992a: 7). Although Museveni was now the president of a sovereign nation, he was keen on maintaining relations with the international media and the transnational non-governmental sector. During his first years as President he regularly met with international staff and editorial boards of the *Washington Post*, *Washington Times*, *USA Today*, and *Los Angeles Times*. Museveni also became popular by breaking taboos, exemplified in his refusal to blame external forces and colonialism for many of the economic failures since independence (Museveni 1992: 51). These efforts were not only rewarded with increasing economic and military aid programs by donors, but also with the goodwill of the transnational sector of media and non-state activists.

Resistance Council elections in 1989

The first nationwide elections since 1980 were held in February 1989. The proclaimed goal was to increase the membership of the NRC from 96 to 278.[1] Underlying this effort was a need to infuse the NRM government with new popular legitimacy as it approached the end of its self-proclaimed four-year interim period. The elections were held over a 30-day period and representatives were elected by queue voting and not secret ballot (Ddungu and Wabwire 1991: 14). In the first stage, all adults over the age of 18 elected the village council (RC I) with nine representatives. In turn, all village committees in a parish elected a parish committee (RC II). The same process applied to the next two levels, the sub-county and the county committees (RC III/IV). The top levels of the council system (RC V and the NRC) were directly elected by RC III representatives. Candidates for the NRC were not required to go through the entire RC election process but stood directly at the RC III level for office.

International observers agreed after the elections that the exercise was largely free and fair, although political party activities remained prohibited. While the UPC leadership had called for a boycott, other UPC members joined DP officials and advocated a strategy of subverting the NRM from within (Ddungu and Wabwire 1991: 28). In the end, a number of former UPC ministers of the Obote regime and many DP leaders were elected to the NRC, but NRM candidates took an overwhelming majority of the elected offices. The elections showed that the political parties maintained control of many of their former strongholds, where party allegiance remained relatively stable. Ten incumbent Cabinet and four deputy ministers lost their positions because they were beaten by other candidates in their respective constituencies (Kasfir 1991: 261).

The elections represented a step toward democracy by turning the majority of the national parliament from non-elective ministers and veterans of the civil war period to a majority of elected officials. However, there were no provisions as to what the relationship between the NRC and lower levels of the RC system should be or how grassroots input on the national level could be extended beyond election day. While the NRM consolidated its domestic control and the NRC became a genuine national parliament, the grassroots level became less significant for decision-making on the national level.

The 1989 elections represented a skilled effort of the Ugandan government to slowly liberalize the political system from a position of strength. On the one hand, these were the first relatively free and fair elections in the country's history. Even the ban on party activities had, at least, one democratizing effect: 'In practice the ban on campaigning succeeded in greatly reducing the opportunity for politicians to corrupt voters' (Kasfir 1991: 268). On the other hand, the elections were not about the NRM, the presidency, or the policies on the national level. The question remained unanswered whether the local RCs should serve as checks against government representatives or should be viewed as extensions of that same government to the local level.[2] Over the next years, it became clear that the NRM had little interest in empowering the local councils against the national government.

In March 1989, the NRM finally embarked on the promised constitutional reform and appointed a 21-member Constitutional Commission under the leadership of Judge Odoki (Waliggo 1995). At the early stages, there was considerable confusion within the NRM government as to how the process of constitutional reform should actually proceed. The commission's mandate included the presentation of a draft constitution after having collected views of the ordinary citizens and stimulated 'public discussion and awareness of constitutional issues.' A majority of its members were NRM-friendly, but a number of critics and independents were also appointed to the commission. There were no provisions as to how the new constitution would ultimately be promulgated, and 'the appointing authorities, the Minister for Constitutional Affairs and the President, were not in *una voce* on this matter' (Furley and Katalikawe 1997: 247). The commission did not commence its work until late 1990.

Extending NRM rule

In July 1989, AI criticized continued human rights problems in its first comprehensive report since the NRM took power in 1986. *Uganda: The Human Rights Record: 1986–1989* opened a series of four human rights reports on Uganda which came out annually until 1992. The main targets were the armed forces and violations connected to operations in the northern insurgency areas. In reaction to the first report, Museveni pledged to investigate the individual allegations and convened a four-day NRA Council meeting in September. During that occasion he reiterated the government's commitment to human rights and pointed out that several dozen NRA soldiers were in detention because of human rights abuses. While the transnational human rights movement began to voice some concern over the ongoing violence in insurgency areas, the 1989 elections had provided enough legitimacy for Museveni to extend his mandate for another five years.

In late September 1989, the NRM government tabled a motion designed to extend its own term of office until 25 January 1995. The Attorney General justified the motion on the grounds of several achievements of the NRM rule since 1986. These included (1) economic growth, (2) the building of a democratic mass movement, (3) the restoration of Uganda's respectability abroad, (4) the re-establishment of the rule of law, human rights and peace in almost all parts of the country, (5) and the rebuilding of an ethnically diverse national army. He noted that some of those achievements were still incomplete and required an extension of the interim NRM rule and a continuation of the broad-based national government. Most importantly, the extension would be used (1) to complete infrastructure rehabilitation programs, (2) the constitution-making process, (3) and to stop the violence in the insurgency areas.[3]

On 10 October 1989, the NRC voted unanimously in favor of the extension of the NRM mandate. Only one NRC member, Wasswa Ziritwawula (DP), resigned in protest. The relationship between the movement and political parties remained unclear and grew increasingly tense. While NRM leaders relied on the alleged sectarianism of party politics as a defense for their non-partisan approach, they faced increasing domestic criticism for repressing the basic human rights of freedom of expression and the right to assembly. As long as moderate critics of the NRM policies were willing to accept the conditions set out by the government, the political opposition remained split. At the same time, there was little outside support for the political opposition which was seen as tainted by years of civil war and tyranny. Museveni's public relations efforts abroad succeeded in winning much praise for his rebuilding efforts and in particular for the first visible results of his government's aggressive HIV/AIDS campaigns (Kirby 2004).

The constitutional reform process

After the 1989 elections and the extension of its rule until 1995, the NRM government was challenged to fulfill its many promises and focused on the three main issues of (1) constitutional reform, (2) peace in the northern part of the country, and (3) rehabilitation of the infrastructure. Shortly before the Odoki Commission began its work, the NRA embarked on a major military effort to end the rebellion in the north. During the campaign, the army forced several thousand civilians out of their villages into guarded camps and held them as the so-called 'lodgers' (ACR, Vol. XXIII, B 407). Officially, the NRA declared that these measures were taken to protect the population from rebel attacks and abductions. Critics argued that these camps deprived civilians of their basic rights. In December, AI published *Uganda: Death in the Countryside: Killings of Civilians by the Army in 1990* (Amnesty International 1990b).

The military campaign in the north contrasted with the deliberations on a new constitution which some observers called 'an integral part of nation-building and a means of establishing common values' (Apter 1995: 171). In the early stages, the Ugandan process of drafting a new constitution was relatively inclusive and broad-based. In late 1990 and throughout 1991, the Odoki Commission traveled around the country, held dozens of seminars, and collected a total of over 25,000 written suggestions for the reform of the constitution. 'Never before has constitution-making been so central and taken so long in the politics of an African nation. Never before have the Ugandan people been so actively involved at every level and placed so much hope for stability and democratization in the constitutional process' (Waliggo 1995: 22). This exercise reaffirmed the NRM's focus extending participation on the local level and providing opportunities for every Ugandan to voice his or her opinions, even if only in a small village forum.

Even though the human rights situation in northern Uganda remained problematic and transnational activists accused the Ugandan army of widespread abuses, Museveni remained popular with the donor community and a majority of Ugandans at home. He meticulously fulfilled economic conditionalities attached to the aid programs, including the privatization of parastatals, the return of property to the Asian community, and the reduction of government spending. In return, the donor community increased aid flows to unprecedented levels, covering more than 60 percent of the government budget in the early 1990s. The total aid committed by the Uganda Consultative Group rose from $550 Mio. in 1988 to $640 Mio. in 1989, and reached more than $800 Mio. annually in the early 1990s. As the political situation in neighboring Kenya was becoming increasingly unstable and donors turned away from President Daniel arap Moi, Museveni was touted as the 'new breed of African leaders' bringing peace and stability to the region and defending Western strategic interests threatened by chaos and an Islamist regime in Sudan.

Continued insurgencies

The failure of the NRA/M to end the insurgency in the northern part of the country with amnesties or violence created a stalemate between increasingly isolated rebel groups and a Ugandan government accused of neglecting the affected population. In the early 1990s, a rebel group called the *Holy Spirit Movement*, led by a self-proclaimed mystic Alice Lakwena (Behrend 1993), emerged as the most visible rebel group in the north. Her successor Joseph Kony turned the rebel group into the LRA and began to invade Ugandan villages from Sudanese territory. While the Ugandan government supported the south-Sudanese rebel group Sudanese People's Liberation Army (SPLA) under the leadership of John Garang, the Islamist regime in Khartoum retaliated by tolerating and supporting the LRA. When indigenous support for the rebels in the northern part of Uganda waned, Kony shifted his strategy away from battlefield action to mass abductions of children, rapes, and killings of innocent civilians (ACR, Vol. XXII, B 375).

When the NRM government detained 18 politicians from northern Uganda and was in the middle of another military campaign against rebels, AI published *Uganda: Human Rights Violations by the National Resistance Army* (Amnesty International 1991) on 4 December 1991. Two weeks later, the Ugandan Minister of Justice claimed that all individual abuses of human rights would be harshly punished and denied that the government sanctioned any of the alleged abuses. In 1991, the government also invited representatives of the International Committee of the Red Cross (ICRC) to visit a total of 23 Ugandan prisons, 26 police stations, and 31 NRA barracks. However, military operations in the rebel areas were off limits for any external observers. Transnational NGO representatives as well as donor governments played a significant role in improving human rights conditions in Uganda by working directly with government officials on issues such as prison reform or the rebuilding of the judiciary.[4] A leading official of the Ugandan Department of Prisons pointed out in an interview that information provided by the ICRC and other NGOs supported his case for increasing his domestic budget.

While the cooperation between the Ugandan government and donors as well as some transnational NGOs had some positive domestic effects on human rights conditions (except for the north), it also revealed a major weakness of such a strategy. Unlike Kenya, the domestic civil society in Uganda was decimated by war and tyranny and not yet emerged as a strong player in balancing the power of an increasingly assertive NRM government. While the government had put in place institutions nominally designed to defend human rights and donors largely paid for their upkeep, those organizations were careful to not challenge the NRM and its monopoly in the domestic realm. When the Deputy IGG Waswa Lule raised in early 1992 concerns about the inability of his organization to fulfill its human rights mandate (Oloka-Onyango 1993), there was insufficient support for his views within civil society and the general public. On 18 August 1992, Lule was removed from his post by NRM hardliners, while donors viewed the issue as not important enough to press Museveni into an intervention on the matter.

In September 1992, AI followed up on its previous publications and released *Uganda: The Failure to Safeguard Human Rights* (Amnesty International 1992b). The Ugandan government called the report 'politically biased and outdated.' Even though it was true that some of the issues raised in the report had diminished in significance due to decreasing rebel activities in the north, the fear that institutional safeguards for human rights in Uganda were still insufficiently developed had been vindicated by the recent events and the Lule affair. Amnesty International took the information collected during the last three years to the UN where the UNCHR decided to investigate the Ugandan situation under the confidential 1503 procedure. For the first time, the NRM government had to officially justify alleged human rights violations in front of the international community.

This was certainly enough to raise alarm in the president's office. In direct response to the imminent threat of international pillorying, in late October 1992, Museveni ordered by presidential decree the establishment of a Human Rights Desk in the Ministry of Justice. As another result of the human rights criticism, the Ugandan government also temporarily changed its hard-line position toward the LRA. The Minister for the North, Betty Bigombe, was authorized to hold secret negotiations with Joseph Kony in order to find a peaceful solution to the conflict.[5] While the security situation improved temporarily and the international attention decreased, the negotiations ultimately failed and did not resolve the underlying differences.

As the Ugandan government felt increasing pressure to complete its mandate, it agreed to the demobilization of its army personnel as one of the major donor concerns of the early 1990s (ACR, Vol. XXIII, B 406). Donor governments covered most of the costs of the demobilization of about 40,000 to 50,000 soldiers. Although critics of the NRM rightly argued that 'Uganda's political grammar [...] has remained essentially the same: soldiers and not civilians form the backbone of those in power' (see also Ddungu and Wabwire 1991: 38–41; Omara-Otunnu 1992: 460), the crucial change occurred within this military regime. While many human rights problems after 1986 were still caused by the armed forces, the political reforms promoted by the NRM slowly but surely changed civil–military relations in Uganda.

In 1991/92, a *de facto* truce as a result of ongoing negotiations had greatly improved the security situation in the north. Amnesty International discontinued its campaign against the NRA, and from 1993 to 1998 published only smaller reports or press releases on Uganda.[6] But this success of the NRM government also became one of its long-term liabilities and undermined the rationale for sustaining a non-partisan regime in violation of basic freedoms and liberties. 'The capacity of the state to restore security destroyed its principal reason for sustaining the essentially soft authoritarian pact with all political parties: the further he moved the country from the civil wars of past decades, the greater the support for the resumption of multipartyism' (Khadiagala 1995: 40). Although the political opposition remained weak, the gaps between rhetoric and reality now offered more numerous opportunities to challenge the all-dominant movement system.

While the NRM started out with an alternative model of democracy and rejected representational systems, the establishment of the NRC and the increasingly ambiguous role of the RC system as a whole indicated a failure of the grassroots model of democratization. As the NRM asserted national control and abandoned its intellectual heritage, it provided its critics with new ammunition demanding a more competitive electoral environment on the national level. The success of the non-partisan strategy undermined its long-term sustainability, and domestic critics of the movement system became increasingly outspoken during the 1990s.

Facing those challenges, Museveni himself resorted to modernization arguments holding that 'some in Africa think if we have multi-party politics we will have prosperity. This is putting the cart before the horse. If we are going to follow Europe's lead, then let us first eliminate the peasants, industrialize and achieve the same level of skilled manpower before embarking on multiparty politics. That is what Europe had to do, why should we be any different?' (cited in Khadiagala 1995: 40). Certainly, Museveni concurred with neighboring Daniel arap Moi on the issue of multipartyism. But while donors forced Moi to re-introduce multipartyism in 1991, no such pressure was put on Museveni. This marked difference can only be explained with reference to the transnational human rights activism and the subsequent de- and re-construction of state images on the international level. As a former progressive activist and ally of the transnational human rights movement, Museveni skillfully cultivated his international image after becoming President of

Uganda. By doing little to encourage the emergence of a critical civil society and political opposition, Museveni left donors with little choice but supporting the NRM and its reform path.

Kenya, 1989–1991: Imposing multipartyism

During 1989/90, the NGO-led reconstruction of the foreign and domestic image of Kenya was completed. This had two major consequences. First, the domestic playing field became increasingly inseparable from the international arena. Domestic and international mobilization reinforced each other in critical ways. Although the rhetoric of Kenyan government officials toward human rights critics was still outright hostile, the government had to accept a significant increase in societal autonomy and resorted to tactical concessions in order to tame the mounting pressure. A whole array of new NGOs sprung up and began to reclaim political space, while the press also became more outspoken in criticizing government officials and supporting the political opposition. Hardliners within KANU resented the growing power of the opposition and revived ideas of ethnic segregation (*majimbo*) while plotting to instigate 'ethnic violence' as a pretext for a return to more repression (Kirschke 2000; Kuria 1994).

Second, diplomatic relations with many Western governments worsened considerably. Within the previously quiet and supportive international donor community voices critical of the Kenyan government's human rights record increased significantly in number and strength. Cracks within the heretofore relatively closed ranks of donor countries emerged as individual countries and their representatives in charge adjusted their images of Kenya at different speeds. During the two years from 1989 until 1991, individual ambassadors and NGO activists played crucial roles in shaping the political future of Kenya.

In October 1989, the conservative US Republican and former journalist Smith Hempstone arrived as the new US Ambassador to Kenya. He was a political appointee and thus less likely to follow the beaten (and rather quiet) path of a life as a career diplomat. During the next four years, he became an outspoken supporter of democratic change who was frequently joined by his German counterpart Berndt Mützelburg (appointed as ambassador in 1991). For Hempstone this meant constant personal attacks by Kenyan government newspapers and KANU officials for allegedly defying the norm of diplomatic neutrality. Initially, he also found little support within the U.S. Department of State for frequently going beyond a rhetorical support for democracy.

The fall of communist regimes in Eastern Europe reinforced the efforts of the international and domestic human rights activists to reconstruct the image of the Kenyan government. While Moi declared early on that the conditions in Africa were vastly different from Eastern Europe, his new image as an unrelenting authoritarian leader increasingly became a liability. From late 1989 onwards, street demonstrations against the regime became more frequent and better organized.[7] Immediately after the fall of the Berlin Wall, an unprecedented 3,000 Kenyan students held a demonstration for democracy in Nairobi. Other major and increasingly violent demonstrations with approximately 10,000 participants followed in February 1990 and around *Saba Saba*[8] in July.

The murder of Foreign Minister Robert Ouko

At the end of 1989, Moi planned another official state visit to the United States in order to secure further financial support for his regime. The White House and the State Department rebuffed this request and Moi was forced to declare his visit a private affair. Nonetheless, Moi traveled with his usual large entourage, including his Foreign Minister Robert Ouko. The US government had made clear for some time that current circumstances in Kenya made it impossible to welcome Kenyan government officials in good faith. 'Following his dressing down in Washington, Moi had returned to the Kenyan High Commission in London in a fury, refusing to have anything to do with Ouko, whom he blamed for the fiasco' (Throup and Hornsby 1997: 59). The Foreign Minister and staunch supporter of Moi, Robert Ouko, was the only exception to that position and rumors in Nairobi had it that the US government favored him as a possible successor of the current president. Ouko had distinguished himself with a relatively moderate position within the Kenyan government and had just begun to confront some of his Cabinet colleagues on the issue of corruption.

Upon return to Nairobi, Moi declared that he 'has received a proper hearing and our relationship with the United States Government has now improved.' However, the rest of the speech and the manner in which Moi repeatedly stopped short of certain remarks indicated that the results of the visit probably did not meet his expectations. '*You know some people take me for granted sometimes because I am a peaceful man.* I have no need to quarrel with anyone. But all this... [changes thought] if only people were patriots, who did whatever they were doing with the purpose of building their country. [...] All these bad things we hear about in this country are spread by those who have made it. Those experiencing hardship and who do not even know where their next meal will come from are not the type of people who incite and bring about chaos. It is the rich ones who board planes and spread rumors to ruin the country. [applause]' (FBIS-AFR-90–026, 7 February 1990, p. 7, emphasis added). Two weeks after the speech, the Foreign Minister Ouko was found murdered not far from his home. Immediately, rumors developed that Ouko was executed because he became a threat to some of his Cabinet colleagues and even to the President himself.[9] In the aftermath, members of Ouko's ethnic group (the Luo) rioted for several days. The unresolved murder of Ouko further alienated donors abroad as well as the Luo community, which had been divided in its support for the Moi government.

The challenge to one-party rule

Despite the increasingly desperate situation of the government, its security officials continued to arrest and harass opposition figures, close newspapers, and thus provoke continuous violence on the streets. Encouraged by the global demise of authoritarianism, the opposition answered the repression with growing defiance. On 3 May, the former Cabinet Ministers Charles Rubia and Kenneth Matiba publicly demanded the end of single-party rule in Kenya (Throup and Hornsby 1997: 61). Prior to their press conference they 'had been carefully coached by Paul Muite and Gibson Kamau Kuria on precisely how far they could go' (Throup and Hornsby 1997: 64). The political opposition tried to take advantage of the global changes and had selected two reputable former ministers to start its campaign for multipartyism. The US ambassador Smith Hempstone had addressed earlier that day the Rotary Club in Nairobi and reminded the audience that 'a strong political tide is flowing in our Congress [...] to concentrate our economic assistance on those of the world's nations that nourish democratic institutions, defend human rights, and practice multiparty politics' (Hempstone 1997: 91).

The Kenyan government subsequently alleged that there was a previous collusion between Hempstone and the political opposition. In his reaction to the mounting political challenges, President Moi denounced Matiba and Rubia as traitors who were paid by foreign sources. Hempstone maintained that the whole affair was a mere coincidence. Two weeks later the US Assistant Secretary of State for African Affairs, Herman J. Cohen, clarified in a Nairobi meeting with Moi that the US government was not making multipartyism a condition for aid as of now. He also refused to meet opposition leaders and left the impression that Hempstone was isolated within his own government (Clough 1992: 100). 'From then on it was the Kenyan government's position that relations between the United States and Kenya were fine [. . .], but Hempstone was a maverick acting on his own' (Hempstone 1997: 95).

The opening created by the Rubia/Matiba press conference led to intensified domestic mobilization for democratic change. On 4 July, the Kenyan police detained Matiba, Rubia, and others who were then adopted by AI as prisoners of conscience (Amnesty International 1990a). Gibson Kamau Kuria took refuge at the US embassy and asked for political asylum. Subsequent street demonstrations in Nairobi and provincial centers culminated on 7 July 1990 when at least 29 civilians were killed during *Saba Saba*. The international response came almost instantaneously. The International Bar Association (IBA) canceled its biannual meeting with more than 3,000 participants to be held in Nairobi in September (Muthoga 1990), citing the general insecurity in the country. Bringing the IBA conference to Nairobi would have been a major success for the Kenyan government in regaining some of its international reputation. Now, the opposite was the case: The cancellation reaffirmed outside perceptions about a serious domestic crisis.

President Moi remained unimpressed by the political developments. On 30 July 1990, Moi declared during a speech in Meru that 'the only thing you hear from Voice of America and BBC are ugly things intended to stir up discord. They say there is war in Kenya. Is there war here in Meru? [Response: No] They say there is war in Meru and elsewhere but we don't have disturbances here or anywhere else. If you Kenyans do not listen well and understand what people are saying, you could be misled by unfair reports. [. . .] If the citizens do what I have told them to do, no one will be deprived of his rights. If a certain law is not observed it is not my fault or the government's fault' (FBIS-AFR-90–147, 31 July 1990, p. 3). On the same day, 34 Kenyan diplomats from Kenyan embassies abroad met in Mombasa to discuss ways of improving the international image of Kenya. Foreign Minister Ayah claimed that efforts to defend Kenya internationally needed to be increased or otherwise it is left to 'foreigners to create views about Kenya' (FBIS-AFR-90–147, 31 July 1991, p. 5).

On 25 August 1990, Moi, upon returning from a state visit to Botswana, attacked human rights activists. 'Many people are using the concept of human rights as their hiding place. They think that if they do evil things, the human rights organizations will cover them.

[laughter] I will get hold of you. Even if you find sanctuary in the human rights organizations, I will drag you out because if you breach Kenyan law you cannot expect to be protected by Amnesty International [applause]. The Kenyan government will never do anything which is contrary to the country's constitutional laws. [...] If you decide to hide yourself in such a place, we will allow them [Moi apparently refers here to foreign donors, HPS] to feed you but we will wait for you here at the airport and all the borders will be closed for you until you get tired and come out' (FBIS-AFR-90–166, 27 August 1990, p. 8). The Kenyan executive came increasingly to the opinion that the 'bid for democracy [was] a movement under the control of the rival Kikuyu ethnic group' (Widner 1992a: 216).

Diplomatic crises and tactical concessions

In October 1990, the Norwegian ambassador Niels Dahl, along with other international observers, attended another trial against Koigi wa Wamwere, after wa Wamwere had been allegedly abducted from Uganda by Kenyan security forces (Saulnier 1997: 30). On Kenyatta Day (20 October), Moi complained that Norway had protested that 'we arrested a criminal (Koigi wa Wamwere), . . . I suppose what he has been planning was at the behest of the Norwegian government. We are not a colony of anyone, let them know that.' In other speeches during 1990, Moi claimed that 'Marxists' were 'plotting armed insurrection' (cited in ACR, Vol. XXII, B 285).

Consequently, Moi interpreted the actions of the Norwegian ambassador as another act of foreign intrusion. Over the next weekend, the inner circle of Moi's personal advisers decided to severe diplomatic relations with Norway without involving the Foreign Ministry or other concerned government agencies (Baehr, Selbervik and Tostensen 1995: 69). The decision was announced on 22 October. In turn, the Norwegian government ended all aid programs. Attempts by the Kenyan foreign ministry to downplay the issue and rescue the aid programs failed.[10]

The outside relationships of the Kenyan government were now openly strained as representatives from Western donor countries reacted to the diplomatic standoff between Kenya and Norway. In October 1990, for the first time, the US Congress attached human rights issues to foreign-aid appropriations for Kenya.[11] Within five years the transnational network had successfully completed its task of 're-mapping' (Brysk 1993: 268) Western perceptions of Kenya. At this point, opposition figures like Gitobu Imanyara or Gibson Kamau Kuria were regularly invited to London, New York, and Washington D.C. by international human rights organizations and met with journalists, members of Congress, and government officials (Human Rights Watch 1991: 43). The global discourse now associated the country with issues like corruption, torture, and insecurity instead of stability and economic development. While the donors were inconsistent in their public pronunciations and altered between the 'stick' of threatening aid cuts and the 'carrot' of releasing partial aid, the human rights issue began to rival their competing strategic and economic considerations.

Apart from the growing international policy relevance of the transnational human rights mobilization and the increase in societal autonomy, the crucial period between the end of 1989 and 1991 was also marked by significant governmental concessions. One of measures taken by Moi to quiet international criticism was the replacement of Attorney General Matthew Greg Muli. On 22 March 1991, Hempstone asked Muli for an appointment to discuss the recently released US State Department Report on the Kenyan human rights situation and an Amnesty report. He complained to Muli about the prison conditions of recently detained opposition activists and the allegedly restricted access for visitors. Specifically, Hempstone demanded a list of prison visits to the three most prominent detainees (Charles Rubia, Kenneth Matiba, and Oginga Odinga) for the last nine months. Muli promised improvements and provided the US embassy with the requested information, but generally held that 'all nations at one time or another in their history employed detention without trial' (Hempstone 1997: 163).

These developments only reinforced Moi's almost paranoid perceptions of his domestic and international environment at that time. When the opposition continued to pressure for change, he proved to be uncompromising. 'Frequently, we hear that Kenya is a bad country. I can only say that Europeans are fools. When a lone African cries, they say he is being oppressed. They do not know the secrets of an African. There are others who go abroad and *demonstrate how people can be tortured* using the television in those countries, and then take it to Europe claiming that Kenyans are being tortured. So they see people being tortured; however that is not happening here. It is portrayed as such to cause chaos in Kenya. [...] No one should shield himself behind human rights. All that is said is being fabricated outside of Kenya through television everywhere and then sent to Europe, America, and elsewhere under the pretext that this is what is happening in Kenya, while it is concocted outside Kenya by others, not even by Kenyans' (FBIS-AFR-91–087, 6 May 1991, p. 4). Moi was intensely aware of the transnational human rights mobilization and how it had become a major liability for his domestic control and aided a political opposition with principled as well as more narrow political objectives.

The end of one-party rule

Considering these frequent rhetorical attacks, the tactical concessions offered by the Kenyan government now failed to make a lasting impression on the donors and other international and domestic observers. To the contrary, the human rights movement countered these efforts by publishing the first comprehensive human rights report on Kenya (Africa Watch/Human Rights Watch 1991). On 30 July 1991, Africa Watch presented 432 pages in 22 chapters (including appendices) detailing accounts of human rights abuses committed by security agencies during the 1980s, discussing some of the background conditions and criticizing the official British and US attitudes toward the country.

The report included extensive documentation concerning the murder of Foreign Minister Robert Ouko and the regular use of sedition laws, detention without trial, and torture to suppress public dissent. It also criticized the lack of judicial independence, horrendous prison conditions, open discrimination of ethnic Somalis in the northern part of the country, and increasing police brutality. While the report contained little new information, it successfully re-emphasized that the human rights violations in Kenya were the result of systematic and intentional government policy rather than isolated acts of individuals. Hence, the report did not solely alert people to new facts; it also brought together the available information and thus supported the case for an actual policy change on the part of the donor governments.

This move was again paralleled by reinvigorated domestic mobilization. On 2 August 1991, the opposition created a broad coalition called the Forum for the Restoration of Democracy (FORD), which was 'inspired by Civil Forum in East Germany and Czechoslovakia' (Throup 1993: 390). The opposition was now strong enough to bypass the government's ban on political parties and represented a loose coalition of clergy, radical lawyers, and individual dissidents. While the NCCK and the LSK had been the main institutional bodies backing opposition dissent during the 1980s, the formation of FORD was a breakthrough in establishing a direct challenge to KANU and Moi. Initially formed as a pressure group, FORD's leadership was an ethnically broad coalition, which included Oginga Odinga (Luo), Martin Shikuku (Luhya), Masinde Muliro (Luhya), Philip Gachoka (Kikuyu), George Nthenge (Kamba), and the Muslim Ahmed Salim Bahmariz from the Coast region. Many of the 'human rights celebrities' such as the former LSK chairman, Paul Muite, and the editor of the *Nairobi Law Monthly*, Gitobu Imanyara, also joined FORD.

The formation of FORD was simultaneously inspired by the fall of Communism in Eastern Europe and Kenya's independence history. In contrast to prior unsuccessful attempts of institutionalizing political opposition, FORD mobilized both international support and also revived the historic Kikuyu–Luo alliance. 'The FORD of 1990 echoed the KANU coalition of the 1960s, not only in its leadership but also in its middle class and urban base and its successful mobilization of rural support from its "ethnic areas." FORD opposed a KANU that resembled the 1960 KADU coalition of minority groups led by largely middle- and upper class leaders whose base remained rural and who were unable to attract an urban following' (Ndegwa 1997: 609). However, in contrast to KANU in the 1960s, FORD was merely an opposition movement that lacked the resources to secure internal cohesion. Already shortly after its formation, internal conflicts about the future role of FORD and the leadership emerged. While one section of FORD advocated the transformation of the movement into a political party a second group wanted to keep FORD as a united opposition movement to press for reforms.

The government and its 'new' KANU (former KADU) coalition reacted to the challenge with a revival of the *Majimbo*-agenda, which had already been part of KADU's political program in the early 1960s. They demanded greater local autonomy and the re-introduction of federal provisions in order to protect the smaller tribes from the dominance of a coalition of the larger Kikuyu and Luo groups.

Essentially, *majimbo* would institutionalize the idea of a 'one-tribe party' and divide Kenya in autonomous regions. In September and October 1991, the minority coalition supporting the current government held five mass rallies in Kalenjin and Maasai areas (Ndegwa 1997: 609–610). During one of those rallies, one of the prominent KANU hawks, Minister for Local Government and Maasai William ole Ntimama, warned the Kikuyus that they would be 'cut down to the size like the Ibo' of Nigeria during the Biafra war.[12] Nicholas Biwott claimed that FORD members would be 'crushed' by KANU youth-wingers.

The main organizers of the rallies called for a *majimbo* system as an alternative to political pluralism and threatened to push for such constitutional changes if multiparty activists would persist in their crusade. The meetings usually openly advocated 'ethnic cleansing' and held that under a new constitution 'outsiders in the Rift Valley would be required to go back to their "motherland"' (Republic of Kenya 1992: 9). Other resolutions included a ban on opposition politicians from entering the area. On 29 October, this counter-mobilization turned violent when the first instance of 'ethnic cleansing' was reported from Nandi District in the Rift Valley. In the next months, the number of violent incidents in border regions between different ethnic groups increased dramatically and hundreds of Kenyans were killed.[13] Beyond the intimidation of suspected opposition voters, the ethnic violence also aimed at closing the ranks of the fragile KANU coalition.[14]

By late 1991, the Moi government had lost control over domestic affairs and even had problems keeping its own ranks closed. The consistent use of violence in dealing with the opposition only strengthened the latter, although it was divided from the start. In early November 1991, Smith Hempstone brokered talks between the Kenyan government and the opposition in order to avoid further confrontation. However, the talks finally broke down on 14 November, and Kenyan security officials arrested several members of the opposition the following night. The next day, the opposition called for street demonstrations against the government. Mützelburg and Hempstone lodged their protests during a meeting with the Permanent Secretary of the Foreign Ministry Bethuel Kiplagat. When the demonstrations turned violent again, the group of the most critical ambassadors (Canada, Denmark, Germany, Finland, Sweden, and the United States) was summoned to the Foreign Ministry on 18 November. They were accused of organizing the demonstrations and of interfering in the internal affairs of the country. Hempstone was personally accused by the minister Ayah of being a 'racist' and 'trying to overthrow the Kenyan government' (Hempstone 1997: 252). The German foreign ministry recalled Mützelburg for consultations and instructed him to issue 'the strongest of protests in the Foreign Ministry in Nairobi' on the human rights situation in the country (FBIS-WEU-91–222, 18 November 1991, p. 17).

In a rare moment of unity, the international community reacted to this crisis on 26 November 1991 by temporarily suspending donor aid. After the joint declaration on democratic governance at the Harare Commonwealth summit in October 1991, even Great Britain finally joined the critical voices, although its High Commissioner Tomkys still refused to carry out the new directives.[15] Prior to the donor decision, last minute efforts by the Kenyan government to avert the crisis failed. Moi even ordered the arrest of his closest aide, Nicholas Biwott, who was accused of being involved in the Ouko murder.[16] These efforts could not make up for the continuous and successful reconstruction of Kenya's international image by non-governmental human rights groups. 'Kenya, the long-time favorite of the West, was being treated as one of Africa's pariah regimes' (Throup and Hornsby 1997: 84).

Shortly after the donor decision, the Kenyan government through its Foreign Ministry published an 85-page response to the July Africa Watch report titled 'Nailing Lies' (Republic of Kenya 1991). Most of the 13 sections directly addressed issues raised in the Africa Watch report. The defense also made reference to criticism contained in British media reports and recently expressed by some of the now internationally well-known Kenyan lawyers. It gave a lengthy (and, at the point of publication, outdated) justification of 'single-party democracy' and argued 'Kenya's situation is entirely different from those African countries now apparently turning to multi-partyism' (Republic of Kenya 1991: 13). The report reaffirmed Kenya's 'commitment to the cause of human rights' and claimed that 'as Kenya's political system evolves, so greater attention is being paid to the rights and freedoms of individuals' (p. 5). In the following sections, the authors cited the full respect for press freedom as a major democratic accomplishment in Kenya. They rejected accusations that the judiciary was not independent, torture was rampant, and refugees were mistreated.

Four days after the donor decision, on 30 November, Hempstone and the visiting US Deputy Assistant Secretary of State for African Affairs, Bob Houdek, met with President Moi and Foreign Minister Ayah. Houdek said that he had been instructed to pursue two essential issues. First, he wanted to know a precise date when the opposition could hold its first legal public meeting. Second, he asked Moi to announce publicly elections with non-KANU candidates. Moi flatly rejected both demands and complained instead about the alleged misconduct of donors and embassy personnel. He asked the United States to 'detach itself from the dissidents and follow diplomatic conventions' (Hempstone 1997: 257). On 2 December, however, Moi announced the end of the one-party era in Kenya. On 31 December, FORD was officially registered as a party.

Comparison

Intensive and sustained transnational mobilization is a necessary but not a sufficient condition for policy and regime change. The case studies show that 'weak' transnational networks cannot impose universal principles on governments or societies, but instead must rely on temporary alliances with more powerful actors such as donor governments or international financial institutions. Not universal principles as such, but their alliance with material pressure promoted significant short-term changes in domestic practices. The case studies also show that transnational mobilization precedes and causes the entrance of donor governments. Transnational mobilization legitimizes material interventions by outside forces, although donors and NGOs usually pursue different agendas and goals.

The process of changing the image of the Kenyan government abroad was completed by 1989. The breakdown of communist regimes in Eastern Europe reinforced the pressure on donor nations to act. While the transnational mobilization pushed successfully for change, it could not determine the kind of reforms implemented by a government still in control of domestic affairs. Donor governments forced multipartyism onto the Moi regime, but refrained from demanding significant reforms in leveling the playing prior to the elections. While donors had previously failed to intervene in situations of gross human rights violations in Uganda, their new found activism remained limited and without a strategy beyond ending one-party rule. Moreover, donor policies were inconsistent in pushing Kenya toward multipartyism, while supporting 'no-party rule' in Uganda.

Donors played a role in supporting the continuation of repressive practices. While the transnational human rights movement played a significant role on the donors' decision to cut aid to Kenya in 1991, the subsequent re-introduction of multipartyism did not promote a greater respect for human rights and democratic participation. Donors were vulnerable to human rights groups and their mobilization, but were also driven by strategic and economic concerns as well as a preference for political stability rather than fundamental political change. With a few exceptions (Hempstone, in particular), diplomats in Kampala and Nairobi were also less likely to challenge their governmental counterparts and more interested in a non-confrontational atmosphere during their limited tenures.

Under pressure for multipartyism, KANU representatives revived the idea of *majimbo* as a challenge to political pluralism. They sought to subordinate national to ethnic citizenship in an effort to counter the threat of a renewed dominance of the larger over the smaller ethnicities. As a result of this counter-mobilization, Kikuyus and Luos became the main victims of 'ethnic cleansing' in areas neighboring the Maasai and Kalenjin heartland. *Majimbo* was the logical preference of the incumbent minority to secure their control of the political process. In contrast, representatives from the larger ethnic groups advocated national unity, liberal values, and majority rule not only for principled reasons but because such a position held the best prospects for their own access to power.

In Uganda, the government was not penalized for its rejection of multipartyism. Unlike Moi, Museveni was perceived as a 'new breed' of African leadership and positively integrated into the international liberal community. The repeated publication of human rights reports by the AI between 1989 and 1992 and the official communication of this information to the UNCHR caused the government to establish a Human Rights Desk within the Department of Justice and reinforced the consideration of an extended Bill of Rights and an independent human rights body in the ongoing constitutional reform process. At the same time, independent domestic pressure for human rights change hardly existed and the government made little effort to support the emergence of an independent civil society. In the absence of significant domestic and international pressure for regime change, the NRM establishment delayed political reforms in the interest of extending its own rule and access to government resources.

Transnational mobilization combines with domestic conditions to produce variation in democratic reform paths. While the Ugandan government promoted the expansion of individual participation in political affairs especially on the local level, Kenya embarked on an electoralist strategy allowing party competition. In both cases, the ruling elites emphasized one dimension of democratization and explicitly or implicitly restricted the other in their efforts to stay in power. In Uganda, a non-partisan movement system suppressed party competition in the name of perpetuating NRM rule. In Kenya, KANU politicians manipulated the electoral playing field and limited the participation of opposition voters in order to secure their political survival in the multiparty era.

6
How Transnational Activism Undermines Democratization

Transnational human rights mobilization targeting Kenya and Uganda during the 1970s and 1980s empowered domestic allies and delegitimized authoritarian regimes. This mobilization effectively challenged repressive regimes and created the basis for fundamental regime change in Uganda and significant political reforms in Kenya. But challenging authoritarian rule is only the beginning of a process aimed at creating sustainable democratic institutions. As the domestic struggle for democratic reforms progresses, the effects of transnational activism change. Targeted governments adapt quickly to the tastes of international human rights groups and devise strategies of deception and counter-mobilization. While previous strategies of conventional, state-led repression were not entirely dropped, new and more subtle efforts of harassment and threats take a prominent place. This chapter also shows how and why transnational mobilization beyond the initiation of regime change has more ambiguous and often negative effects on the political opposition.

First, transnational networks tend to be limited to urban-based, professional elites primarily residing in the major capitals. This is unproblematic as long as a common enemy of authoritarianism defines joint interests and goals. But beyond regime change, external connections can become a liability and distraction for local activists, who may not represent larger segments of society and fail to see their personal struggle as part of a larger effort. Second, transnational interventions based on universal principles of human rights are vulnerable to political co-optation by domestic actors engaged in political, religious, or ethnic struggles. Transnational activists are frequently focused on a narrow agenda driven by their mandate, rather than by the political realities and local needs expressed in their target. Their interventions may have a principled intention, but as they become part of the domestic political discourse, local actors use them to further more narrow personal, political, or ethnic agendas. Third, transnational interventions can benefit not only their domestic allies, but also their political enemies. Domestic elites resisting those interventions successfully use nationalist and anti-colonial frames to undermine the legitimacy of domestic supporters of democratic change. Transnational activism empowers those capable of appropriating and framing external interventions for their political gain at home. These groups are not necessarily allies of transnational groups and may have entirely different and opposing agendas.

Uganda, 1993–1997: The re-emergence of authoritarianism

The Odoki Commission charged with presenting a draft constitution presented its 700-page final report on 31 December 1992 (Odoki Commission 1992). It recommended the convening of a constitutional assembly for further deliberations, presidential elections, and an extension of the no-party system until a national referendum would decide on the future shape of Uganda's political system. The commission ascertained a majority within the population against the immediate introduction of multipartyism. The NRM government was naturally pleased with the results and announced elections for a CA, although such a measure would further side-line the RC system. 'Oddly, after putting great energy into developing RCs in every village and at higher levels, the NRM quietly handed over the shaping of Ugandan democracy to a state-appointed Constitutional Commission and a Constituent Assembly' (Kasfir 1998: 51). Museveni himself immediately began to campaign and announced plans to revive the traditional kingdoms as cultural (but not political) entities. This move was designed to secure the Baganda vote for the upcoming elections.

The CA elections transformed the movement system and shifted attention away from the grassroots to the national level. The original enthusiasm of this bottom–up perspective was increasingly substituted by a bureaucratic top–down approach. By early 1992, the Ugandan democratic experiment was basically abandoned. The parties, originally identified as 'the main problem' of Ugandan politics, had survived. The political competition in the 1990s now pitted 'movementists' against 'multipartyists,' even if everyone running for office had to do so as an individual member of the NRM.

On 14 July 1993, the NRC reversed Obote's constitutional ban on kingdoms from 1967. Although a total of four kingdoms were reinstated, the measure mainly benefited Buganda as the largest and still relatively well-organized entity. Two weeks after the decision, the Buganda parliament (*lukiiko*) was reopened, Ronald Mutebi was officially named *kabaka* (king) and the property (palace and other buildings) was officially returned. While the NRM and Museveni had always maintained that all questions of national significance should be decided directly by the people, the crucial issue of Buganda's status within Uganda was now removed from the process of constitutional reform.

The CA elections and constitutional reforms

The number of constituencies for the CA elections in March 1994 increased by about 25 percent based on updated population figures. One CA delegate represented an average of 70,000 residents.[1] Voters' interest and participation was exceptionally high[2] with 85 percent of eligible voters registered and 87 percent of those registered voting.[3] A total of more than 1,120 candidates ran for 214 seats. 'The opportunity afforded to the electorate to question the candidates, both stellar political figures and unknowns alike, *produced the most dramatic levelling of the playing field of the campaign, ...*' (Geist 1995: 96).[4] In the whole exercise the RC system played a minor role as a platform for the opposing candidate's non-partisan campaigns, which were required to tour in groups from parish to parish. The NRM secured an absolute majority of the 214 seats, while about 70 candidates supporting multi-partyism and 10–20 'independents' were elected. The NRM lost in most constituencies of the North, where its candidates were rejected in favor of UPC's prominent multipartyists. A total of nine cabinet and assistant ministers lost to competing candidates, while 24 won their respective electoral race.[5]

The elections did not fully test 'the rulers' commitment to democracy,' but there was more at stake than 'simply the preparation of a new constitution' (Kasfir 1995: 151, 154). The NRM government succeeded in holding reasonably free and fair elections, which enhanced its domestic and international legitimacy. Candidates were forced to present their credentials with respect to substantive issues rather than resort to mere electoral campaigning. 'This was an unprecedented development in political education. In previous Ugandan elections, party rallies had been the main form of public campaigning, making it virtually impossible for prospective voters to convey their issue preferences to candidates' (Kasfir 1995: 165). Although the CA elections were held as a means to constitutional reforms, the logic of electoral competition had important repercussions for the NRM. It not only effectively undermined the RC system as an alternative to party politics, but it also put the NRM on track to transform itself into a political party.

The newly elected CA appointed a close associate of Museveni, James Wapakhabulo, as its speaker. Within the first few weeks of deliberations the original timetable of seven months was overturned and the CA deliberated for a total of 17 months before returning a draft constitution. While smaller issues were open for debate and some influence by the opposition, the NRM leadership rejected any serious consideration of multipartyism and federalism. At the international level, the 'constitutional' year 1995 began with the discussion of Uganda's belated response to the allegations made by AI under the 1503 procedure. After hearing the Ugandan representative, the UNCHR decided to discontinue the investigation. The 49-page response (Republic of Uganda 1995c) defended Uganda's human rights record (1) by pointing to the economic situation of the country, particularly after 20 years of civil war, (2) by attributing abuses to ignorance instead of intention,[6] (3) by blaming rebel groups or criminals for committing the abuses, (4) and by questioning the full application of international standards disregarding the peculiar situation of the country.[7] The report further highlighted the fact that the Ugandan government had not only 'accorded maximum co-operation to Amnesty International' and that the NGO used to have a 'proper appreciation of the country's human rights situation' (Republic of Uganda 1995c: 2), but also admitted individual cases of human rights abuses, even torture, committed by government agencies and mentioned the payment of compensation to victims and families (39f.).[8] During the rest of the year, the Ugandan government made further efforts to show the international community, at least in rhetoric, a strong commitment to human rights. In late May 1995, the Ugandan government acceded to the International Covenant on Civil and Political Rights (ICCPR) and in September it signed the first protocol which provided for an individual complaint procedure (Republic of Uganda 1995b).

In June 1995, the CA voted 199 to 68 against an amendment aimed at an immediate restoration of multipartyism.[9] Instead, the NRM majority within the CA secured another extension of the movement system until 1999/2000 (Art. 273, Sect. 3). The final product (Republic of Uganda 1995a) contained an expanded Bill of Rights, which went far beyond the 1962 and 1967 constitutions (Chapter IV, Arts. 20–58).[10] In addition, the constitution provided for a UHRC charged with investigations 'on its own initiative,' 'visits of jails, prisons, and places of detention and related facilities,' human rights education, and monitoring of the 'Government's compliance with international treaty and convention obligations on human rights' (Art. 51). The UHRC 'shall publish periodical reports' and provide an 'annual report to parliament on the state of human rights and freedoms in the country' (Art. 52, Sect. 2). In order to fulfill these functions it was given the powers of a court (Art. 53).

The constitutional provisions restricting party activities stood in stark contrast to the model character of the Bill of Rights. In Article 269, political activities were sharply limited by (1) outlawing the opening of branch offices, (2) the holding of delegates' conferences (3) or public rallies, (4) the support for a candidate for any public elections, (5) and any activities that may interfere with the movement political system for the time being in force. The political opposition strongly protested the restrictions contained in the new constitution, which was finally promulgated on 8 October 1995. However, the international community did little to support the domestic opposition and remained largely quiet on the extension of the no-party rule. International observers found the opposition still tainted by their connections to Obote and Amin, while Museveni made significant strides in areas of economic development and the battle against HIV/AIDS. 'It is, in fact doubtful whether the multi-partyists' irrational suspicion of anything to do with the NRM government could have been set at rest' (Furley and Katalikawe 1997: 250).

The constitution did little to clarify the symbiotic relationship between the movement and the state institutions. The NRA became the UPDF, while the RCs were renamed as Local Councils (LCs). The constitution confirmed the NRM as a 'transitional government' which was 'continue in office until a new government is elected' (Art. 263). Despite the extension of the movement system and *de-facto* one-party rule, most donor representatives were content with the economic advancements and felt that the process as a whole was a step in the right direction. Open criticism with respect to the limits on freedom of assembly and party activities came only from the British and the US embassies. The US ambassador called those sections of the constitution a 'serious defect' and a 'blot on the face of this constitution [...] which we urge Ugandans to correct at the earliest possible date.'[11] Although this statement expressed the dissatisfaction of the US government, it also made clear that it was up to the Ugandan people and not the donor community to bring about the desired changes. The United States and other governments had no intention of pressing its Ugandan counterpart on this issue. Donors and domestic critics hoped that the first presidential and parliamentary elections planned for 1996 would begin to loosen the grip of the NRM on national politics.

Resurgence of armed rebellions

During the CA deliberations, the LRA stepped up its attacks in the north, while on 13 November 1995 a new rebel group, the Allied Democratic Forces (ADF), opened another front by attacking villages in southwestern Uganda from Zairian territory. Soon the rebel attacks caused a major diplomatic standoff between the Ugandan and the Sudanese governments. Since early 1994, the latter had supplied the LRA with arms (Amnesty International 1997: 6) and used the rebels as a militia to fight the South SPLA, which controlled large parts of southern Sudan. After a massacre of Ugandan civilians in Atiak, just north of the Sudanese border, the Ugandan government accused the Sudanese government of complicity and severed diplomatic relations.

The ADF in eastern Zaire mainly recruited former Hutu soldiers who had been responsible for the 1994 genocide in Rwanda and had fled to Zaire after being defeated by the Rwandan Patriotic Front (RPF). After some of the Hutu militia (*Interahamwe*) had regrouped in the refugee camps of Zaire, they attacked Rwandan and Ugandan villages. This threat of a second front in the West became a major incentive for Museveni and the NRM to support the rebel movement led by Laurent Kabila against the Zairian dictator Mobutu Sese Seko. Museveni hoped that a Kabila government would reassert Kinshasa's control of eastern Zaire and help Uganda in destroying the rebel hideouts in the area.

In the following three years, Ugandan forces repeatedly invaded the neighbor to the west and ultimately occupied some of the most mineral-rich areas in the eastern part of the newly renamed Democratic Republic of Congo. The growing military engagement became an increasingly contentious domestic issue, which NRM hardliners exploited to consolidate their domestic power. While the NRM was running out of reasons to limit basic freedoms of association and party activities, government officials increasingly blamed domestic human rights critics for strengthening the armed rebellions.

Presidential and parliamentary elections, 1996

The first presidential and parliamentary elections after the NRM victory took place in May 1996. In contrast to the deep divisions within the opposition in Kenya, the main Ugandan opposition parties UPC and DP presented the DP leader Paul Ssemogerere as joint challenger to Museveni. He had previously stepped down as a government minister in order to focus on his electoral campaign. UPC and DP also formed the Inter-Political Forces Cooperation (IPFC) to break the NRM's dominance in electoral contests. The campaigns of all presidential candidates were state-financed, but the incumbent used government resources to supplement those funds. The opposition primarily focused on the issue of multipartyism, while Museveni emphasized the accomplishments of his government and promised free education for at least four children from every Ugandan family.

Although Ssemogerere was a popular political leader and united the political opposition, Museveni overwhelmingly won the presidential race with 74.2 percent of the vote against Ssemogerere's 23.7 percent. This victory carried over to the parliamentary elections two weeks later, where the NRM was able to maintain its overall dominance. Only the north remained solidly in the hands of the opposition. Ssemogerere carried the UPC strongholds of Lira (85.5 percent), Kitgum (88.4 percent), and Gulu (90.5 percent).

In late July 1996, the LRA launched a major attack on smaller villages in the Ugandan/Sudanese border region and killed more than 100 civilians and UPDF soldiers. The LRA began a campaign of directly targeting civilians and abducting children, which were forced to become child soldiers or slaves. For the first time since 1986, the army command, represented by Museveni's brother, Maj. General Salim Saleh, imposed censorship on journalists reporting from the insurgency area. The UPDF succeeded in pushing the rebels back into Sudanese territory and began to (re)establish the so-called 'protected villages.' Museveni himself defended this measure in parliament as the only way of saving innocent Ugandans from abduction and rape. Despite the strong presence of the UPDF, hundreds of civilians were tortured and killed by the rebels and thousands of children were abducted since the mid-1990s. The issue soon became a new focus of transnational human rights activism.

The UPDF was also unable to contain the ADF in western Uganda, whose fighters sought refuge in eastern Zaire. After Zairian President Mobutu Sese Seko rejected Museveni's request for military cooperation to fight the rebels in the border region, Uganda began to support the anti-Mobutu coalition led by Laurent Kabila. Rwandan and Ugandan troops soon followed the march of the rebels on Kinshasa in 1997.[12]

Entrenchment of the movement system

In early 1997, the NRM became 'the Movement' and a new act provided that every Ugandan was automatically a member of that organization. The act created movement organs for all administrative levels (parish, subcounty, municipal, and district movement committees) with the highest decision-making organ (National Conference) scheduled to be convened biannually. For day-to-day decisions, responsibility rested with the National Executive Committee (NEC) and the Movement Secretariat led by a National Political Commissar (NPC). The NPC and its officers were not set up as an independent entity within the movement system, but Museveni had the power to appoint and remove anyone in the Secretariat. The majority in parliament rejected motions by the opposition to give parties direct representation and influence in the movement system. While movementists defended the principle of 'election based only on individual merit,' one critic stated in a heated debate that the Movement is nothing but 'state-level thuggery by which the people of Uganda are being held at ransom by a corrupt group who call themselves strugglists' (*New Vision*, 10 July 1997). Most of the multipartyists boycotted the final debate and voting. The DP representatives declared that they would also call for a boycott of the 2000 referendum, which would for the first time put the question of the political system to the Ugandan people.

The formal institutionalization of the movement system stood in stark contrast to the more or less successful completion of the major reform projects (e.g. the new constitution and the LC system) promised by the government (Kjaer 1999). The apparent exhaustion of the NRM agenda after 10 years in power began to strengthen the position of the domestic civil opposition. Despite convincing electoral victories and strong outside material support, the refusal of the NRM to allow party activities and restrict basic political freedoms came increasingly under pressure. As the old leadership of the UPC and DP was increasingly replaced by younger faces, the political opposition gradually gained legitimacy against an increasingly unresponsive government.

Those intensifying domestic conflicts had little effect on Museveni's reputation abroad. The opposite was true. In April 1997, Uganda was selected as the first country to benefit from the World Bank's newly established Highly Indebted Poor Countries Debt (HIPC) Initiative. The total package initially reduced Uganda's debt by $338 million and ultimately exceeded $700 million.[13] Museveni and other examples of an alleged 'new breed' of African leaders attained a high profile in the foreign media during this time.[14] Within the donor community, only US ambassador Michael Southwick took a principled line against the entrenchment of the movement system and the idea of holding a referendum to determine the fate of political parties. 'You don't have a referendum on religious or press freedom, so why have it on freedom of association and assembly' (*New Vision*, 20 July 1997). On the same occasion, Southwick ruled out that the US government would provide funding for the 2000 referendum and labeled the 1996 elections as 'transitional' rather than 'free and fair in the sense that they meet international norms.'

In contrast, the newly elected Labour government in Great Britain declared in early October 1997 that it had no intention of pressing for multiparty reforms in Uganda. The British Secretary of State for International Development, Clare Short, clarified that the question of political parties was to be decided by Ugandans alone in the 2000 referendum. 'I don't think it is necessarily right for Uganda to have the same kind of political system like Britain' (cited in *New Vision*, 8 October 1997). Museveni clearly reaped the benefits of his social and economic policies, which showed significant progress in the areas of universal primary education, combating the HIV/AIDS epidemic, and lowering the number of Ugandans living in poverty from more than 50 to less than 35 percent during the 1990s. Apart from a few critical voices, the international support reached a high point during this time period and allowed Museveni and the movement leadership to increase repression at home and become generally less responsive to the growing domestic criticism. Increasing violence in the North and the military engagements in neighboring nations further contributed to a growing disconnect between an entrenched government enjoying significant international support and a domestic society unable to challenge repression and push for more meaningful democratic reforms.

Shifting targets: Rebels and gross human rights abuses

Intense transnational activism returned to Uganda after rebel groups in the north stepped up their attacks and began to target the civilian population with abductions and gross human rights violations. Museveni himself moved temporarily to the northern town Gulu to command the counter-insurgency operations against the main rebel group, the LRA. He refused to open talks with the rebels accusing them of committing crimes against humanity. International human rights observers such as the AI and also UNICEF had just begun to target the LRA for its practices of abducting children, forced recruitment, and widespread rape. On 18 July 1996, the AI condemned 'callous and calculated killings' by the LRA following a massacre of more than 300 civilians on 12 and 13 July in northern Uganda (Amnesty International News Release, AFR 54/14/96). In December 1996 and March 1997, the UN Department for Humanitarian Affairs published reports on the humanitarian situation in northern Uganda criticizing both sides for violating basic human rights.

In early to mid-1997, international interest in Uganda solidly focused on the situation human rights abuses committed by the LRA as well as the unfolding power struggle in neighboring Zaire. While the donor community supported Museveni in his regional policies, the transnational human rights community supplemented that support by targeting the rebels for their widespread human rights abuses. In June 1997, an AI delegation followed up on its 1996 report and visited northern Uganda for two weeks. Afterwards, the Amnesty representative Andrew Mowson declared that he was 'shocked at the systematic nature of gross abuses the rebels are perpetuating.' He added that the Ugandan army committed fewer human rights abuses than the rebels, but was still guilty of many violations committed in the course of military action (*Daily Nation*, 17 June 1997). During the rest of the year, international human rights groups compiled more reports on the situation in northern Uganda.

On 18 September 1997, AI, HRW, domestic human rights groups, and UNICEF presented their respective reports in a joint press conference in Kampala. The AI claimed that the LRA abducted more than 8,000 children during the last three years (Amnesty International 1997). The AI and HRW simultaneously published reports on the LRA's conduct in the north and accused Joseph Kony of gross human rights violations (Human Rights Watch/Africa 1997b). They also blamed the Sudanese authorities for supporting the LRA and failing to stop the violence. The AI went into the history of the conflict and questioned Museveni's sincerity in helping the north and admitting to own human rights abuses. 'An inquiry set up in 1988 into alleged human rights violations in Gulu District spluttered in and out of existence until 1991 when it produced a confidential work in progress report and asked government for more funds. Since then it has collapsed' (Amnesty International 1997: 32). The Amnesty report requested a full investigation of abuses committed by all sides. 'So far, there has not been a focused, public confrontation of the human rights experience of people in northern Uganda during the 11-year long war' (Amnesty International 1997: 33). The graphic description of torture methods used against children had a strong impact in the Western media (*Washington Post*, 14 October 1997, p. A14), but the targets of international outrage were primarily the rebels and not the Ugandan government.

In light of the new quality of the northern rebellion, local leaders and domestic human rights groups stepped up their demands for a dialogue with the aim of ending the rebellion in the north. Reports on secret talks between Kony and government representatives claimed that these had broken down after Museveni gave the rebels an ultimatum of seven days to turn in their arms. Critics blamed ethnic animosities within the government for the deadlock and alleged that the army was unwilling to stop the rebellion because the north had overwhelmingly voted for the opposition in the 1996 elections. The government rejected these accusations and warned its critics that their claims could be misunderstood as undermining national security and a support for the rebels.

The transnational human rights groups blamed both sides for human rights abuses, but the international public focused almost entirely on the atrocities committed by the LRA, in particular the abduction and abuse of children. The US government supported Museveni in his refusal to (re-)open talks with the rebel groups and used the international human rights issue for its own narrow strategic interests. During an official visit to Gulu in December 1997, US Secretary of State Madeleine Albright declared, 'the US government will stand by the Ugandan government to contain the threat of Sudanese sponsored terrorism and improve security in the region, especially of children' (*New Vision*, 15 October 1997). Western government support was easily mobilized because the NGOs' concern for children coincided with the short-term strategic interests in containing the Islamic regime in Khartoum as well as establishing a new government in Zaire. Museveni's growing military engagement in Zaire was justified as a struggle against the remnants of the *Interahamwe* militia, the perpetrators of the Rwandan genocide of 1994.

During a March 1998 visit to Africa, US President Bill Clinton reaffirmed the close cooperation between the United States and the Ugandan government. The focus was clearly on questions of common interest in regional affairs rather than the US position on multipartyism. In a joint statement with the presidents from Ethiopia, Kenya, Tanzania, Rwanda, and Uganda, Clinton agreed that there was 'no fixed model for democratic institutions and transitions' (*New Vision*, 28 March 1998). In a speech at Makerere University, First Lady Hillary Clinton focused on the gross violations committed by the LRA and condoned by the Sudanese government. She told the audience 'when I met President Museveni he told me about the 10,000 children abducted by the LRA. One of the children was Charlotte who has never returned. Her mother came to see me in Washington and told me what happened that night when she was abducted. They broke the windows, tied up the girls, beat them up as they cried and took them away into a life of unspeakable horror' (The *Monitor*, 26 March 1998). Mrs. Clinton went on to promise financial support for indigenous children NGOs such as the Concerned Parents' Association (CPA).

In early 1998, UNICEF brought the conduct of the LRA in northern Uganda to the attention of the UNCHR. The UNICEF based its report on the information contained in non-governmental reports and claimed that the rebels fought 'a psychotic war on children' abducting an estimated 6,000 to 8,000 children over the last five years. The UNICEF representative in Uganda, Leila Takkala, declared that about half of the abducted children had returned home while the other half was still missing. She also estimated that about 80 percent of the LRA soldiers were abducted children. During 1997 and 1998, UNICEF representatives regularly visited northern Uganda and cooperated with newly established local NGOs such as the CPA. UNICEF's Executive Director, Carol Bellamy, said that the 'world must take responsibility instead of taking cover' because 'whatever the origins and complexities of these intricate and tragic crises [are], there is no 'just cause' for the death or torture of a child.'

A number of domestic and international NGOs, such as World Vision, set up health and counseling centers for traumatized children mainly in the Gulu and Kitgum districts (Muhumuza 1997). During that time, dozens of international TV teams, journalists, and representatives from international organizations or governments passed through Gulu. The problem of child soldiers in general and the atrocities committed by the LRA continued to catch the attention of mainstream international media (Rubin 1998). On 22 April 1998, the UNCHR demanded 'the immediate cessation of all abductions and attacks on all civilian populations and in particular women and children, in northern Uganda by the Lord's Resistance Army' (Resolution 1998/75; 24 in favor, one against, 27 abstentions). In a letter to the parents of abducted children, Secretary General Kofi Annan promised that the 'UN will do all in its efforts to rescue the children held in Sudan.'

The LRA initially reacted to the international accusations by declaring all Western NGOs active in the North as 'legitimate military targets because they support the Government policy of extermination.' A spokesman of the rebel group accused Western NGOs of not condemning the practice of setting up 'protected villages,' which he referred to as 'concentration camps' (cited in *New Vision*, 13 April 1998). However, within only a few weeks, the international campaign had discernible effects on the LRA and the Sudanese government. In mid-May, the leadership in Khartoum admitted for the first time that the LRA was indeed based in Sudan. The Sudanese government also promised that it would push for the release of abducted children.

The same month, the British Secretary of International Development, Clare Short, used the example of the LRA to criticize international human rights groups for spending too much time on 'carping' about illegal arrests and torture while ignoring health, education, and economic issues. In an interview for an AI publication, she warned that ignoring economic and social problems would ultimately result in 'losing an audience in a large chunk of the world.' She specifically rejected a recent Amnesty report, which 'seemed to treat the Lord's Resistance Army – which kidnaps children, and turns boys into soldiers and the girls into sex slaves – and the government of Uganda as equally bad people' (cited in *The Guardian*, 15 May 1998).

The international focus on the LRA's gross violations of human rights reinforced the domestic hard-line approach by the Ugandan government. While the Ugandan government maintained its offer of amnesty to individual rebel soldiers, it remained adamantly opposed to peace talks with the rebel leadership. Rather, it suggested that those leaders should be tried for their alleged crimes against humanity. During the whole period, northern politicians repeatedly introduced motions in parliament that asked the government and rebels to immediately stop hostilities and open talks (*New Vision*, 4 September 1998). After watching the parliamentary debates for some time, an angry Museveni declared in mid-September that 'these barbarians (rebels, HPS) are supported by some politicians here, receiving wonderful allowances from the state. But the NRM has got a very long hand; we shall one day get to the root cause of the problem. [...] I want you (MPs, HPS) to visit the 30 mass graves in Luwero Triangle, each with 2,000 skulls. There are skulls of small children and those who killed our people in cold blood are here' (cited in *New Vision*, 17 September 1998).

In September 1998, the Ugandan government received additional international support for its counter-insurgency operations in the northern and western parts of the country. The World Bank accepted a 26 percent increase in defense expenditures (for a total of 10 percent of the annual budget) for 1998/99 (from about $100 million to $131 million). 'The [World] Bank's representative in Uganda, Mr. Randolph Harris, told the East African, that although a reduction in the defense budget would be welcome, the current security threat cannot be ignored' (*East African*, 7 September 1998). At the same time, the World Bank offered Uganda additional financial support from a special fund set up in 1997 to enable peace initiatives and facilitate transitions from protracted violence to peaceful conflict resolution. Only a few days earlier, the Ugandan government had officially declared the rebels as terrorist organizations.[15]

In September 1998, the CPA appealed to the British government to close the LRA's London office and expel all supporters from the country. In its response, the LRA representative in London asked the British government to refrain from closing down its offices and claimed that the group 'is a liberation movement that is now observing the tenets of civilized conduct.'[16] In mid-October, a section of the LRA declared that it would no longer support its leadership's attacks on civilians and children and form its own breakaway group. The ICRC announced in late October that more than 400,000 Ugandans had been displaced by the ongoing insurgencies in the north and the west. The organization registered 1,800 Sudanese POWs, which were held in 36 Ugandan prisons and detention centers. It helped 300 of those detainees to communicate with their families in Sudan. The ICRC also continued its practice of monitoring prisons and military barracks throughout Uganda (*The Monitor*, 27 October 1998).

The effects of regional insecurity on Uganda became even more pronounced when the relations between Mobutu's successor Laurent Kabila and his erstwhile supporter Museveni soured within a short period of time. In early 1998, Museveni ordered his troops to occupy eastern parts of the Congo and support a rebellion against Kabila. In mid-1998, Kabila accused Rwanda and Uganda of backing a rebellion against his government, while the two countries alleged that Kabila's troops were responsible for genocide against the Banyamulenge, an ethnic group living in the border regions of Rwanda, Uganda, and the Congo. Soon, Kabila received military support from Angola and Zimbabwe and the conflict threatened to turn into a major regional war. Ugandan troops were deployed deep into Congolese territory and established the eastern capital of Kisangani as their headquarters from 1998 until their withdrawal in 2004. During this time period, Ugandan military officers profited from their control over a mineral-rich area by smuggling resources from the region to Uganda (Clark 2001; Tangri and A.M. Mwenda 2003).

How did transnational mobilization affect democratization in Uganda? While transnational human rights organizations blamed both sides for abuses committed in northern Uganda, the international media and western governments tended to focus primarily on the atrocities committed by the rebels. This shift in international attention provided the Ugandan government with ample room to justify a tightening of domestic control and a rejection of any significant democratic reforms. Some international observers also argued that the rebel atrocities deserved far greater attention and that the Ugandan government had successfully advanced social and economic rights. The weakness of the Ugandan civil society and the political opposition was not only blamed on the past rather than on government control, but it also served as a convenient excuse to throw one's support behind Museveni. While statements calling for multipartyism and increasing electoral contestation were infrequent, the majority of external voices preferred to focus on the successes of Museveni as a 'benign' dictator. Donors promoting the HIPC initiative needed Museveni's success as much as Museveni needed the financial aid flow. The motives for this joint position were diverse and included the principles of basic human rights driving transnational activism, the desire of international aid agencies to present Uganda as a model case, and the strategic interests of the United States and European governments. Underlying those rationalizations were also more deep-seated and hardly admitted doubts that Ugandans were ready for governing themselves in a multiparty system. The failures of multipartyism in neighboring Kenya, described in the next section, did little to change those opinions.

Kenya, 1992–1997: Manipulating electoral democracy

The December 1991 decision for multipartyism relieved some of the pressure on the Moi government, but also opened up societal space for the civil society sector and a more critical domestic media. The *Daily Nation*, the dominant national newspaper, began to exploit new found freedoms, while a whole array of new dailies and weeklies emerged on the streets of Nairobi. Newly created domestic NGOs and action committees with specific human rights mandates or political agendas joined existing societal organizations such as women's groups, unions, and church organizations. This process was strongly supported by an influx of donor money shifting aid packages away from state agencies toward the non-governmental sector.

The more restrained attitude of the Kenyan government toward the civil society sector and the almost immediate usurpation of the societal space had its first major consequence when a coalition of domestic and international NGOs mobilized against governmental legislation designed to establish control over the NGO sector through registration and a permanent regulatory framework (Ndegwa 1996: 31–54). During this period, the NGO sector not only exploded in numbers, but also increased transnational ties with external actors such as donors and transnational groups (Widner 1992b: 188). In June 1992, the government lifted the ban for representatives of the AI to visit the country.

In September of that year, the KHRC emerged as the first domestic human rights watchdog essentially copying working methods of the AI and other international human rights groups. It simultaneously opened offices in Nairobi and Boston, US. As KHRC was officially registered by the government, the same authorities refused registration for a number of other human rights groups, including RPP and the *Center for Law and Research International* (CLARION).

While parts of the opposition were now busy building a strengthened civil society, others turned into politicians preparing to challenge Moi by the end of 1992. KANU and Moi himself focused on ensuring their political survival in the multiparty era. As the external pressure deflated and the domestic opposition began to split in separate camps, Moi reasserted domestic control using many of the tools of repression which had served him well during the 1980s (Kenya Human Rights Commission 1994: Appendix). In the period leading up to the December elections, the Kenyan police used detention without trial (Preservation of Public Security Act), required licenses for any public meeting (Public Order Act and Public Collections Act), and enforced a registration of all parties and other organizations under the Societies Act. The opposition was regularly threatened with sedition laws contained in the Penal Code, and the free movement in urban areas was regularly restricted to prevent large gatherings in support of the opposition (Vagrancy Act). Those laws were not only extensively used by the executive during the 1992 election campaign, they also continued to play an important role in repressing the opposition until mid-1997 (Ndegwa 1998: 197–201).

After 1991, court cases of prominent opposition figures were moved away from Nairobi in order to avoid domestic and international media attention. Prominent critics such as Koigi wa Wamwere were no longer charged with political offenses or detained without trial, but they were charged with criminal offences and evidence for capital crimes was fabricated by the police. Opposition figures could now 'legally' be kept away from the public as long as the government deemed it necessary (African Rights 1996: 131; Article 19, 1995). KANU also made strong efforts to manipulate the electoral playing field. Locally, the provincial administration regularly banned opposition meetings and harassed opposition politicians. Soon, harassment became open violence and local leaders supporting KANU mobilized youths to attack voters in opposition areas (Amisi 1997; Haugerud 1995: 38). The organization 'Youth for KANU'92' became particularly infamous for sending truck loads of KANU supporters into opposition areas, ultimately killing several hundred civilians and displacing many thousands (Lafargue

1996: 228–234). This politically directed 'ethnic violence' had started with the first *majimbo* rallies organized by KANU politicians in September 1991 and intensified until the elections approached in December 1992 (Klopp 2001; Throup 1993: 391). The violence spread from the Western part of Kenya (Nyanza and Western Province) to the Rift Valley, and mainly affected districts where Kalenjin as well as Maasai lived close to Kikuyus and Luos (e.g. Nakuru, Kisumu, Trans-Nzoia, Kisii).[17]

On 13 May 1992, parliament voted to appoint a select committee charged with the investigation of the 'ethnic clashes.' In September, the committee presented its conclusions arguing that 'the ethnic clashes invariably pitted the Kalenjin and Maasai in the Rift Valley Province against virtually all other ethnic groups residing in Western Kenya. [. . .] The evidence further received indicates that the target or victims at whom the clashes were directed were the ethnic groups of Kikuyu, Luo, Abaluhyia, Abagusii, Teso, who were not *only suspected and presumed to be supporters of the multi-party crusade, but to whom also the main proponents of multi-partyism belong*' (Republic of Kenya 1992: 68, emphasis added). The so-called Kiliku report also named high-level KANU representatives like Nicholas Biwott as responsible for the violence (Lafargue 1996: 248). In October, the KANU majority in parliament voted against an official recognition of the findings and the report was shelved. The government maintained that only 365 people were killed and about 7,000 displaced during the violence. The Kiliku report put the numbers at 779 and 54,000, respectively. Church representatives and international human rights NGOs claimed that between 1,000 and 2,000 were killed and 100,000 to 150,000 displaced (Africa Watch/Human Rights Watch 1993).

The violent attacks on the opposition diverted attention away from other measures taken by the government to secure KANU's electoral victory. While the period for voter registration had lasted longer than five months at the last elections in 1988, the government now shortened the period to only one month. After sharp opposition protests, the period was extended by ten days, but still gave a clear advantage to the much more well-organized KANU machinery. As a result, areas supporting KANU averaged higher levels of registration than opposition areas. In districts where KANU candidates faced serious challengers, KANU 'imported' supporters from other areas for registration (Throup 1993: 392). Constituencies in support of KANU were on average smaller than in the opposition areas (Fox 1996), and KANU further increased the number of constituencies in its stronghold areas prior to the December elections (Ndegwa 1998: 208). On election day, the opposition parties had to gain an average of three to four times more votes than KANU for each parliamentary seat. The gerrymandering of constituencies reaffirmed that *majimbo* was hardly a new idea in Kenyan politics, but already a guided official government policy.

Moi also appointed all members of the Electoral Commission and used these powers to keep the body under his control. The chairman and former judge Zacheaus Chesoni twice had been forced to declare bankruptcy and quit judicial positions before Moi appointed him to his new position.[18] He was a typical representative of the patronage system who owed his political and economic survival solely to the president.

In July 1992, KANU completed its efforts to secure its victory prior to the election date. A majority in parliament voted for constitutional amendments, which made it virtually impossible for the opposition to remove KANU or Moi from power. These amendments required the winner to attain a minimum of 25 percent of the vote in five out of the eight Kenyan provinces. Furthermore, the elected president was only allowed to appoint ministers from his own party. Finally, the maximum tenure for a president was limited to two terms in office. The first measure emphasized the representative character of the presidency, but really gave an advantage for Moi and KANU. None of the other major candidates were likely to become 'truly' national leaders within the next few months, and their appeal was likely to be limited to their respective ethnicity and home region. The second measure simply outlawed a coalition government, making it impossible for a divided opposition to take power. The third amendment was the only unambiguous democratizing measure in the package, although it seemed of little relevance to Moi who was 70 years old.

Although the opposition continued to sharply protest 'ethnic violence' and the bundles of measures taken in favor of KANU, it failed to develop a united position to avert the looming electoral defeat. The donor community repeated its general calls for a level playing field and a peaceful campaign, but shied away from publicly commenting on any of those specific issues. Until mid-May 1992, the Luhya Martin Shikuku, the Kikuyu Kenneth Matiba, and the Luo Oginga Odinga, had officially declared their intention to run as FORD candidates for presidency. The former Vice President and Kikuyu Mwai Kibaki had already announced in January the formation of the DP. In the next few weeks, intense internal wrangles within FORD paralyzed its work and no single challenger to Moi emerged. The FORD split into two factions, one led by Martin Shikuku and Kenneth Matiba, and the other by Oginga Odinga.

In October, the Attorney General threatened that FORD would not be allowed to run in the elections because of those internal divisions. Shortly thereafter, FORD broke apart and Oginga Odinga announced the formation of FORD-Kenya. Martin Shikuku and Kenneth Matiba formed the competing FORD-Asili. The fragile coalition between Luhyas, Luos, and Kikuyus disintegrated even before election date.[19] While Matiba took parts of the Kikuyu community to FORD-Asili and faced Kibaki's DP as the main inter-ethnic competitor, the human rights activist Paul Muite and the publisher Gitobu Imanyara joined FORD-Kenya. Secret attempts by US ambassador Hempstone, German ambassador Mützelburg, and other diplomats to unite the opposition behind one candidate ultimately failed (Hempstone 1997: 304). Within months after the re-introduction of multipartyism, the spectrum of new parties developed along ethnic lines. In December, eight parties and candidates contested the elections. Apart from KANU and Moi, they included FORD-Kenya (Odinga), FORD-Asili (Matiba), the DP (Kibaki), the Kenya National Congress (Chibule wa Tsuma), the Kenya Social Congress (George Anyona), the Kenyan National Democratic Alliance (Mukaru Ng'ang'a), and the Party of Independent Candidates for Kenya (John Harun).

Multiparty elections in December 1992

Moi and KANU won the multiparty elections, even though opposition forces accounted for about two-thirds of the votes both in the presidential and in the parliamentary race. Due to the gerrymandering of constituencies, KANU won a majority of 95 seats in the new parliament (53 percent) with an average of 14,138 votes. FORD-Kenya ended up with only 31 seats, but averaged 32,152 votes, while FORD-Asili gained 29 seats with an average of 38,220 votes. The DP was allotted 23 seats, but the average of 43,779 indicated that its total number of votes was almost as high as KANU's (Ndegwa 1998: 207). A large contingent of foreign observers was present during election day and subsequent counting procedures. The Commonwealth Observer Group gave the exercise and not an 'unqualified rating as free and fair' but declared the elections as ultimately an 'expression of the will of the people' (Commonwealth Observer Group 1993: 40).

The opposition's initial refusal to accept the election results lasted only for a couple of weeks. Western governments pressed the opposition to acknowledge their defeat (Mair 1994: 122), as they feared violence and instability more than an obviously rigged election. Donors were also directly invested in the exercise, since they financed large parts of the elections. The disintegration of the opposition continued and resulted in the emergence of more mono-ethnical parties. The Luhya–Kikuyu alliance of FORD-Asili broke apart shortly after the elections and seven FORD-Asili MPs defected to KANU. In 1993, a total of 14 opposition MPs (re-)joined KANU and were rewarded for their decisions with government positions (Tostensen, Andreassen and Tronvoll 1998: 19).

In 1993, an observer of Kenyan politics would have to conclude that the results of the mobilization against Moi's authoritarian regime were dismal. Even the suspension of financial aid to Kenya did not decisively change the domestic power balance. To the contrary, Moi and KANU emerged strengthened by the multiparty contest that had been forced on them by the donor community. The isolation and confrontation led to a 'rally around the flag' effect, rather than a disintegration of the ruling party into hard- and soft-liners. The KANU leadership rejected the demands for democratization with even greater confidence in 1993 than in 1989.

At the same time, all hopes that the political opposition would unite its forces to remove Moi were in vain. Instead, the new parties were in disarray and split along ethnic lines. The focus had been shifted from democratic reforms and human rights towards electoral competition and securing a place in Moi's patronage system. While donors had been responsible for the introduction of formal electoral contestation on the national level, they did little to insure a level playing field. Worse, after the flawed elections, donors preferred political stability and discouraged the opposition from challenging the results. Still, below the surface of electoral defeat and governmental rhetoric, the process of strengthening civil society actors represented a crucial development with long-term effects on the Kenyan political system.

The expansion of civil society

Until 1995/1996, the skeptics' warnings of continued governmental repression and opposition failure were largely vindicated. But unlike the pre-1992 period, the rise of a strengthened civil society represented a significant new challenge to the Moi regime. The mushrooming of political NGOs during the 1991/92 period supplemented the activities of the churches and individual human rights activists in pressing for political reforms. While virtually all registered NGOs in the 1980s were active in traditional development sectors, this picture changed completely in the early 1990s. 'A majority tended not only to address community development and institution building, but also human rights issues with civic education constituting the core of their activities' (Tostensen, Andreassen and Tronvoll 1998: 33). At the same time, transnational activism became less significant overall and had more ambiguous effects locally. Outside pressure and support actually undermined democratization during this time period, because it distracted domestic activists from networking at home and provided crucial mobilizing opportunities for entrenched KANU elites. Progress made during this period took place despite, and not because of, external pressures.

When the parliamentary opposition was weakened by ethnic divisions and defections, the thriving NGO sector became the major source for a sustained and credible challenge to KANU dominance. Newly formed action coalitions reunited the human rights activists, who had been the main challengers of Moi's regime in the 1980s. The human rights lawyer Kivutha Kibwana created the CLARION, and Willy Mutunga became a founding member of the KHRC as well as the Citizens' Coalition for Constitutional Change (the 4C's). Other long-time human rights activists such as Paul Muite, who had joined party politics prior to the 1992 election, now returned to the NGO sector to lobby for constitutional reforms. Efforts by the government to contain the (re-)formation of the opposition had little success. While the executive refused registration of CLARION, others were able to get past the government or operated as 'projects' as part of already registered NGOs.

Although civil society showed growing strength, it's transnational ties turned now out to be a frequent liability. By the early 1990s, individual NGOs were well connected to donors outside the country, but neglected networking within Kenya or with other African human rights groups. The most prominent organizations were based in Nairobi and had little capacity to reach beyond their urban and elitist base. Activists were often more well known in Europe and the United States than at home. While donors frequently complained about the ineffectiveness of the organizations they now supported, Kenyan NGO representatives resented excessive reporting requirements, lack of funding for their core activities, and a tendency of donors to come up with new issues every year. It was not only government repression, but also the unintended consequences of outsider support, which undermined the effectiveness of Kenyan civil society during this time period.

The civil society challenge as well as the ongoing international mobilization paralleled continued governmental efforts to repress dissent and delay political reforms. In the inter-election period, Koigi wa Wamwere became again a symbol for continued mobilization. Several international groups, including the Kenya Human Rights Initiative

(KHRI), based at Cornell University's Center for Religion, Ethics, and Social Policy, lobbied the US administration, Congress, and the embassy in Nairobi. The organization's home page 'Free Koigi' was prominently featured in many US newspapers and magazines (Saulnier 1997: 30). For the first time, Kenya now became subject to a confidential 1503 investigation by the UNCHR. Information by human rights NGOs and a defense by the government were presented at its 49th session in early 1993. After a brief discussion, the members of the commission were satisfied with the government's response and the investigation was discontinued without further action. When Koigi wa Wamwere was finally released on 19 January 1993, his release reflected the usual government tactic to pre-empt the application of serious international pressure. An official at the US embassy in Nairobi confirmed that Koigi's case frequently trumped all other human rights issues, simply because human rights activists in the United States would inundate the embassy and the State Department with calls inquiring about their efforts to secure the release of wa Wamwere. This focus on celebrity cases of human rights activism did little to address the structural causes of human rights violations and the lack of democratic reforms.

In late 1993, the donor community returned to business as usual in working with Kenyan authorities. The World Bank and the IMF were the first to end the aid freeze, while other donor governments later followed. Only the US government continued its ban of aid to government agencies and supported civil society actors only. While the World Bank and the IMF, supported by Italy, France, Great Britain, and Japan, stuck to a relatively narrow understanding of 'good governance,' Scandinavian countries, Germany, and the United States preferred even stricter criteria (Prunier 1997). The World Bank and the IMF were satisfied with promised anti-corruption measures and the overall political stability in the country. Others remained more pessimistic and highlighted the manipulation of the election process and ongoing human rights abuses. In November 1993, the community pledged a total of $850 million in aid (Human Rights Watch 1995: 24).

The donor decision was sharply criticized by domestic human rights advocates. The KHRC began in early 1994 to publish *Quarterly Repression Reports*, which monitored the human rights situation in Kenya in much the same way transnational groups did before. The reports invariably invoked international human rights law at the beginning and closed with recommendations to the Kenyan government and the international community. The KHRC was funded by outside donors including the Ford Foundation,[20] the Swedish NGO Foundation for Human Rights, and the National Endowment for Democracy. The information gathered by KHRC was later frequently reproduced in Amnesty reports and the annual US State Department report on the human rights situation in Kenya.

Donor governments disagreed about the wisdom of supporting specific political agendas promoted by Kenyan NGOs. While KHRC represented one of the most professional organizations operating in Kenya, it used human rights issues to further a partisan agenda against the Moi government. KHRC's work was dominated by a concern for Kikuyu interests and skillfully used principled activism as a way of masking a political and also ethnic agenda. While the US embassy was more likely to tolerate such partisan views within civil society and support direct challenges to Moi, the British High Commission preferred a strategy aimed at strengthening the moderate sections within the government (including Attorney General Amos Wako) and KANU.

The inter-election period

Despite the strengthening of civil society organizations in the human rights area, direct repression of dissent only slowly decreased. In early 1995, the offices of the legal aid organization *Kituo Cha Sheria* were the targets of fire-bombings on six separate occasions. These attacks followed the expansion of the organization's mandate to include more advocacy-oriented activities, which created greater tensions with government officials. Two members of human rights organizations, including a member of KHRC and the Secretary General of RPP, were killed under mysterious circumstances in 1995 and 1996. In early 1995, police and unknown attackers systematically raided the offices of critical newspapers and police officers broke into the offices of Colourprint, the printer of many opposition papers. The officers damaged the presses and charged the owner, Anil Vidyathi, with sedition.

The repression was accompanied by unchanged human rights rhetoric of the president and continued refusal to accept substantive political reforms. On 24 April 1995, Daniel arap Moi addressed the issue of human rights in a statement disseminated by the state-run Kenya Broadcasting Corporation (KBC). 'His Excellency President Daniel arap Moi today criticized human rights organizations for employing double standards when dealing with human rights issues in Kenya. President Moi observed that human rights organizations have made a habit of attacking the Kenyan government on human rights violations when the situation in a number of countries of the region was pathetic. The president wondered why Kenya should be criticized by such organizations when wanton killing of innocent people is taking place unabated in countries such as Rwanda and Liberia' (FBIS-AFR-95–080, 26 April 1995).

Returning from the 31st ordinary session of the OAU Heads of State in June 1995, Moi defended Kenya's human rights record upon arrival at Jomo Kenyatta Airport. 'His Excellency President Daniel arap Moi today defended the country's human rights record, saying that there was no Kenyan refugee who had fled the country to seek refuge elsewhere. President Moi noted that some powerful Western countries were accusing Kenya of flouting human rights, because the government had refused to dictated upon' (FBIS-AFR-95-126, 30 June 1995, p. 5). Moi was reacting to substantial diplomatic irritation that emerged after the government-sponsored newspaper *Kenya Times* had accused opposition member and former Director of the Kenyan Wildlife Service Richard Leakey of coordinating efforts by British and American businessman as well as the KKK to 're-colonize' Kenya.

Only eight months after Koigi wa Wamwere had been released in early 1993, he and five others were arrested on 22 September 1993 in Nakuru. After an alleged attack on a police station, the Attorney General charged the group with murder. The trial against Koigi wa Wamwere and his friends commenced in early 1995 and became a major focus of international attention during that year. On 20 May 1995, two Norwegian journalists were detained and charged with going to police stations without authorization, photographing police stations, and resisting arrest. After 13 hours they were released on bail and left the country. In July, the Kenyan government censored a BBC report that detailed a violent attack on Richard Leakey and a BBC reporter in front of the courthouse in Nakuru. In the aftermath, President Moi called the British Minister for Overseas Development Administration, Baroness Lynda Chalker, a 'village headmistress' after she had declared that new aid commitments would depend on progress in the area of good governance. In an official statement, Moi called Chalker's behavior 'impolite and contemptuous' because she made the statement before talking to Moi about future British aid. Kenya's Information Minister Johnstone Makau declared that the government would not renew a contract with BBC unless the tone of its reports on Kenya changed.

The continued clashes with international media and donor governments threatened to put the Kenyan executive back into a precarious position prior to the annual Paris donor meeting on 24 July 1995. Although an aid freeze was highly unlikely, the Kenyan government resorted to its strategy of empty tactical concessions. Two days ahead of the meeting, Moi announced the creation of a domestic Human Rights Committee (FBIS-AFR-95-143, p. 4). The donor community raised the usual issues of good governance, but did not press the government further on these issues. A few days later, Moi appointed KANU MP Moses Wetangula as head of the newly created human rights body. However, in early August, Wetangula declared that there was no national human rights body, but only a committee within KANU, which would focus henceforth on human rights issues. Wetangula said that no one had been appointed other than him. The *Daily Nation* claimed that Moi's announcement was only meant to pacify the donor community and was later buried or shot down by KANU hardliners (*Daily Nation*, 10 August 1995).

Whereas the donors failed to follow-up on the democracy agenda they had been purportedly pushing in the early 1990s, transnational human rights groups remained actively engaged on human rights issues. Following a new report on widespread torture in Kenya published in December 1995 (Amnesty International 1995b), two Amnesty delegations visited the country in 1996. In March, the Kenyan government presented a detailed response to the allegations and repeated that the use of torture was illegal in Kenya. For the first time, the government admitted problems in this particular area. 'These cases of torture are not unique to Kenya and should therefore be seen in proper context. [...] In Kenya such incidents are treated as criminal offences and [...] if established, the culprits, be they security officers or the ordinary public, are dealt with in accordance with the law' (cited in *Daily Nation*, 10 January 1997). In his reaction to the report, the Attorney General Amos Wako, called the organization 'unethical' and the report an 'ambush' because Amnesty failed 'to give a draft copy of the report to the government.'

In April 1996, the Government responded for the first time to KHRC's *Quarterly Repression Reports* and a 210-page memorandum 'Death Sentence: Prison Conditions in Kenya' also published by KHRC (Republic of Kenya 1996). In contrast to its prior responses to international human rights criticism, the unsigned copy was simply dropped off by a vehicle from the Office of the Vice President at a hotel where members of the opposition held a meeting (*Economic Review*, 13 May 1996). The first sentence admitted, 'Kenya, like all countries in the world, does not possess a perfect human rights record.' The main defending line taking in the report indicated growing concern about the human rights image of the country abroad but little appreciation for the emergence of domestic human rights monitors. The authors emphasized that Kenya's human rights record should be viewed as comparatively positive considering the economic constraints and the situation in neighboring countries. The authors also claimed that Kenya faced a number of more important problems including threats to national unity by tribal clashes.

In their defense of the government's human rights record, the authors also questioned the motives of KHRC and attacked their working methods. 'Unlike other human rights reports, which detail in what respect the State has failed to discharge its responsibilities under international human rights instruments, the KHRC Report does not approach the subject as a specialized legal subject requiring the creation of a nexus between the incidence and State culpability! It is embarrassing to the sponsors (Western donors, HPS) of the project and it is hoped that they will analyze the professionalism of the KHRC' (Republic of Kenya 1996: 2). The KHRC's work was dismissed as an 'unprofessional and mediocre propagandist catalogue of criminal incidents' to 'justify to sponsors that something has been done with the donor funds.'

The same year, the UN Special Rapporteur on Torture, Nigel S. Rodley, cited the Government of Kenya as having categorically denied that police systematically used torture because this would be in contradiction to the constitution of the country. In two out of six individual cases transmitted to the Government of Kenya replies were received,[21] whereas other cases remained without response.

Whereas the government became more responsive to international human rights criticism, it showed still little tolerance for similar domestic activities. Rude attacks on members of the AI, common during the 1980s, were now absent from the government's rhetorical repertoire. With the emergence of KHRC and other domestic NGOs in the 1990s, some of these attacks were now directed at these groups. Behind the principled human rights advocacy of KHRC and other NGOs, the Kenyan government suspected a Kikuyu conspiracy and showed resentment toward the existence of a donor-driven patronage system rivaling its own control over national politics. The 1996 response to KHRC's work also alleged that Maina Kiai, the Executive Director of the organization had turned KHRC into a 'heckling family-incoming-generating venture' (Republic of Kenya 1996: 6).

In the midst of sharp domestic confrontations and unchanged rhetoric, the government continued its policy of combining tactical concessions with continued refusal of substantive reforms. The human rights body created within KANU in 1995 began its work in early 1996 and now was made up of ten individuals appointed by Moi. Any reports the Standing Committee submitted were not public and went directly to Moi himself. On the occasion of the 48th anniversary of the Universal Declaration of Human Rights on 10 December 1996, Attorney General Amos Wako announced during a luncheon that the government would 'implement all the recommendations you [the Standing Committee, HPS] made in your first quarterly report, which you handed to the president.' The invited Executive Director of KHRC, Maina Kiai, interrupted Wako and demanded open access to the Standing Committee's work. Wako responded with a promise that Kenya would soon begin submitting periodic reports on the human rights situation in the country to international organizations. The chairman of the committee, Prof. Onesmus Mutungi, replied to Kiai, 'one of the greatest democratic rights is the right to be wrong. Just go and lodge your complaints officially and we shall investigate' (*Daily Nation*, 11 December 1996).

The international and domestic non-governmental human rights community continued its pressure on the Kenyan government. On 12 December, the *Daily Nation* carried a special report on the release of 'Kenya: Shadow Justice,' a 300-page human rights report published by the London-based NGO African Rights (African Rights 1996). The report detailed how the Kenyan executive continued to abuse the judiciary and human rights after the 1992 elections. On 16 December, the Kenyan chapter of the ICJ followed suit and published its annual report titled 'State of the Rule of Law.' It accused the government of continued human rights violations and lack of respect for established human rights safeguards (International Commission of Jurists (Kenya Chapter) 1996). The *Daily Nation* regularly reprinted these reports in full length, which gave ordinary Kenyans access to the information collected by domestic and international human rights groups.

The failure of the opposition parties to decisively challenge the KANU government in 1992 represented the background for a renewed domestic and international mobilization for political reforms in the mid-1990s. The weak parliamentary opposition as an institutional challenger of KANU was increasingly replaced by those newly established extra-parliamentary forces within civil society. In late 1996 and early 1997, the upcoming second multiparty elections became a catalyst for further mobilization and a more united approach of the opposition. At last, domestic pressure became a major force for democratic reforms.

The mobilization for constitutional reforms

The domestic and international mobilization had distinct effects during the run-up to the second multiparty elections in December 1997. International pressure secured the release of Koigi wa Wamwere on 13 December 1996 and was also largely responsible for Kenya's accession to the UN Convention against Torture and other Cruel, Inhuman or Degrading Treatment or Punishment in February 1997. Both of these measures were tactical concessions designed to keep the donors happy without undermining the domestic power of Moi and KANU. But the domestic opposition now used its newly acquired organizational capacities to challenge this recalcitrant position and press for meaningful democratic reforms and a more level playing field for the elections.

In January 1997 the wave of domestic mobilization gathered momentum when the government engaged in early manipulations of the electoral process similar to the 1991/92 period. This time, the President's Office announced the issuance of new ID cards as a requirement for voting in the general elections, which would have given an unfair advantage to KANU. Immediately, the NCCK protested the decision with advertisements in the national press. The NCCK also demanded minimum constitutional reforms prior to the elections, including the reform of the Electoral Commission, equal access to financial resources for all parties, and the protection of all candidates by state security forces.

After the *Nairobi Law Monthly* had published proposals for a model constitution by KHRC, the ICJ, and the LSK (Issue No. 51, pp. 8–32) in early 1995, the opposition began to mobilize for these reforms prior to election day. In the intensified struggle for political reforms, the newly established NGOs eclipsed the opposition parties and led a renewed challenge of KANU's dominant role in domestic politics. The demands of civil society actors went well beyond the parliamentary opposition, which was mainly interested in an election environment favorable to their success and not necessarily in fundamental democratic reforms. Only to the extent that constitutional reforms were perceived as increasing their chances to be part of the next government were these politicians in favor of such a process.

The tension between democratic principles and electoral self-interests expressed itself on both sides of the political divide during the public exchange of arguments for majoritarian multipartyism versus *majimbo*. This debate did not merely pit an authoritarian regime against the 'forces of democracy,' but also highlighted exclusionary self-interests disguised as different visions of democracy. *Majimbo* would insure that the minority groups remained in control of their home areas and retained at least a veto position in national politics. The ethnic group and not the individual was claimed to be the basis of democracy. Politicians within the ruling coalition defended this position, because it was most likely to further their political survival.

In contrast, the civil society groups and churches referred to ethnic groups only in the context of violence and non-democratic conduct. Instead, the suggested reforms and the new constitution were expected to 'facilitate the expression of the will of *All* by merely aiming at facilitating the exercise of sovereignty by all governed' (cited in Ndegwa 1998: 611). Consequently, the NCCK and others called for a referendum as main mechanism of constitutional reform and the application of majority rules to arrive at important national decisions. In this vision, protection against possible state intrusion was extended to individuals but not to ethnic groups. While this reflects liberal values and principled advocacy also promoted on the international level, the position was also likely to give an advantage to the larger ethnic groups, which, incidentally, dominated the organizations lobbying for constitutional reforms.

The upcoming elections did more than merely mobilize the vibrant extra-parliamentary realm. Both KANU and the opposition parties also continued to regroup, as did the donor community. Bilateral donors enhanced their coordination efforts by expanding a small group of like-minded embassies to create the Democratic Development Group (DDG), which now included 26 foreign missions present in Nairobi. While its joint statements carried greater weight than individual interventions, the size of the group also led to the frequent need for compromise language and the release of 'balanced' statements. While donors began in the mid-1990s to speak with a more unified voice, their contributions to democratization remained ambiguous and weak (Brown 2001).

On 1 January 1997, the opposition further split when Raila Odinga and many of his followers left FORD-Kenya and revived the dormant National Development Party (NDP).[22] The NDP was now a party representing the Luo community in Nyanza, while FORD-Kenya under the leadership of the Luhya Michael Wamalwa was reduced to a regional force in the Western Province. Moi's preparations for the general elections included the return of the infamous Nicholas Biwott to the center of national politics.[23] The *Financial Times* commented that 'Kenya's chances of persuading donors that it is tackling official corruption took a battering yesterday when a former minister associated with some of the country's worst scandals was re-appointed to Moi's cabinet' (*Financial Times*, 16 January 1997, p. 4)

The National Convention for Constitutional Reform

In spring 1997, efforts to unite the opposition on the issue of constitutional reforms prior to the elections finally bore fruit. From 3–6 April, a coalition of 13 opposition parties, churches, and NGOs held the first National Convention for Constitutional Reform in Limuru (*Daily Nation*, 7 April 1997). The organizations formed the National Convention Assembly (NCA) and the National Convention Executive Committee (NCEC), which was in charge of daily operations (Ndegwa 1998: 196). The meeting reiterated long-standing reform demands, and added the threat of mass action if the government would not change its position on political reforms (Tostensen, Andreassen and Tronvoll 1998: 34). The date for the first street demonstrations was set for the 31 May, the day before an AI delegation led by the organization's General Secretary Pierre Sané was expected to arrive in Nairobi. In the following months, the NCEC became an established domestic political actor and the main force behind the demands for constitutional reforms. In turn, the leaders of KHRC, the 4Cs and the other political NGOs were the main driving force behind the NCEC. These included activists like Gibson Kamau Kuria, Kivuta Kibwana, Paul Muite, and Willy Mutunga.

On 8–9 May, 20 Kenyan and international human rights groups held a two-day meeting in Nairobi. Participating organizations included KHRC, the 4Cs, the ICJ (Kenyan Chapter), the churches, and the British organization Article 19. The meeting resolved that existing Kenyan laws could not secure a level playing field for the elections. The demands echoed the NCEC agenda and included a more independent Electoral Commission, the abolition of licenses for public rallies, and the opening of the electronic media to the opposition. In early May, the AI launched a 'Human Rights Manifesto for Kenya' that had been developed in cooperation with 17 domestic human rights NGOs. The manifesto reiterated the specific demands for constitutional reform and the strengthening of the press and the judiciary. The donor governments also followed up on these issues and presented their expectations concerning the upcoming general elections. The list included, *inter alia*, a fair resolution of the ID card issue, registration of all eligible parties, equal access to print and electronic media, and transparent counting procedures on election day. Leaders of the Catholic and Protestant churches added on 22 May an ultimatum to their demands for minimal reforms.

Moi immediately rejected the attempts to press him into political change as 'dictatorship' and warned the opposition of 'causing chaos to attract coverage by the BBC and other international media as a way of winning sympathy' (*Daily Nation*, 24 May 1997). However, his attitude changed when the visit of the AI delegation approached and the NCEC's call for demonstrations brought thousands of protesters to the streets. On 1 June, Moi offered to replace the Public Order Act with a Peaceful Assembly Bill, but still continued to dismiss all demands for minimal reforms prior to the elections. On the second day of its visit, Amnesty representatives welcomed Moi's willingness to repeal the Public Order Act, but pointed to the reality of human rights conditions and a whole range of repressive laws not mentioned by Moi. The same day, the IBA in London published a critical report on the state of the Kenyan judiciary (International Bar Association 1997). Within the next two weeks, the HRW released two additional human rights report on Kenya (Human Rights Watch/Africa 1997a). As the general elections in December were approaching, international human rights groups used the spotlight to increase their pressure by releasing reports and mobilizing the international public.

During its visit, the Amnesty delegation held extensive talks with high-level Kenyan government officials. A request to meet with President Moi was rejected. Instead, Vice President Saitoti, the Attorney General Amos Wako, the Commissioners for Prisons and Police, and the Ministers for Health and Education attended the meetings. Saitoti clarified that the government was willing to openly discuss shortcomings, but would reject all recommendations 'couched in peremptory and prescriptive terms which are usually employed in master–servant relationships. The government hopes that Amnesty International will in future be sensitive to our national sovereignty.' Saitoti requested Amnesty to inform Kenyan government officials prior to the release of new reports. He also defended the government's refusal to go ahead with constitutional reforms, saying, 'It is a time constraint, rather than unwillingness to embark on the constitutional review.' Saitoti pointed out that all laws criticized by Amnesty were already under review and promised that the Amnesty memorandum would be given to the Standing Committee for Human Rights for further consideration (*Daily Nation*, 6 June 1997).

On 19 June, opposition parliamentarians disrupted the annual budget speech of Finance Minister Musalia Mudavadi by chanting 'Moi must go' and waving placards in favor of political reforms. Opposition and KANU MPs began to punch each other in front of a patiently watching Daniel arap Moi and many Western diplomats. The next day,

Moi blamed 'foreign-funded NGOs' for the chaos in parliament and threatened to de-register them. 'There are some NGOs such as the ones that have been engaged in feeding famine victims, but there are others which have gone against their mandate and are seeking to influence political developments in this country. [. . .] They were not allowed here to play politics, because that is how Africa has become the experimental ground for everything' (*Daily Nation*, 21 June 1997). In another speech on the same day, Moi suddenly indicated a change of mind on the political reform question and announced that he would meet the newly installed Catholic Archbishop Ndingi Mwana'a Nzeki to discuss the issue. 'I hope that after the meeting he will be able to understand my position. [. . .] I am not an obstacle to peaceful discussions relating to the future of Kenya.' However, Moi refused to talk to the NCEC, because it was not an elected body but just a 'congregation of self-styled leaders.'

The international and grassroots support for the opposition encouraged the NCEC to announce another street demonstration for 7 July, again a symbolic day in remembrance of the *Saba Saba* violence in 1991. Hard-line government officials such as KANU Secretary General Joseph Kamotho declared that no such rallies would be tolerated. When the demonstrators began to chant 'Moi must go' and 'Moi-butu' (in reference to the deposed Zairian leader), the riot police dispersed the crowds and left 12 people dead (*Daily Nation*, 8 July 1997). Several dozen persons were injured when the police stormed Nairobi's All Saints Cathedral during a service, threw tear gas canisters, and beat up many parishioners. International and domestic outrage flared up again. Once again, the news made it to the headlines of international media and the Kenyan government had maneuvered itself into international isolation.

Western envoys in Nairobi requested a meeting with President Moi on the next day. During the 90-minute encounter at State House, Moi accused the group of eight envoys[24] of being 'pro-opposition' and rejected all demands for reforms. In response to the documents by the Donor's Democratic and Development Group, the Kenyan government explicitly refused the registration of new parties. According to the *East African*, Moi repeated that he was only willing to talk to the Catholic Church about reforms (*East African*, 8 July 1997). On the next day, riot police stormed the dormitories of Nairobi and Kenyatta Universities after students had announced more street demonstrations. The universities were closed. Two executives of the formally independent TV station Kenya Television Network (KTN) were fired, following a critical report and video coverage of police brutality against the students.

On 10 July, the opposition failed to agree on a proposed election boycott conditional on the government's refusal to implement minimal constitutional reforms. The parliamentary opposition rejected such a plan and seemed confident that it could remove Moi from power this time round. In contrast, the more principled extra-parliamentary groups sustained the boycott demands. Moi reaffirmed his rejection of reforms and used the example of Uganda to accuse Western governments of double standards. 'Our friends who are telling us about democracy have no moral authority to tell us to do things which they do not do. A set of double-standards of democracy have been established for each country by the Western world.' Moi reacted to a statement by US Secretary of State Madeleine Albright who blamed for the political violence in Kenya 'not just the Government's unacceptable "strong arm" tactics, but its failure to take the essential steps to create a free and fair electoral climate' (*Daily Nation*, 11 July 1997). At the request of the Kenyan government, a donor meeting scheduled for late July in Paris was postponed. In two strongly worded editorials, The British *Times* accused Moi of being 'adept at giving just enough ground to split the opposition and placate his international critics, only to reclaim it later. [...] The West used to champion Moi, but now it is horrified by the brutality meted out over the last weeks' (cited in *Daily Nation*, 22 July 1997).

Between early 1997 and the aftermath of *Saba Saba*, the isolation of the Kenyan government resembled the situation in 1991/92. The NCEC had become the leading organization lobbying for reforms within the opposition and mobilizing the people to the streets. With some transnational pressure as support, the domestic civil society emerged as the only viable challenger to the government. Although Moi's resistance grew again with the amount of pressure on him, the violence finally forced him to accept reform talks.

Pressure from above and below

In a first hint of the things to come, Moi declared on 11 July that he would soon convene the KANU National Delegates Conference and the Governing Council to deliberate on the issue of constitutional reforms. 'I am not a dictator. [...] When they ask me to change the constitution who am I to change it? I was elected by Kenyans and it is them who must give me the mandate to change the constitution' (*Daily Nation*, 12 July 1997). The last time these two bodies met together in December 1991, Moi used the occasion to announce the repeal of Section 2A of the constitution, which declared Kenya a one-party state. On 14 July, the European Parliament called upon the European Union 'to suspend financial co-operation for structural adjustment programs under the Lomé Convention with Kenya, in the event the Kenyan government persists in not respecting human rights.' The same day, the Permanent Secretary in the Foreign Ministry, Sally Kosgei, flew to the United States to reassure the Clinton administration of the Kenyan government's democratic commitment. She held meetings with Undersecretary of State for Political Affairs Thomas Pickering, Assistant Secretary of State for Human Rights John Shattuck, and various Members of Congress. Kosgei defended Kenya's human rights record and said that it was portrayed unfairly in the Western press (*East African*, 23 July 1997). Important individual donor governments such as Germany and Great Britain officially declared that they would review their aid commitments.

On 15 July, Moi met 17 religious leaders on the question of political reforms. During the meeting, Moi agreed that 'a comprehensive review of the administrative and legislative framework' was needed, but left the timetable open. The following day, Moi made the first major concession and announced that licenses for public rallies would now be granted automatically. 'KANU and opposition politicians are expected to apply and only under special circumstances will they be denied licenses. The reasons for denial will be explained to the applicant' (*Daily Nation*, 17 July 1997). After a one-day meeting, the KANU NEC announced on 17 July that it recommended the immediate establishment of a commission to review the constitution and certain other acts. It insisted that only representatives from the parties represented in parliament should be members of the commission. KANU Secretary General Kamotho refused talks with NCEC, echoing Moi's arguments that it was not elected by the Kenyan people.

The conditional offer for talks split the opposition. The group dominating the NCEC demanded all-inclusive talks about constitutional reforms, which would also recognize the contributions of the civil society sector. Subsequent efforts by extra-parliamentary groups and church representatives to unite the opposition against the KANU conditions failed. While the main leaders of the opposition parties (Mwai Kibaki/DP, Michael Wamalwa/FORD-Kenya, and Martin Shikuku/ FORD-Asili) saw this as an opportunity to come back into the political game and agreed to the conditions set out by KANU, the leadership of the NCEC rejected the offer as 'piecemeal negotiations.' The NCEC called for a general strike on 8 August to press for the inclusion of the civil society groups.

On 30 July, the Kenyan Ambassador to the United States Benjamin Edgar Kipkorir defended the Kenyan human rights record in front to the US Senate Subcommittee on African Affairs which held a hearing on 'Kenya: Election Crisis.' Kipkorir presented several documents purport-edly proving the government's willingness to implement serious polit-ical reforms. One of the documents he submitted carried the name of the Attorney General Amos Wako, but represented the NCEC blueprint for constitutional reforms. The NCEC memorandum included the release of political prisoners, the resettlement of victims of ethnic viol-ence, the registration of all parties, and equal access to the media for all parties.[25] Much to the embarrassment of the Kenyan government, Amos Wako declared later that Kipkorir had submitted the wrong documents.

On 31 July, the IMF suspended a $220 million low-interest loan saying that the Kenyan government had not taken the previously agreed upon steps to combat corruption and strengthen management in the energy sector. Kenya became the first victim of new IMF guide-lines on corruption, which were approved by the IMF board on 5 August. An IMF official declared that there was 'absolutely no political motivation in consideration of the decision.' A few days later, the *Daily Nation* reported that Finance Minister Mudavadi had originally agreed to the conditions of the IMF one day shy of the deadline, but that Moi himself withdrew this letter the next day. Moi claimed that the conditions were political rather than economic. The Ministry of Foreign Affairs was completely kept off the issue. Similar to the 1990 decision to break diplomatic relations with Norway, Moi and a small number of advisers around him were responsible for this decision (*Daily Nation*, 3 August 1997). A few days later the World Bank followed suit and cited corruption as a reason for withholding about $70 million in aid.

The general strike on 8 August brought more violence and led to the death of three Kenyans, although the strike was barely followed by the general population. Without the support from popular political leaders, the NCEC's strategy of mass mobilization failed, because its leaders were much better known in Western capitals than in Kenyan rural villages or the slums of Nairobi. The counter-mobilization by KANU sympathizers initially targeted the coastal region and those who had moved to the area to work. One week after the failed general strike, a police station in Likoni close to Mombasa was raided and six police officers killed. Leaf-lets appeared on the streets demanding that 'non-coastal people' should leave. Over the course of the next few months, about 100 violent deaths were reported and thousands of Kenyans fled the region south of Mombasa (Kenya Human Rights Commission 1997).

By the end of August, the government and the NCEC exchanged increasingly hostile accusations. Moi and his ministers claimed that the

NCEC was 'backed by foreigners to start a revolution in Kenya' (*Daily Nation*, 31 August 1997). The President warned that the NCEC was about to stage a 'civilian coup' and intended to subvert the elected government. This statement followed an opposition meeting held from 25 to 28 August where NGO representatives decided to constitute the NCEC as a parallel government if KANU did not enter a dialogue with civil society actors. The meeting also resolved to call for two more major rallies on 9 September (*Tisa Tisa*) and 10 October (*Kumi Kumi*). This increasing pressure convinced moderate sections within the KANU government to enter into a dialogue in order to prevent further violent confrontations.

Minimal reforms

Vice President Saitoti took the lead in breaking the political deadlock and invited opposition MPs to jointly form the Inter-Party Parliamentary Group (IPPG), which would be charged with kicking off the constitutional reform process. Within a few days, the group agreed on minimum legal reforms, including a reform of the Electoral Commission and the deletion of the ban on forming a coalition government. The IPPG created three committees on (1) legal and administrative issues, (2), the electoral reform (3), and problems of domestic security. KANU and the opposition parties each took half of the seats in those committees. However, civil society groups were excluded from this reform effort. Efforts by the NCEC to force its inclusion by organizing street demonstrations ended with much the same dismal results as earlier in August. Unlike the elected leaders, the civil society groups had hardly any popular following, represented a narrow urban elite of lawyers and other professionals, and received most of their support from external sources. The moderate opposition in parliament accepted KANU's refusal to allow non-elected NCEC representatives at the negotiating table.

On the day of the first IPPG talks, the AI launched a six-month campaign called *Kenya – The Quest for Justice* which was organized in cooperation with domestic human rights groups. During the entire period, the AI brought Kenyan activists working for RPP to Europe and organized meeting and briefings with governmental representatives, parliamentarians, and the general public on the human rights situation in Kenya. At the domestic level, the reform process progressed quickly as the second multiparty elections approached in late December. Within only two months' time, the committees completed their work and the reforms were tabled by the Attorney General Amos Wako in parliament. The AI cautiously welcomed the progress made on constitutional reforms, but maintained that many issues were still unresolved.

Hardliners within KANU, including Moi himself, did not support the IPPG talks and every effort was made to prevent their success. Kenyan police briefly detained prominent opposition MPs, including the leader of the DP, Mwai Kibaki and NDP chairman Raila Odinga. Vice President Saitoti apologized in parliament for the attacks and reassured that opposition rallies will 'never again be disrupted. [...] I am saying in no unmistakable terms that this will never happen again. I've never made this kind of statement of reassurance to fellow MPs and recanted the next day. Investigations will commence immediately and action will be taken against those who perpetrated it' (*Daily Nation*, 8 October 1997). In contrast to those well-intentioned statements, hardliners within the executive and KANU rejected political change and even the imminent minimal reforms.

On 30 October, parliament voted with more than the required two-third majority in favor of the IPPG package (156 in favor, 26 against, one abstention). On the same day, Moi appointed ten new members to the enlarged Electoral Commission. They were added to the 11 existing commissioners and were all proposed by the opposition in parliament. One week later, Moi signed the IPPG proposals into law (*Daily Nation*, 8 November 1997). Apart from the strengthening and enlargement of the Electoral Commission, the constitutional reforms declared Kenya a 'multi-party democratic state,' abolished all licensing requirements for public rallies, abolished 'detention without trial' from the Preservation of Public Security Act, deleted all references to 'sedition' from the Penal Code, empowered the Electoral Commission to monitor the election coverage of the state-run media outlets, and required the Kenyan police to be neutral on political matters.[26] The compromise also provided that all pending applications for broadcasting licenses should be processed within 30 days and that all political parties seeking to compete in the upcoming elections should be registered immediately. Finally, the Constitution of Kenya Review Commission (CKRC) Bill set up a commission that would undertake a comprehensive review of the constitution immediately after the elections.[27]

The NCEC rejected the compromise as insufficient. On 11 September, the NCEC stated, 'the recommendations of the IPPG Sub-Committee change NOTHING whatsoever of real substance concerning reforms towards free and fair election in Kenya' (cited in Tostensen, Andreassen and Tronvoll 1998: 37). Similar statements followed from critical church representatives. Later, the NCEC published a document listing the democratic deficiencies of the IPPG package and comparing it with their own proposals. However, an initial resolution by the NCEC to boycott and disrupt the elections was shelved on 11 November 'pending public feedback.'

The fast and successful completion of the IPPG talks would not have been possible without the presence of a strengthened domestic opposition. This result had little to do with transnational mobilization, which played only a minor role in the completion of the reform process. The domestic allies of the transnational human rights groups and many donor governments had little support among the public and were easily pushed to the side by moderates within KANU and the parliamentary opposition. KANU hardliners held back for the time being, but had no intentions of accepting the reform process.

The 1997 elections

On 10 November, three days after the enactment of the IPPG reforms, Moi dissolved parliament and set the date for the general elections in late December. The KANU rejected a move by opposition MPs to have parliament discuss the implementation of the reforms prior to the elections. Immediately, suspicions arose that the government would now renege on some of the promised reforms and simply not implement them. Indeed, the government still refused to register one of the political parties (Safina), and the media coverage of the ongoing campaign remained biased (Tostensen, Andreassen and Tronvoll 1998: 42). The executive also refused to look into the issue of licensing more private TV and radio stations. While opposition rallies were now largely tolerated by the provincial administration, there was still no level playing field (Human Rights Watch 2002). Nonetheless, the donor community was satisfied with the progress and agreed to finance the electoral exercise as well as monitoring. Donors gave about $1.5 million to the NCCK, the Catholic Justice and Peace Commission, and the Institute for Education in Democracy (IED), which deployed together about 27,000 volunteers as poll watchers. Following the prior mixed experiences with charging foreign observers the donors now concentrated their resources on enabling indigenous monitoring efforts.

A total of 32 MPs had defected from their parties in the inter-election period, primarily from the opposition to the governing KANU (Tostensen, Andreassen and Tronvoll 1998: 19–22). FORD-Asili had now split into three sections: the remaining FORD-Asili led by Martin Shikuku, the Asili-*Saba Saba* led by Kenneth Matiba (who eventually boycotted the elections) and FORD-People headed by Kimani wa Nyoike.

FORD-Kenya had already lost Paul Muite and his comrades, who now played a major role in the NCEC and had formed Safina. Raila Odinga had quit FORD-Kenya and taken the Luo community into the NDP. Finally, a third group around Peter Anyang' Nyongo left FORD-Kenya for the Social Democratic Party (SDP). They were joined by the Kamba Charity Ngilu, who defected from the DP and took the Kamba vote to become the presidential candidate for SDP. In the end, the vast majority of opposition parties represented one ethnic group only. Twenty-six parties and fifteen presidential candidates were running in 1997 compared to eight each in 1992. Roughly 900 candidates for 210 parliamentary seats were cleared by the Electoral Commission, including the long-time political prisoner Koigi wa Wamwere.[28] On 26 November, the government belatedly also registered Safina party. Attorney General Wako declared that the allegations for the original decision to refuse registration might still be valid, but he was 'giving the said individuals the benefit of doubt over the allegations' (*Daily Nation*, 27 November 1997).

On 29 December, the elections almost ended in disaster because the newly empowered Electoral Commission proved incapable of managing the event. While the IPPG compromise gave the EC complete control of the electoral process, the government had failed to allocate sufficient funding to the EC. 'Ironically, the managerial problems might also be traced to the barring of the Provincial Administration, for obvious political reasons, from any involvement in the electoral process' (Tostensen, Andreassen and Tronvoll 1998: 53). Many ballot boxes did not arrive on time or were misdirected. Voting papers and even election officials were often missing so that poll watchers at about half of the polling stations reported that the voting exercise could not start on time. In light of the general chaos, the Electoral Commission extended the elections for an additional day. A total of eight were killed in election-related violence.

Despite those difficulties, voter participation was high. The final joint statement of the Kenyan NGOs observing the elections concluded, 'the results do on the whole reflect the wishes of Kenyan voters.' However, it also held in its conclusions that the 'institutional bias in favor of KANU, such as domination of the state media and unfair delineation of electoral constituencies, needs to be seriously addressed' (cited in Tostensen, Andreassen and Tronvoll 1998: 75). The 1997 elections were not yet free and fair, but they showed clear improvements compared to the 1992 exercise. 'In summary it may be said that neither the 1992 nor the 1997 elections were fair. [. . .] However, the belated IPPG reform package no doubt made the electoral environment measurably fairer than it had been five years ago' (Tostensen, Andreassen and Tronvoll 1998: 53).

Serious irregularities were identified in nine out of the 210 constituencies. Subsequently, a number of candidates contested the results in
court, but none of those applications were successful.

While the opposition was able to blame KANU manipulations of the
1992 election process for its failure to remove Moi from power, these
arguments were less convincing in 1997. There was still no level playing
field, but the continued fragmentation of the opposition had made a
defeat of KANU even more unlikely. In the presidential race, Moi was
re-elected in the first round with 40.4 percent of the total vote (1992: 37
percent). He also gained more than the required 25 percent in five out
of the eight provinces (Coast, Eastern, North-Eastern, Rift Valley, and
Western). Mwai Kibaki (DP) came in second with 31 percent of the vote
(1992: 19 percent). The remarkable increase was mainly due to Matiba's
boycott. The Kikuyu vote now went almost entirely to Kibaki who was
also the only candidate, apart from Moi, attracting voters outside of his
home province (Central: 89, Nairobi: 44, Eastern: 28, Rift Valley: 21,
North-Eastern: 21). Three other candidates won their home provinces,
but remained largely insignificant outside (except for the 'melting-pot'
Nairobi). Raila Odinga (NDP) took the Luo vote in Nyanza (nationwide:
10.8 percent), Michael Wamwala (FORD-Kenya) mobilized the Luhya in
Western (8.1 percent nationwide), and Charity Ngilu (SDP) in Eastern
(nationwide 7.9 percent). All other candidates remained below one
percent, including the internationally celebrated Koigi wa Wamwere
with 14 percent.

In the parliamentary vote, the race between KANU and opposition
was undecided until weeks after the elections. After both sides had
added their nominated MPs, the ratio was 113 KANU to 109 opposition
MPs. The DP now led the opposition with 41 seats, NDP followed with
22, FORD-Kenya with 18, and SDP with 16. Despite its late registration
Safina was able to gain six seats, while smaller parties gained a total of
another six seats. Uniting the Kikuyu vote had strengthened DP, while
FORD-Kenya was reduced to a Luhya party and NDP emerged as the
most successful newcomer based on the Luo vote in Nyanza Province.
From the larger ethnic groups, the Kamba, Kisii and Luhya were split
and voted in significant numbers for KANU and opposition candidates.

All opposition parties and the NCEC initially rejected the election
results as seriously flawed. KHRC, other advocacy NGOs, and the Catholic
Church called on 2 January for the immediate formation of a coalition
government that would also include religious and civil society organizations (*Daily Nation*, 3 January 1998). After the NGO observers had
announced on 3 January that the elections reflected the will of the

Kenyan people, Michael Wamwala and Raila Odinga declared their acceptance of Moi's victory. The president was sworn in for his fifth and final term on 5 January. Mwai Kibaki continued to reject the results but said his party would cooperate in the parliament. On 8 January, Moi announced his new cabinet, but left the crucial position of the vice-president open. Its former occupant Saitoti was punished for his cooperation with the opposition and demoted to the Ministry of Planning and National Development.

How did transnational mobilization affect democratization in Kenya during the inter-election period between 1992 and 1997? While external human rights groups continued to publish reports and build links with domestic allies, the effects of those activities were less significant and more ambiguous than in previous periods. Transnational mobilization had created in the late 1980s a powerful coalition for political change in Kenya. But when donors finally gave Moi no choice, they limited their efforts to demanding multipartyism and little else. Issues long demanded by human rights groups, including meaningful constitutional reforms, were ignored. This gave the KANU government sufficient room to manipulate two electoral contests and avoid any significant loss of power until the IPPG talks started in late 1997. While external support was crucial to protect domestic dissidents during the 1980s, it became a liability in the multiparty era. The domestic activists pushing for political reforms were unable to mobilize people to the streets and failed to create broad-based domestic coalitions. External support for celebrated individuals took on entirely different meanings as it entered the domestic realm. While donors and transnational human rights groups were focused on principles such as human rights, the legitimacy they conferred on their domestic allies was frequently used to further ethnic and personal agendas. The political opposition was more divided along ethnic lines in 1997 than it was in 1992.

Comparison

Transnational mobilization plays a less important and more ambiguous role in the period following the initiation of regime change. In both cases, transnational activism was still a significant, but no longer a driving force of political change. In Uganda, the narrow human rights mobilization focused on the rebel atrocities became a supporter of the Museveni government despite increasing domestic repression and an entrenchment of elites. In Kenya, a much stronger and more visible civil society became the main challenger of the Moi regime after the first multiparty elections, but the domestic legitimacy of activists was weak and their mobilization was based not only on principles but also on ethnic and personal power interests. Transnational mobilization naturally dropped off more quickly in the case of Uganda, where a complete change of guards took place. In Kenya, transnational activists remained more vigil and continued to monitor the government's human rights record in the multiparty era.

Transnational mobilization decreased markedly in Uganda after 1986 and only Amnesty International remained a regular observer for about a decade until the mid-1990s. In 1995/96, the international human rights movement returned again in full force and reported on gross human rights violations committed by rebel groups active in northern and western Uganda. This new mobilization coincided with strategic interests of the United States in the region. While the issue of child abductions was a major public relations success for the international human rights community and organizations such as UNICEF, this mobilization has given the Museveni government significant room to slow down the reform process and further strengthen its domestic control. While the media enjoys formal freedom from government censorship and consti-tutional guarantees to free speech, journalists critical of the government were regularly harassed and occasionally killed by security forces or under questionable circumstances.[29] The courts also display their independence by frequently acquitting journalists charged by the government, but the actions of the executive still result in intimidation and a practice of self-censorship in the media as well as in the broader civil society where 'non-political' NGOs avoid open clashes with the government.[30]

The principled human rights mobilization in Kenya remained narrow and created more ambiguous effects on the inside. Domestic activists have been distracted by their outside connections and ruling elites have successfully mobilized against 'foreign interventions.' Donors' efforts to channel more funding to NGOs were hardly coordinated and embassies frequently jockeyed for exclusive control over the more prominent domestic NGOs. Donors themselves undermined further democratiza-tion by endorsing flawed elections, preferring stability over substantive political change, and by privileging other priorities such as economic and strategic interests (Brown 2001; Hook 1998; Olsen 1998; Schraeder Hook and Taylor 1998).[31] Having invested heavily into the electoral exercise, donors were unlikely to admit a failure. A prevailing hope at the time was that greater contestation through the ballot box would improve governance and fight corruption, no matter what government emerged on electoral day. Moreover, Moi was for donors a known and predictable entity, while many in the opposition camp were not.

At the same time, the agendas of the most visible urban-based civil society groups were partly driven by a mix of donor preferences, personal aspirations, and the mandates originally set out to govern their activities. During the 1990s, transnational activism aligned with a narrow ethnic base in Kenya and failed to broaden its appeal beyond a few urban-based professionals in Nairobi. These defects of the domestic civil society were only slowly recognized by the donor community, which began in the mid-1990s to diversify its support and become more active in the rural areas. Only by the end of the decade, domestic civil society had begun to spread to the countryside and embraced issues of economic and social inequality. Democratization now progressed slowly and frequently despite the outside interventions by transnational activists and donors.

Beyond those internal problems within the political opposition, the Moi regime is responsible for ethnic violence and continued repression during the 1990s. As the government lost external support it reverted to the mobilization of its ethnic base and created conditions approaching civil war during the periods leading up to general elections. A divided opposition combined with official 'electoral despotism' (Klopp 2001) secured the survival of the Moi regime. The counter-mobilization by KANU representatives based on a revived *majimbo*-agenda brought ethnicity back to the forefront. Although the *majimbo* debate raised valid questions about the future role of different ethnicities in Kenyan politics, its blatant abuse by the government undermined any progress on constitutional reform or a transition to more democratic practices.

7

The Limits of Multipartyism

The most recent political reforms in Kenya and Uganda have addressed previously neglected aspects of participation and contestation. The 1997 constitutional reforms in Kenya created a more level electoral playing field and prepared the ground for an opposition victory in 2002. While multipartyism and electoral contestation are now well established in Kenyan politics, the constitutional reforms have begun to address issues of participation and the constitutional balance between different institutions of the government. In Uganda, the recent political reforms have addressed the issue of contestation and are likely to result in a return to multipartyism by 2006. Transnational activism played again a diminished role in shaping the direction of regime change. After a period of mobilization focused on atrocities committed by rebel groups in northern Uganda, NGOs begun more recently to challenge the authoritarianism of the Museveni government.

In Kenya, the 2002 electoral victory of the political opposition resulted in the appointment of several former civil society members to government positions. Human rights protections and democratic institutions have since been strengthened. In both cases, the pressure for sustaining the reform process came primarily from an increasingly confident domestic civil society sector. The recent development in both cases also confirms the pitfalls of a focus on multipartyism and contestation. In Kenya, the current Kibaki government took more than three years to bring a comprehensive constitutional reform package to parliament. Significant demands of civil society actors, such as a reconfiguration of the president's powers, have been watered down by the new government. In Uganda, the move toward multipartyism has only been possible, because the opposition accepted constitutional changes allowing Museveni to run for a third term as President.

Uganda, 1998–2005: The politics of multipartyism

The 1996 parliamentary and presidential elections did little to solidify the domestic control of the Museveni government. With the conclusion of the constitutional reform agenda and an emerging representative democracy on the national level, pressures for lifting the ban on party activities increased. Parliament, the judiciary, and civil society actors began in the late 1990s to assert their independence and challenge the tutelage of the NRM leadership. As a result of the 1996 elections, the dominance of older 'movement' leaders weakened, and younger representatives with less ties to the established regime entered the political realm. The Young Parliamentarian's Association (YPA), a new pressure group within the 'movement,' quickly developed a profile for its anti-corruption campaigns and its challenges to the old NRM guard. In February 1998, YPA led parliament to censure the former chief of the Internal Security Organization (ISO) and Minister of State, Brig. Jim Muhwezi, for corruption. YPA also sought to influence the first Movement National Conference held in July 1998, but failed to push its candidates past Museveni's handpicked choices. During the five-day meeting of 1600 delegates in Kampala, Museveni was elected unopposed as chairman. The Speaker of the former CA and the current parliament, James Wapakhabulo, was elected unopposed as the first NPC. Museveni also pre-selected all other members of the new secretariat and carefully balanced the influence of moderates and hardliners. Prominent critics included in the secretariat were Winnie Byanyima[1] (Director of Information) and Obiga Kania who had introduced an unsuccessful motion to remove restrictions on party activities during the CA deliberations in June 1995. Despite those concessions to the opposition, the Movement conference was little more than a confirmation of the complete control Museveni exercised over the political system and society at large.

A few days after the conference, Museveni rejected allegations that the Movement was slowly turning Uganda into a one-party state. 'The Movement isn't a one-party system because the decision to allow parties to function fully or not is with the people, that's the big difference between the old one-party system and the movement system. [...] Some people are saying that the whole question of asking people whether or not they want parties is out of order. Their real argument is that parties are a human right, that whether the people want them or not, they should be here. [. . .] Why don't partyists go and convince the people to vote for parties and leave me alone' (cited in *The Monitor*, 22 July 1998). This statement indicated a significant rhetorical shift in Museveni's position as well as a sign that multipartyism was on the horizon. While Museveni previously used to blame parties for the 'sectarian violence' of the past, he and the NRM now held that the will of the people should decide the question of multipartyism.

A rhetorically strengthened domestic opposition within and outside of the 'movement' led to frequent standoffs of government and 'movement' officials. Senior government advisors and Museveni regularly referred to their domestic critics as 'traitors' and accused them of conspiring with outside enemies (*New Vision*, 21 October 1998). Apart from the press, the main targets of government attacks were groups challenging Museveni's dominance, such as The Free Movement (TFM). When the former member of the Electoral Commission and Vice Chairman of TFM, Charles Owor, declared at a seminar of his organization that the 1996 elections were rigged, Museveni personally called for his arrest (*The Monitor*, 28 October 1998). Domestic repression further increased in the aftermath of the August 1998 bombings of the US embassies in Nairobi and Dar es Salaam. Ugandan security forces arrested and mistreated dozens of suspects and charged several with treason (*The Monitor*, 27 October 1998), and the government later introduced an anti-terrorism bill severely limiting free speech and other fundamental rights. During this period, only the peace accord between Uganda and Sudan, signed in December 1999 in Nairobi, brought some relief of domestic pressure. Both sides declared that they would withdraw their support for rebel groups in the neighboring nation.

Referendum and 2001 elections

In the lead-up to the 2000 referendum on the future of the movement system and the 2001 elections, the donor community became increasingly alarmed about the military engagement of the Ugandan army in the Congo and the delay of political reforms. But the donors were divided on the issues and failed to create a united front that pushed beyond occasional diplomatic interventions. The Dutch government was most explicit by threatening with freezing aid, if Uganda would not cut military spending and end its occupation in the Congo.

The referendum in June 2000 brought the predictable extension of the party ban. The political opposition had called for a boycott, which dropped the participation to slightly above 50 percent of registered voters. After the votes were counted, the government declared that over

90 percent of the voters supported the ban. Both sides could claim victory based on this outcome.

After the referendum, the government continued to harass journalists and dissidents calling for a boycott of any elections under no-party rules. Typically, one or two individuals were picked up by the security forces and detained for a few weeks to send a message to other journalists or the general public. In the March 2001 presidential elections, Museveni was re-elected with almost 70 percent of the popular vote, while his closest competitor and former ally Kizza Besigye, garnered a respectable 27.3 percent. The parliamentary elections for 214 seats were dominated by NRM candidates, although more than 50 percent of those elected ran for the first time for office. The number of 'official' opposition members in the new parliament increased from 12 to 35. Political parties were still prevented from holding public meetings, opening branch offices, or sponsoring a candidate for elections. After the elections, opposition leaders claimed electoral fraud and called for a repeat vote under free and fair conditions. The HRW supported those claims by challenging the voter registration process and claiming that the government had manipulated the results (Human Rights Watch 2001a). In August, Kizza Besigye, fled the country after being repeatedly threatened and harassed by the police and government officials. In September 2002, a parliamentary investigation of the elections called on the government to stop using its security organs for partisan purposes prior and during voting procedures. Museveni appointed a CRC to counter the growing internal and external criticism of his *de facto* one-party rule.

The attacks of 11 September 2001 provided Museveni new opportunities to delay the reform process and undermine the emergence of a viable political opposition. Following the peace with Sudan, Museveni opened again talks with rebels in northern Uganda, but soon reverted to military operations under the label 'Operation Iron Fist.' The HRW reported that the 'rebel Lord's Resistance Army (LRA) has abducted nearly 8400 children and thousands more adults' since mid-2002 (Human Rights Watch 2003). A limited ceasefire in early 2003 failed and the Ugandan army stepped up its efforts now securing the support of the Sudanese government in seeking to apprehend the LRA leader Joseph Kony. This cooperation between Sudan and Uganda intensified when the South Sudanese rebel movement, led by John Garang, ended its violent struggle and in 2004 became a part of the Sudanese government.

In early 2002, the HRW joined with the Ugandan Foundation for Human Rights Initiative to brief a committee of the Ugandan parliament on proposed legislation combating terrorism and regulating the operation of NGOs and political parties. HRW and FHRI expressed grave concern that the impending legislation would further strengthen the government and weaken individual rights, civil society, and the political opposition. This intervention along with strong resistance from other domestic NGOs did not prevent the passing of some regulatory legislation, but considerably weakened the provisions and preserved the independence of the civil society sector. Unlike the 1980s and 1990s, the government now faced serious domestic challenges to its rule, which pushed successfully for greater political freedoms.

The Political Organizations Act of May 2002 permitted, for the first time since the 1980s, party activities in the capital of Kampala. The law required a renewed registration of existing parties, a provision strongly rejected by the opposition leaders. In 2003, the Supreme Court sided with opposition and struck down as unconstitutional two provisions of the Political Organizations Act, which prohibited parties from holding rallies, taking part in voter mobilization, and maintaining branches outside of Kampala. The government reacted to the decision by declaring that Uganda would return to multiparty democracy by 2006.

The political opening for political parties was paralleled by the continued efforts of the government to limit dissent. The 'Suppression of Terrorism Bill' proposed in 2002 defined terrorism as any type of violence committed for political, religious, cultural, or economic ends. It also threatened journalists with 10 years in prison, if they publish news 'likely to promote terrorism.' In October 2002, the main independent newspaper, the *Monitor*, was temporarily closed by the police after it published a government-critical report on the war in northern Uganda. Museveni has framed the conflict since 2001 as a 'war on terrorism' and continues to receive support by the United States which has put the LRA on its list of terrorist organizations.

While Museveni called in early 2004 on the International Criminal Court (ICC) to prosecute the LRA, international and domestic observers continue to be highly critical of the army's anti-insurgency efforts. In May 2004, the International Crisis Group claimed that Museveni was fuelling the conflict as an excuse to evade substantial security reform and cuts in military spending (International Crisis Group 2004: 10). When the ICC's prosecutor Luis Moreno-Ocampo opened a formal investigation of the LRA leadership in January 2004, transnational human rights groups demanded that the conduct of members of the Ugandan army should also be made subject to the ICC's jurisdiction. The ICC agreed to investigate crimes committed after 1 July 2002.

Throughout 2004 and early 2005, the ICC held meetings and workshops in Uganda to prepare for the investigation and familiarize local officials from northern Uganda with the jurisdiction and procedures of the ICC.[2]

As the return to multipartyism became inevitable, the movement leadership sought to turn its agreement to such a move into a bargaining chip. Officials close to Museveni demanded a change of Article 105 of the constitution in order to give the current president an opportunity to run for a third term in office. The opposition rejected this demand, arguing that a return to multiparty rule was a question of basic human rights and not of political bargaining. Museveni himself reneged by late 2004 on his election promise made at the beginning of his second term to step down prior to the next contest. Instead, he entered the campaign trail in full force, promising hikes in salaries and scrapping an unpopular tax on motorcycle taxis (commonly know in Kampala as *boda boda*). The government also rewarded every parliamentarian with almost US$3,000 for 'discussing' the issue of a third term for Museveni in their constituencies.

In April 2005, the British government suspended a small amount of aid to Uganda, citing dissatisfaction with the transition to multiparty rule. By June 2005, the majority in parliament accepted a government proposal to drop the term limit from the constitution. In return, the leadership now announced the support for a referendum on multipartyism two months later. The opposition rejected the parliamentary vote as a fraud and called for a boycott of the referendum. While the 'movement' and Museveni now actively campaigned for what they had rejected for the past 19 years, the opposition resisted what had been its major objective in the past decade. The referendum question put to the voters on 28 July 2005 asked 'Do you agree to open up the political space to allow those who wish to join different organisations/parties to do so to compete for political power?' Only 47 percent of the registered voters went to the polls and turned out a 93 percent support for the multiparty proposal. Five years earlier, a similarly low turnout of barely 50 percent had voted against multipartyism with a similar margin.

While Uganda is now on track to return to multiparty rule, there are serious doubts about the democratizing effects of such a step. Donor governments have put some pressure on the government, but lack a comprehensive and long-term strategy of promoting democratization beyond the introduction of multipartyism. Strategic and commercial concerns rival a desire to promote democratic governance. Threats to domestic stability are relatively high in a country still engaged in a war with insurgents in the north and bordering Rwanda and the Democratic Republic of Congo. While Museveni's rule has brought some stability and peace as well as impressive economic recovery to large parts of the nation, the 'movement' system prevented the emergence of viable alternatives to him. A much weaker civil society in Uganda (Dicklitch and Lwanga 2003; Goetz 2002) will be less capable of challenging Museveni in his next term and may even face a much less 'benign' successor in the future.

Kenya, 1998–2005: Elite turnover without change?

The constitutional reforms of 1997 split both the opposition and the KANU leadership. Moderates on both sides accomplished a limited set of changes, which sidelined KANU hardliners and civil society groups. In December 1997, the opposition failed to remove Moi from power for a second time and had to take most of the blame on itself. While the 1992 contest had neither been free nor fair, the opposition now lost primarily because it had disintegrated into more than 20 parties and offered 14 presidential candidates. While this defeat gave KANU another five years in power, it also prepared the ground for the first peaceful handover of national power in 2002. Since 1991, donor governments did little to support the democratization process and were more concerned with political stability, economic reforms, and a desire to maintain friendly diplomatic relations. Their primary contribution to democratic reforms during the next few years was a successful veto of Moi's aspirations to run for an extra-constitutional third term in 2002.

Two days after the major opposition parties had been pressured by donor governments to accept the 1997 election results, 'ethnic violence' returned to the Rift Valley. By late January 1998, more than 100 people were killed in Laikipia and Njoro, most of them Kikuyu opposition voters. The response by the government, as well as the provincial administration and police force, was slow and showed little interest in identifying the responsible parties. The head of the Church of the Province of Kenya (Anglican Church) Archbishop David Gitari suspected that 'the government does not seem to have the will to end these clashes at the earliest moment possible' and demanded an independent investigation by the UNCHR (*Daily Nation*, 9 February 1998). US President Bill Clinton sent the Reverend Jesse Jackson as a special envoy to the Rift Valley's largest city of Nakuru to hold talks to end the violence. Moi declined an invitation to join Jackson on a tour to the affected areas. Donors remained largely quiet on the issue, fearing that pressure on the

government would only spark more violence and create political instability. Only the U.S. Department of State report on Kenyan human
rights practices for 1997 made a strong claim of identifying 'indications
that the violence had political roots, with local KANU political leaders
reportedly involved in the planning' (U.S. Department of State 1998).
Other statements by the donor's DDG consistently refused to take sides
and condemned both sides for the violence (Democratic Development
Group 2000).

The politics of violence

The NCEC called the violence a sign of continued repression by the
government and a failure of the moderates agreeing to minimal constitutional reforms. A few days later, on 19 January 1998, the NCEC
spokesman Kivutha Kibwana was abducted in front of his home. He was
released the same night, but was told by his assailants that they came
'to kill him' (*Daily Nation*, 15 February 1998). The parliamentary
opposition threatened to boycott the opening session of the new parliament until the government committed to ending the violence. NCEC
representatives (re-)joined with popular political leaders and repeated
their demands for an all-inclusive Constitutional Conference. After
remaining silent for weeks after the elections, Moi declared on 29
January that the law enforcement agencies had been instructed to
'firmly' deal with the instigators of the violence. He blamed the opposition for the renewed violence. When the eighth parliament held its first
session on 3 February 1998, opposition MPs used the occasion to
protest the violence by waving placards and chanting 'Moi must go,'
'No peace, no *Bunge*' (parliament), and '*Hatutaki Majimbo*' (We don't
want federalism). On 10 February 1998, the government relented and
accepted the creation of a parliamentary commission of inquiry to
probe the recent violent clashes.

Transnational NGOs were successful in influencing individual donor
decisions on Kenya. After the 1997 *Saba Saba* violence, the British
Section of AI had focused on the issue of selling anti-riot equipment to
Kenya. By early 1998, the British government announced that it refused
to deliver such equipment to the Kenyan police, because it was 'particularly concerned about the persistent police brutality and the evidence of
torture and extra-judicial killings' (*Daily Nation*, 7 February 1998).

Two weeks after the opening of the Kenyan parliament, KANU
formed its first informal coalition with Raila Odinga's NDP. Odinga
declared that the last five years showed a need for change in order to
break the gridlock in the political arena. This move enlarged the KANU

majority in parliament from four to 26 seats. On 19 February, the Catholic and Protestant leadership held that the new government had 'no moral legitimacy to lead.' In a joint statement they supported the NCEC's rejection of the IPPG package and the demands for a constitutional conference. NCCK Secretary General Mutuva Musyimi appealed to donors to support the idea of 'all-party constitutional conference.' Moi reacted immediately to the demands and said, 'a Philippine-like revolution would not succeed in Kenya.' He accused the church leaders of joining 'the many shady and illegal groupings opposed to the formation of a Constitutional Review Commission' (*Daily Nation*, 21 February 1998). While Moi insisted that only elected representatives should participate in the constitutional review process, the NCEC demanded full participation of the extra-parliamentary forces.

On 25 February 1998, the London-based NGO Article 19 repeated its accusations of 'endemic torture' and other human rights abuses. The organization asked the Commonwealth Ministerial Action Group (CMAG) 'to add Kenya to its list of serious and persistent human rights offenders' (which included at that time Nigeria, Sierra Leone and the Gambia) at its 2–3 March meeting in London. However, the CMAG meeting passed without any actions on Kenya. During the same time period, the IMF extended its suspension of aid based on inadequate measures against corruption.

Domestic NGOs as well as the parliamentary opposition continued to clash verbally with the government. Moi threatened NGOs supporting the 'illegal' NCEC with de-registration, while the NCEC called for an escalation of general strikes beginning in early April 1998. KANU ministers responded by accusing the NCEC of preparing a coup 'at the behest of foreign governments,' while others openly warned NCEC activists that 'they would regret it if they dared to set a foot in Nakuru, Kapsabet or Eldoret towns' (*Daily Nation*, 27 March 1998). On 1 April 1998, the Attorney General Amos Wako appointed 12 members of the opposition and 13 KANU MPs to form the Inter-Party Parliamentary Committee (IPPC) to supervise the constitutional reform process. The general strike called by the NCEC failed to elicit significant support from the general public.

The disintegration of KANU

The repeat failure of the general strike tactics convinced the NCEC to withdraw further plans for any mass action. But KANU hardliners and the president also found themselves increasingly isolated. No senior KANU officials were invited when the US embassy, the World Bank, and Germany's Friedrich-Ebert-Foundation hosted donors, government officials, and MPs to discuss Kenya's economic problems (*Daily Nation*, 24 April 1998). While Moi roundly rejected the meeting and its recommendations, 160 MPs (including 82 from KANU), many key cabinet ministers, and ambassadors followed the invitation. In his keynote address, Finance Minister Nyachae echoed many of the international demands for economic and administrative reforms and frankly admitted that 'Kenya was broke and corruption was rampant.'[3]

In an official statement two days after the meeting, Moi declared that the results were 'inconsequential' because it pretended that there was 'no constitutionally elected government in Kenya' (*Daily Nation*, 28 April 1998). The president also declared that he would intensify cooperation with Raila Odinga's NDP in parliament to combat 'illegal' domestic groups and foreign intrusion. Moi continued to refuse to name a Vice President and call KANU party elections, because both issues would have focused attention on the question of his successor. While the KANU–NDP alliance made Moi less vulnerable to dissent within KANU and prevented a rapprochement between Kikuyu and Luo elites, the NDP leadership reaped the economic benefits for its home region.

When Moi convened in April 1998 a KANU meeting, several MPs openly challenged his position on the recently held economic forum. A majority of MPs rejected a proposal in which KANU would have officially distanced itself from the recommendations of the meeting. An anonymous source attending the meeting told the *Daily Nation* that defiant KANU MPs declared toward Moi: 'It was not lost to us that while the Mombasa seminar was on, you and Mr. Odinga were in Nyanza celebrating the marriage between their parties' (*Daily Nation*, 29 April 1998). Only a few days later, Moi gave in to domestic and IMF pressures and agreed to economic reforms largely in line with the donor expectations and the Mombasa recommendations.

The second major defeat for Moi occurred shortly afterwards in parliament, when the opposition prevailed over KANU in a motion to create a commission investigating human rights abuses and the causes for the ethnic violence since 1991. Although KANU MPs outnumbered their opposition colleagues, the motion for the commission won a 54 to 49 majority. KANU MPs had deliberately abstained or voted in favor of the opposition proposal. On 1 July, President Moi appointed Justice Akilano Molade Akiwumi as head of the Judicial Commission of Inquiry into Tribal Clashes between 1991 and 1998.

Moi's negative attitude toward the participation of civil society groups in the process of constitutional review was also now challenged from within KANU. The KANU members within the IPPC invited political, religious, and NGOs leaders to debate constitutional reform issues. Attorney General Amos Wako chaired the meeting at 'Bomas of Kenya' on 11 May, which initially only confirmed the differences on the role of the IPPC. While KANU representatives insisted on its current form, NCEC speakers demanded their inclusion into the review process. Gibson Kamau Kuria and Kivutha Kibwana repeatedly walked out in protest and the participants ultimately only agreed to continue the dialogue.

Before the second round of the Bomas talks planned for 8–9 June, 36 participating groups led by the Catholic Church, the NCEC, and the NGO Council threatened to boycott the meeting if their demands for greater inclusiveness were not met. They were supported by 42 MPs including 5 from the ruling party. Apart from civil society participation, the demands included the complete implementation of the IPPG package, as well as security of tenure and financial independence of any body concerned with the issue of constitutional reform. Catholic Archbishop Ndingi Mwana'a Nzeki declared during a sermon in late May that the government would 'waste its time if it did not expand the committee on constitutional reform.' The following day, Moi gave in to the continued pressure and announced an expansion of the review committee. During his annual Mandaraka Day speech, he declared that 'the stakeholders should make the appointments and my role should only be to formally sign on' (*Daily Nation*, 2 June 1998). Moi also asked all dissidents within KANU to leave the party and repeated his rejection of any foreign intrusion. A few days later, Moi announced a cooperation with FORD-Kenya by telling KANU followers that the FORD-Kenya leader Wamalwa 'is not your enemy. Your enemies are within the party' (*Daily Nation*, 5 June 1998).

On 22 June, 33 civil organizations and all Kenyan political parties met to decide on the future of the constitutional reform process. The NCEC was now officially included in the talks. During the meeting, KANU representatives suggested enlarging the IPPC on the basis of district representation, a modus that would have secured continued KANU dominance. The NCEC rejected the plan as 'tribalist,' and demanded representation based on existing civil society organizations. After intensive debates, both sides agreed one week later to set up a three-tiered structure topped by a CRC. One of the two other bodies would consist of representatives from the 65 districts, while the third tier would bring in a broad range of politically active domestic organizations.

A week after Moi's political concessions, domestic and international outrage again engulfed the Kenyan executive. On 10 July, the government banned the newspaper *Star*, and the magazines *Finance* and *Post on Sunday*. Editors and owner of the *Star* were arrested and charged in court with publishing articles likely to 'cause fear.' An editorial in the *Daily Nation* called the measure a 'heinous, intimidatory and retrogressive tactic used only by undemocratic regimes' (*Daily Nation*, 11 July 1998). The KANU Secretary General defended the measure saying that 'malicious and irresponsible journalism undermines press freedom.' On 15 July, the *Nation* management complained about increasing attempts to intimidate its reporters, in particular the journalists developing Internet services. The statement highlighted threats to journalists investigating corruption cases and a recent clash between the *Nation* and members of Raila Odinga's NDP. Seventeen MPs from the party had publicly threatened to stop the circulation of the newspaper in their constituencies in Nyanza District. The same day, the donors' DDG also condemned the press ban in a joint statement.

The Akiwumi hearings

On 20 July, the Akiwumi Commission began its hearings on the ethnic clashes. A police officer explained in the first hearing that the 'Kalenjins, who mainly supported KANU, did not understand multi-party politics and did not want neighboring communities to vote for the opposition.' The chairman of the LSK, Nzamba Kitonga, said that senior politicians were behind the coastal violence. He alleged that they misused the *majimbo* debate to recruit unemployed youths from the area for attacks on upcountry communities, which had come to the coast because of employment opportunities in the tourism industry. A member of KHRC also presented evidence based on their own investigations to the commission. Finally, the chairman of the Standing Committee for Human Rights, Onesmus Mutungi, confirmed the political nature of the clashes. He said that in both cases unemployment and ethnic animosity prepared a fertile ground for political violence related to the upcoming elections of December 1997 (*Daily Nation*, 21 July 1998).

In his testimonies, Mutungi explicitly rejected explanations advanced by the local administration, which tried to downplay the political nature of the attacks. Mutungi held that 'the administrative authorities must have been aware or should have been aware of the impending clashes,' and 'Given the security of the country, it is not possible for ten people to meet for a period of time without the security personnel knowing' (*Daily Nation*, 14 October 1998). On 22 October, Binaifer

Nowrojee from the Africa Watch/HRW office in New York testified and reiterated the findings of her organization, which identified government officials close to President Moi as responsible for the violence. Full-length transcripts of the hearings were regularly printed in the *Daily Nation*.[4]

The hardliners within KANU refused to accept the compromise on the three-tiered constitutional reform process and Moi himself insisted on the territorial principle as the only basis for representation. The president also declared that he was only willing to accept church organizations as civil society representatives in the constitutional debates. The imminent standoff between the opposition and the government was temporarily suspended when bomb explosions targeting US embassies in Nairobi and Dar es Salaam on 7 August killed more than 250 people and wounded many more. As the two sides in the constitutional reform process returned to the negotiation table, Moi no longer insisted on the exclusion of the civil society sector and also agreed that the new constitution should significantly limit presidential powers. The three-tiered structure of the review process was now implemented and consisted of a 25-member Review Commission, a National Constitutional Consultative Forum (NCCF) and at the District Consultative Forum (DCF). The success of the civil society sector was most visible in the composition of the Review Commission, where all political parties (including KANU) together appointed 13 representatives and the civil society sector named the other 12 members. On 8 December, the Constitutional Review Bill was passed in the parliament.

The compromise highlighted the profound changes that Kenyan domestic politics had undergone since the early 1990s. 'The fact that "radicals" such as Prof. (Kivutha, HPS) Kibwana were sitting on the same committee with Mr. Sunkuli, an ultra-right wing KANU politicians shows just how much transformation Kenyan politics has undergone over the past few months' (Githongo 1998). While the DCF secured representation according to the *majimbo* ideas advanced by the incumbent minority groups supporting the government, the NCCF represented the liberal ideas of the civil society sector. The former preferred constitutional reform based on ethnic communities and their representation in the parliament. In contrast, the NCEC preferred a majoritarian process which also gave greater weight to the larger ethnic communities dominating the ranks of the civil society sector. The struggle for national power intensified as the Moi government faced growing internal dissent and renewed pressures for substantive political reforms.

When the deadline for the nomination of representatives for the CRC approached in mid-February 1999, KANU reneged on the compromise to nominate five of the 13 seats allotted to parties and claimed seven instead. Intense struggles over the nomination of commissioners erupted within parliament as well as the civil society sector. When no compromise was reached and the stakeholders sent a total of 41 instead of 25 names to the Office of the Attorney General, Amos Wako called for a consultative meeting with two representatives from each of the 19 nominating parties and organizations. On 18 February, this meeting failed when KANU sent 21 delegates including 11 ministers (*Daily Nation*, 19 February 1999). During the following weeks, the 10 parties began to hold behind-the-door negotiations to break the deadlock.

Departure of Daniel arap Moi

Moi's absolute control over Kenyan politics ended long before the 2002 elections. Although the president increased his slim parliamentary majority by including FORD-Kenya and the NDP in his government, the eighth parliament had little resemblance with its predecessors. Only one MP from the pre-multipartyism (1988–92) period was still in the parliament and only 38 out of 210 elected had been in the 1992 assembly. The turnover in the legislature and the constitutional end of his second term severely restricted the president's control of the legislature. Over the term of the parliament, basic compensation for MPs increased sevenfold to the equivalent of US$5,000. The 2002 parliament increased salaries again to about $6,000 (Barkan 2003). Non-partisan cooperation across party lines increased in the 1998 parliament and was facilitated by the activities of more policy-oriented Kenyan NGOs such as the Institute for Economic Affairs or the Institute for Policy Analysis and Research. Institutionally, parliament established in 1999 the Parliamentary Service Commission, which accompanied efforts to end the dependence of day-to-day operations of the National Assembly on the Office of the President. Parliament now controlled its rules of operations, budget, staff appointments, and compensation. Moi's system of patronage lost crucial tools of controlling the policy-making process.

After another round of standoffs between the opposition and the KANU establishment on the composition of the Review Commission, the civil society actors quit the constitutional reform process and created a parallel process named the Ufangamano Initiative. Domestic and international pressures forced the parliamentary and the civil society process to merge again in March 2001. The CKRC was now led by the internationally renowned lawyer Yash Ghai and submitted its first draft proposal to parliament in September 2002.[5]

In the summer of 2002, the opposition finally succeeded in uniting its forces and was also aided by Moi's decision to choose the son of Jomo Kenyatta, Uhuru, as his successor. While many within KANU were pushing for Moi to run for a third term, donors made it very clear that they would not tolerate such a move. In selecting a Kikuyu as presidential candidate, Moi hoped to divide the opposition, but miscalculated both the resolve within the opposition and the level of dissent within his own party KANU. With Moi no longer running for presidency, KANU officials openly defied his choice. When Moi presented Uhuru Kenyatta as his candidate for the December elections, 13 opposition parties countered with the creation of the National Alliance Party of Kenya (NAK). Within KANU, Vice President Saitoti and Raila Odinga openly resisted Moi's choice, created a breakaway faction called 'Rainbow' within the party, and demanded a secret ballot to choose the candidate (Ajulu 2001). When Moi declined to follow their demands, the KANU dissenters left the party in October and created with NAK the NARC. Former Vice President Mwai Kibaki emerged as the single opposition candidate challenging KANU's Uhuru Kenyatta.

The December 2002 elections ended with a decisive victory of NARC and Mwai Kibaki (Anderson 2003). NARC gained an absolute majority of 133 seats, while KANU was reduced to 67 seats. Election-related violence decreased considerably. The handover of power was peaceful and Kibaki immediately took legislative steps to strengthen the judiciary and human rights provisions. The areas of activities for the Office of the President were sharply reduced from 48 to 25 and functions such as immigration and airport security were handed back to governmental ministries (*Daily Nation*, 16 January 2003). The first US State Department report (2004) on the Kenyan human rights situation was cautiously optimistic and emphasizes many of the still existing institutional conditions conducive to human rights abuses.

Within a few months after taking power, the NARC coalition faced intense international and domestic criticisms for its lack of political reforms and the continuation of patronage politics under a new leadership. Several high-profile corruption scandals erupted in 2003 and led the British Ambassador, Sir Edward Clay, to declare in July 2004 that corrupt ministers were 'eating like gluttons' and 'vomiting on the shoes' of donors. The situation became worse when internal dissent within NARC prompted Kibaki in October 2004 to bring in opposition-KANU politicians into his cabinet. Although Kibaki had included the former head of the Kenyan chapter of Transparency International, John Githongo, into his first Cabinet, donors soon raised alarm about corruption and threatened to suspend aid. Githongo resigned from his position in February 2005 saying that the government was no longer committed to fighting corruption. Githongo went into exile to London after receiving credible death threats. The government also faced increasingly intense criticism for its handling of the constitutional reform process.

When Mwai Kibaki won the December elections, he promised a new constitution within 100 days. However, by late 2005, the NARC government was embroiled in a deep controversy over the contents of the new constitution. While Kibaki himself now insisted on preserving a strong presidency and was unwilling to share powers with a newly appointed prime minister, his critics charged him with following Moi's path by concentrating too much power in his own office. Violent street protests in July 2005 led to deep rifts within the NARC government, which plans to hold a referendum on the constitution in November 2005.

The most recent political developments in Kenya confirm the limitations of multipartyism as a tool for sustained democratization. Kibaki came to power with the help of senior KANU politicians breaking ranks with Moi shortly before the 2002 elections. By maximizing his electoral chances, Kibaki severely limited his room for political reforms after becoming president. By relying on many senior officials from the previous regime, Kibaki (himself a former Vice President of Moi) is an unlikely candidate for pushing serious political reforms.

Comparison

Multipartyism has not created conditions of sustainable democratization in Kenya and Uganda. In Kenya, the experiences with the new government in place since late 2002 are sobering, and indicate that the logic of electoral success can effectively undermine democratic reforms beyond election day. Mwai Kibaki and the opposition made a rational choice of including KANU dissenters into their ranks to improve their electoral chances. But after winning the elections, the legacy of corruption and patronage carried over from the past to the current government. A peaceful handover of power to new elites, frequently celebrated in the democratization literature as a sign of democratic consolidation, has not created conditions for sustainable democratic reforms in Kenya. In Uganda, multipartyism is unlikely to sweep in a new government, and the politics around it have already undermined important constitutional provisions such as the two-term limit for the president.

In both countries, transnational mobilization for human rights and democracy continued to play a role in domestic politics, albeit it remains less significant for democratization overall and focuses on specific aspects of reforms such as judicial independence and laws regulating the civil society sector. In Uganda, the continued insurgency in the north and the atrocities committed by the LRA provide the platform for the most high-profile involvement of transnational groups. While transnational activists primarily targeted the rebels during the 1990s, more recent reports reflect more scrutiny of the Ugandan army and its gross violations of human rights. Musveni lost much of his international standing as a result of the military involvement in the neighboring Democratic Republic of Congo, the failure to end the insurgency in the north (despite a peace accord with Sudan), frequent reports about government corruption, and his repression of a political opposition and a viable power alternative to the 'movement.' The donor focus on multiparty politics is unlikely to remedy those issues in the short or medium term. Most importantly, Ugandan civil society remains weak. A recent study of Ugandan NGOs confirmed that a combination of government and donor policies have limited the ability of domestic activists to attain financial independence as a requisite for an increased role on the democratization process.[6] While donor governments and transnational activists have frequently called on Museveni to accelerate political reforms, their interventions in support of civil society have only marginally strengthened the sector.

8
Conclusions: Transnational Mobilization Beyond Multiparty Rule

The results of transnational activism directed at Kenya and Uganda challenge prevailing scholarly views of democratization and external human rights mobilization. Transnational activism plays a more prominent and effective role in challenging authoritarian rule than in building sustainable democratic change after the fall of a repressive regime. In challenging authoritarianism, transnational mobilization succeeds in drawing attention to the situation, forcing the government to react with denial or concessions, pressuring donor governments to address the situation, and protecting domestic activists. Beyond initiating regime change, transnational mobilization plays a diminishing role and has more ambiguous effects on democratization.

Unlike the standard story told in the transnationalist literature, networks of activists are less integrated by shared principles, and mobilization takes on varied meanings among different international and domestic stakeholders involved in the politics of transition. While transnational NGOs focused on human rights conditions in their mobilization, affected donor governments diluted those pressures by adding their own concerns for political stability as well as strategic and commercial interests. The transformation of principled activism into a pressure for multipartyism substantially hindered further democratic reforms in Kenya. While donors acted based on the mobilization by human rights groups, they narrowed the goal to the issue of formal electoral contestation. Moreover, when elections were flawed donors regularly called on the opposition to accept results and preferred political stability to democratic change. Transnational activism put Kenya on the agenda, but could not determine the outcome and failed to adapt well to changing domestic conditions.

Transnational mobilization and its translation on the domestic level not only strengthens human rights allies, but also provides mobilizing opportunities for the attacked elites. The human rights mobilization directed against rebel groups in Uganda allowed Museveni and his government to increase societal control and delay democratic reforms during the 1990s. The Moi regime was particularly skilled in turning outside interventions into a domestic asset. Based on a nationalist and anti-colonial rhetoric, the KANU government framed external interventions as illegitimate and questioned the democratic legitimacy of domestic allies. Moi's rhetoric of rejecting civil society participation in the reform process was supported by references to principles of legitimate democratic participation and national sovereignty. While external actors had a rhetorical advantage during the late 1980s by contrasting universal human rights principles with domestic practices, the Moi government was able to mobilize recognized democratic principles in the debates of the 1990s.

External interventions may not only strengthen the wrong parties, but also weaken allies. Transnational activism does not necessarily strengthen domestic groups beyond protecting them from repressive governments. Domestic NGOs in Kenya formed a significant force, but they were not always strengthened by outside contacts. Competition for funding and recognition can distract and undermine horizontal networking and coalition-building at home. Vertical connections compete with the domestic presence of activists. Many in the opposition in Kenya wrongly believed that donors and outside pressure would do their work and remove Moi from power. The task of building a strong coalition for sustainable political change remained frequently unfulfilled, disappearing behind political ambitions and a need to maintain a good standing with external supporters.

Transnational mobilization also fundamentally changes its meaning as it crosses into the domestic realm. Outside support may be driven by human rights principles or a desire to promote democracy, but as these ideas make their way into a society they become part of existing ethnic, political, and social divisions. Domestic activists are also frequently driven by entirely different agendas than what they express in their pledges to cooperate with external actors. In Kenya and Uganda, AI and other transnational NGOs have often defended the rights of a few elite activists and given less attention to the immediate social and economic needs of the majority population. A focus on the roots of repression in poverty and corruption would have created a broader base for democratic change and empowered larger sections of the domestic society. Such a strategy may have gotten less media attention at home, but it would have created a more sustainable basis for transnational support of democratic change beyond the breakdown of authoritarian rule.

Research implications

The results of this analysis have implications for future research on transnational activism as well as the comparative study of democratization. They point well beyond the human rights area and the two East African cases presented here. Transnational activism is a significant factor across regions and issue areas. Studying the role of those non-state actors creates new research avenues aimed at understanding the sources, institutional bases, and effects of global processes driven by transnational activism.

The transnational dimensions of democratization

The African experience is a central part of understanding the spread and effects of formally democratic reforms on a global scale. Just as the fall of Communism in 1989/90 reinvigorated academic and policy debates on democratization (Bunce 2000; Thomas 2001), the current African experiences with regime change promise to further advance our understanding of social change driven by local and transnational factors. Most African nations are undoubtedly more vulnerable to external influences, because they rely on foreign aid for significant parts of their public policies. Since the end of the Cold War, donors have become more willing to engage in the rhetoric of democracy promotion and targeted Sub-Saharan Africa with greater consistency than areas where more significant commercial and strategic interests may compromise a push for democracy.

Regime change in sub-Saharan Africa provides a preview of a world where transnational influences are strengthened and interact relatively unhindered with local and domestic processes. Despite their comparatively low level of economic development, these nations experienced significant political reforms and took distinct paths of regime change. Domestic conditions prior to the onset of transnational mobilization play a role in determining the direction of initial reforms. While external actors were effective in challenging authoritarian rule, national leaders determined on their own to implement constitutional reforms in Uganda and multipartyism in Kenya. More crucially, both regimes effectively restricted the complementary aspects of contestation (Uganda) or participation (Kenya) in order to secure their domestic power. The governments did not engage in deceptive practices and empty rhetoric, but reframed transnational mobilization for human rights and democracy to effectively bolster their claims to domestic control.

Subsequent to the initial opening, external actors played a less significant and sometimes negative role in the transition process. Partly this was a matter of donors' actively undermining reforms based on competing strategic interests or a desire for political stability, and partly it was an unintended consequence of efforts to strengthen domestic civil society and promote human rights. The lessons from these two cases show that donors not only frequently follow the lead of non-governmental mobilization, but are inconsistent and unreliable external promoters of democratic change. Moreover, democratic donor governments not only deal with conflicting principles and interests on the national level, but must also balance domestic pressures at home with what officials perceive to be effective methods of promoting democracy abroad. The case of Koigi wa Wamwere is a telling example of a domestic audience in the United States and Norway focusing on an individual victim, rather than the larger socioeconomic and political causes of abuses affecting millions of others.

But domestic factors, in particular elite choices, play the crucial role in explaining the direction of regime change. Variation in the type of authoritarian rule prior to transnational mobilization determines the availability and composition of potential domestic allies of global activists. In Uganda, the opposition to Museveni was tainted by association with the previous Obote and Amin regimes. The rest of civil society was either part of the new government, remained in exile, or elected to remain 'non-political.' The Museveni government did nothing to encourage the emergence of alternative political forces outside of the movement system.

In Kenya, a vibrant civil society quickly took advantage of the political opening in 1991, but it had also limited success in pushing for reforms during the multiparty era. Donors were partly responsible, but the weakness of a nominally strong Kenyan civil society was largely due to internal ethnic divisions and failures to create sustainable domestic coalitions. In addition, the logic of multiparty rule and electoral contestation privileged the creation of short-term 'winning coalitions' integrated by patronage rather than a common desire to create sustainable democratic institutions. While Ugandan civil society lacked basic capacity to challenge the state, its Kenyan counterpart had larger capabilities, but was unable to mobilize its potential. Therefore, the issue is not if countries have a 'strong' or 'weak' civil society, but how the different parts of domestic society relate to each other, the government, and external actors.

In both cases, transnational mobilization played a significantly different role after the onset of initial reforms. The Moi and Museveni governments adapted quickly to the preferences not only of donors, but also of transnational human rights organizations. Museveni successfully diverted attention away from his own human rights record by actively lobbying international NGOs and the UN to focus on the atrocities committed by the LRA. Moi rhetorically resisted human rights pressure, but changed the modes of repression after 1991 in order to prolong his power without having to face another showdown with donors. The politics of 'ethnic violence' and the practice of moving trials of dissidents outside of Nairobi were some of the efforts taken to cover up responsibilities and avoid international detection and blame.

Beyond the contribution made to the democratization literature, a focus on transnational dimensions of regime change challenges the very separation between countries 'in transition' and 'established' democracies. Non-state organizations such as AI regularly target authoritarian or less than democratic regimes, but they also mobilize against human rights abuses in democracies. Examples include the long-standing campaign against the death penalty in the United States or the targeting of immigration policies in Western Europe. A transnational perspective offers new opportunities to explore new and less common comparisons across regions and countries. Integrating the role of transnational activism into the study of regime change is not a one-way street. The results of this analysis offer to comparativists an opportunity to look beyond the nation state and find additional areas of comparative research, including the democratization of international institutions and the study of non-state actors not only as agents of change, but also as domestic structures with significant variation among themselves. Comparative methods are the tools needed to further our understanding of the global and the local roles of transnational activism.

The domestic dimensions of transnational activism

The study of transnational activism is a rapidly evolving research area. During the 1990s, a first generation of scholars primarily focused on establishing norms and NGOs as significant factors in a discipline dominated by state-centrism and concerns for material power. As a result, scholars emphasized the differences between transnational actors and states by focusing on the principled character and the network strategies of NGOs. These studies showed how principled actors 'beat the odds' and became influential in areas such as human rights, environmental protection, and global security. Beyond those trail-blazing efforts, the next generation of scholarship today takes the importance of transnational NGOs for granted and explores more systematically their origins, motives, the context of their activism, and the conditions of success as well as failure.

This study makes four central contributions to the study of transnational activism. First, it shows that the effects of transnational mobilization vary over time and place depending on domestic conditions. Challenges to authoritarian rule create very different demands for effective transnational action than the creation of sustainable democratic institutions in a contested domestic arena. Second, the evidence suggests that mobilization does not necessarily strengthen domestic allies, but may undermine their position by competing for local ties and weakening their legitimacy. Third, the results show that any domestic group can appropriate external influences, even if those are explicitly aimed at strengthening allies of transnational networks. Ruling elites frequently are successful in framing external interventions as 'neo-colonial' and inappropriate to counter mobilization for human rights and democracy. Fourth, researchers cannot assume an identity of principles and interests among those participating in transnational networks. Transnational activism reduces the complexities of domestic politics to categories of 'perpetrators' and 'victims,' which frequently ignored the multiple roles individuals and groups play. Ethnic and social identities may be powerful influences on regime change, but tend to be ignored by transnational human rights activists and the scholars following their mobilization. While some of these results challenge earlier assumptions of the transnationalist literature, they also confirm the relevance of those actors for domestic and international change.

The results also suggest promising new research avenues exploring the interactions among different transnational actors as well as the 'domestic' politics within individual organizations. Just as domestic activists compete among themselves for outside attention and funding, transnational organizations compete for media attention and support. Competition among and within those entities remains underexplored, and its study promises to answer some of the questions about their choices of goals and strategies. The professionalization of activism in recent decades as well as shifts toward more campaign-style and media-driven mobilization suggest additional variables to account for the specific forms of today's transnational activism.

Transnational networks and their participating NGOs are not merely vessels for universal norms and principles, but they exhibit significant variation with regard to their internal organization. Amnesty International is a membership-based organization with sections in more than 50 countries of the world, while HRW mobilizes without individual membership and relies almost entirely on media and lobbying strategies. A membership base not only provides organizations with greater independence from large donors, but may also limit their flexibility as they balance the demands of their base. Looking more closely at the 'domestic' of transnational activism will also allow scholars to detect issues that are likely to gain wider global recognition in the future. Debates about mandates and strategies conducted within NGOs may not have immediate effects on the outside world, but they foreshadow the subsequent publicity of transnational campaigns and mobilization. Decisions such as AI's focus on 'prisoners of conscience' and letter writing campaigns have long-term implications as the organization expands its reach and attains global recognition.

Policy implications

The evidence presented here highlights important policy lessons. Above all, there is a need for greater coordination among external actors seeking to positively influence democratic reforms. The 1990s saw improved donor coordination in dealing with governments, but there is no similar effort to coordinate interactions of donors as a whole with civil society or transnational groups. While coordination always carries the risk of stagnation and a failure to act quickly, those issues have to be weighed against the harm of uncoordinated action. External actors need to carefully evaluate how their partners are affected by the cooperation. Transnational activists should be at least open to the idea that the risks of an intervention may outweigh the potential benefits.

Policies designed to promote democracy abroad should be based on a more coherent and proactive plan beyond challenging and ending authoritarian rule. Many of the problems described here stemmed from a failure of external actors to understand all the consequences of their actions, a reactive approach to their counterparts in Kenya and Uganda, and a lack of vision beyond initial reforms such as multipartyism. Transnational human rights groups primarily reacted to abuses after the fact, were limited by their narrow mandates, and failed to review the results of their interventions as they became part of the larger domestic political context. Donors also largely failed to develop a proactive approach. During the 1980s, they reacted by appeasing domestic and international human rights critics and used their material power to force political reforms. In Kenya, the push for multipartyism became a smallest common denominator with unfounded hopes that other reforms would follow more or less automatically. During the 1990s, donors returned to sending mixed messages to East African governments and continued to operate by managing and balancing demands from the outside rather than developing consistent policies toward their partners. The reactive nature of both transnational NGOs and foreign governments compromised consistency and the emergence of more coordinated and comprehensive approaches to democracy and human rights promotion.

There is a wide range of models regarding transnational ties in support of democracy and human rights. While donors and some civil society actors such as the German *Stiftungen* maintain a presence in the countries, many transnational human rights groups do not have the resources to do the same. Until recently, AI had rules explicitly barring any activities of local groups directed at their own government and society. This kind of distance between watchdog and target was promoted to insure political independence and legitimacy as an impassionate advocate. This approach finds support in the tendency of local embassy and donor representatives to be less outspoken and more concerned with creating friendly inter-governmental relations. Moreover, the German *Stiftungen* and other external actors with a local presence are subject to the laws of their host nations and have to negotiate explicit frameworks regulating their presence and activities. This can severely limit their ability to effectively promote democratic change. The advantage of a local presence is a greater ability to work directly with societal groups and adjust policies to local needs. Some of the problems of transnational mobilization identified in this book were caused by a lack of local knowledge and a failure to understand that 'apolitical' interventions based on human rights norms can have unintended consequences in a highly charged political battle on the local level. While global human rights groups should enhance their regional presence in order to better grasp the different human rights needs of local populations, external actors with a local presence should enhance cooperative arrangements among themselves and be as transparent as possible about their goals and strategies.

Coordination among external actors facilitates the creation of a common framework, even if not everyone can agree on every goal. For donors, it is unrealistic to expect a principled policy void of strategic and commercial interests. Rather than focusing on the issues preventing donors from being more principled, domestic and transnational groups should build more pragmatic strategies cognizant of those limitations. For domestic groups, reliance on outside support should be limited and serve a specific purpose. For external actors, the aim should be to create favorable conditions for domestic mobilization rather than to support individual organizations. Democracy and respect for human rights cannot be sustained from the outside, but external actors can play a role in creating favorable conditions for domestic supporters of democratization.

Appendix: List of Interview Partners

NB: Positions identified as at time of interview

Kenya

Wolfgang Ahner-Tönnis, Resident representative, Konrad-Adenauer-Stiftung, Nairobi.
Dr. Anyang' Nyong'o, Friedrich-Naumann-Foundation.
Ove Christian Danbolt, Chargé d'Affaires, Norwegian Embassy.
Daniel Davis, Institution Development Officer, Overseas Development Administration, British High Commission.
Marguerite Garling, Ford Foundation.
Rev. Jephthah Gathaka, The Ecumenical Centre for Justice and Peace.
Bettina Gaus, Foreign correspondent, *Tageszeitung* (TAZ, Berlin).
Nancy Gitau, Program Officer, USAID.
Grace Githu, Institute for Education and Democracy.
Peter Gitonga, Outreach Officer, Kituo Cha Sheria.
Sally Healy, First Secretary (Political), British High Commission.
Christian Hegemer, Resident Representative, Hanns-Seidel-Stiftung.
Gitobi Imaraya, *Nairobi Law Journal*.
John Ngure Kabutha, Program Officer, UNDP.
Maina Kiai, Executive Director, Kenya Human Rights Commission (KHRC).
Kivutha Kibwana, Executive Director, RECAP.
Connie Kiplagat, Executive Director, International Commission for Jurists (Section Kenya).
Mirete Kituyi, writer.
Dr. Erich Kristof, Deputy Head of Mission, Embassy of the Federal Republic of Germany.
Wachira Maina, Institute for Economic Affairs.
Kathurima M'Intoni, Chairman, International Commission for Jurists (Section Kenya).
Dorothy McCormick, Institute for Development Studies, University of Nairobi.
Mundia C. Muchiri, Chief Sub-Editor, *Sunday Nation*.
Christopher Mulei, Executive Director, Center for Governance and Democracy.
Willy Mutunga, Citizen's Coalition for Constitutional Change (CCCC).
Githu Muigai, International Commission for Jurists (Section Kenya).
Karega Mutahi, *The Standard*.
Alfred Ndambiri, Legal Resource Center.
Dr. Maria Nzomo, Institute for Diplomacy and International Studies, University of Nairobi.
Kwendo Opanga, Associate Editor, *Daily Nation*.
Nicholas Otieno, Chief Executive Officer, Civic Resource and Information Centre (CRIC).
Tina Ottenburger, BMZ/GTZ-NGO support programme.
Elizabeth Owuor-Oyugi, Director, African Network for the Prevention and Protection Against Child Abuse and Neglect (ANNPCAN), Kenya Chapter.

Christoph Plate, *Der Spiegel* (German weekly).
Anne Marie Rosenlund, First Secretary, Danish Embassy.
Lena Schildt-Herring, First Secretary, Swedish Embassy.
Paul Wamae, Chairman, Law Society of Kenya.
Joseph M. Young, Second Secretary (Political), U.S. Embassy.

Uganda

Harold E. Acemah, Director, Multilateral Organizations & Treaties Department, Ministry of Foreign Affairs.
Solomy Bbosa, President, Uganda Law Society.
Mrs. Janet Beik, Political Officer, Embassy of the United States of America.
Albrecht Bossert, Resident Representative, Konrad-Adenauer-Stiftung.
Judy Butterman, Public Affairs Officer, United States Information Service.
Lesley Craig, Third Secretary Chancery/Information, British High Commission.
Joseph Etima, Commissioner for Prisons.
Josephine Harmsworth-Andama, HURINET.
Günther Haustedt, Resident Representative, Friedrich-Ebert-Stiftung.
Prof. George Kanyeihamba, Senior Presidential Adviser on Human Rights and International Affairs.
Dr. Khiddu-Makubuya, Director of Human Rights & Peace Center, Faculty of Law, Makerere University.
Thomas Kurz, Embassy of the Federal Republic of Germany.
Anton Mair, Resident Representative, Austrian Regional Bureau for Development Cooperation.
Apollo Makubuya, Board of Directors, FHRI.
John Nagenda, *Sunday Vision*.
Apolo R. Nsimbambi, Makerere Institute for Social Research and Presidential Candidate.
Justice Fred M.S. Egonda Ntende, Judicial Training Commission, High Court of Uganda.
S.L. Nsamba, Director, African Center for the Treatment and Rehabilitation of Torture Victims (ACVT).
Justice Arthur Oder, Supreme Court.
Jacob Oulanyah L'Okori, Law Reform Commission.
Omara-Atubo, Minister of State for Defense and Finances (1987–1991).
Charles Onyango-Obbo (*The Monitor*).
James A. Otto, Human Rights Focus, Gulu.
Justice Harold Platt, Law Reform Commission.
Livingston Sewanyana, Executive Director, Foundation for Human Rights Initiative.
Friedrich Steinemann, ICRC.
Lucian Tibaruha, Human Rights Desk, Commissioner for Legal Advisory Services Attorney General's Chambers, Ministry of Justice.
Father Dr. John Mary Waliggo, Executive Secretary of the Catholic Commission for Peace and Justice, Member of Constitutional Commission 1989–1993.
Fleming West, DANIDA.

Notes

Chapter 1: Introduction

1. A recent survey of foreign aid effects on Ugandan civil society confirms that 'donor funding for civil society policy advocacy has not made a major impact' (Robinson and Friedman 2005). For similar arguments with regard to donor–NGO relationships in other regional settings, see Henderson (2002); Lynch (2004); Mendelson and Glenn (2002); and Stiles (2002).
2. 'The lack of broader theoretical perspectives and of the empirical testing of existing approaches is particularly evident when we try to answer the question of the interaction between domestic politics and international factors' (Dimitrova and Pridham 2004, p. 104).
3. While democratization is most frequently studied as a form of transition from authoritarian rule, even established democracies regularly face significant external pressure to expand participation and improve modes of democratic governance. Despite more than a century of sustained economic growth and a formally established democracy in the United States, minority groups did not enjoy the formal recognition of their civil rights until well after World War II. In many other democracies, women only attained the right to vote in the early 20th century. While the struggles for women's rights and civil rights were largely fought and won domestically, their transnational dimensions have been well documented (Borstelmann 2001; Dudziak 2000; Layton 2000) and further strengthen the view that the process of democratization includes significant external and ideational components.
4. Clifford Bob explores other limits of the 'boomerang model' by elaborating the difficulties encountered by domestic activists in attracting outside support in the first place (Bob 2005).
5. For two sharply contrasting assessments of Museveni's policies, see Kannyo (2004) and Mughisa (2004).

Chapter 2: Transnational dimensions of democratization

1. An extended version of this chapter was previously published under the title 'Domestic and Transnational Perspectives on Democratization,' *International Studies Review* 6(3), pp. 403–426.
2. 'Strategically powerful players may develop normative commitments to democracy, or they may become persuaded that the ancien régime was unjust or illegitimate in ways that will cause them to accept frustration of their interests to a degree' (Shapiro 1993: 131).

Chapter 3: From repression to democratic reforms in Kenya and Uganda

1. Kenya's ethnic communities were purposefully created by leaders in the middle of the last century to further specific economic and political interests. Before political independence, inter-ethnic relationships were frequently symbiotic and there were few reports of 'ethnic violence' (Haugerud 1995). Only after independence, ethnicity was politicized and 'ethnic clashes' erupted for the first time in October 1991 during the run-up to the first multiparty elections during the Moi presidency.
2. In response to Odinga's dissent Moi stated 'I am the only "father" of or Head of Government in this country. If over the last three or so years you have not mended your ways, you are too late. Time is not on your side' (ACR, Vol. XIV, B 184).
3. The Swahili word means 'dirty' or 'untrustworthy' person.
4. In his famous 'parrot' speech on 13 September 1984, Moi demanded from 'all Ministers, Assistant Ministers and every other person to sing like parrots in issues I have mentioned. During Kenyatta's period I persistently sang the Kenyatta tune until people said: "This fellow has nothing to say except to sing for Kenyatta". I say: "I didn't have ideas of my own. Who was I to have my own ideas? I was in Kenyatta's shoes and, therefore, I had to sing whatever Kenyatta wanted. [. . .] Therefore, you ought to sing the song I sing. [. . .] The day you become a big person, you will have the liberty to sing your own song and everybody else will sing it" ' (cited in ACR, Vol. XVII, B 262).
5. In his writings, Mutesa explained that Obote was a 'herd boy' who decided, 'life was too vigorous to him' (quoted in Martin 1974: 101).
6. The British press was full of chauvinist praise for the coup. The *Daily Telegraph* wrote on 26 January 1971 that 'one good reason that might be advanced for holding Commonwealth conferences more often is that the number of undesirable rulers overthrown as a result of their temporary absence, as has now happened to Dr. Obote in Uganda, would thereby be increased.' The *Spectator* held on 30 January that 'if a choice is to be made between quiet military men and noisy civil dictators then I prefer, in Africa at least, the military' (quoted in Martin 1974: 61).
7. The first number in the Freedom House ranking represents a ranking from 1 to 7 measuring political rights, the second measuring civil rights. A low score indicates a high respect for political and civil rights. Some of the improvements on civil rights recorded were caused by changes in how Freedom House evaluates civil rights rather than improvements in the country itself (see www.freedomhouse.org).
8. Kenya's Freedom House scores are 6,6 (1987 to 1991); 5,4 (1992); 5,6 (1993); 6,6 (1994); 7,6 (1995 and 1996); 6,6 (1997); 6,5 (1998–2001); 4,4 (2002); 3,3 (2003).
9. Uganda's Freedom House Rankings are 5,4 (1986–1988); 6,4 (1989); 6,5 (1990); 6,6 (1991); 6,5 (1992 and 1993); 5,5 (1994); 5,4 (1995); 4,4 (1996–1998); 5,5 (1999); 5,5 (2000 and 2001); 6,5 (2002); 5,4 (2003).
10. For a background on the causes for the ethnic tensions in the Rift Valley, see Brown (2003).

11. For an exemplary account on the conditions in Kenyan police stations and prisons, see *Nairobi Law Monthly*, No. 14, 1989, pp. 17–19.
12. 'Despite all the evidence that torture of detainees is endemic and systematic throughout the country, the Kenyan authorities prefer to deny that these abuses take place . . .' (Amnesty International 1995c: 5).
13. The UHRC opened regional branches in Gulu (1999), Soroti (2000), Mbarara, Fort Portal, and Jinja (all in 2002).
14. Based on Anderson (2003) and Ndegwa (2003: 148); for in-depth reviews of the 1992 and 1997 elections, see Barkan (1993) and Throup and Hornsby (1997).
15. 'Provided that socioeconomic and political realities in Uganda perpetuated existing fundamental inequalities and injustices, the law by itself can do little to implement a regime of genuine grassroots democracy' (Oloka-Onyango 1989: 478).

Chapter 4: Successful challenges to authoritarian rule

1. Four years earlier, on 27 May 1970, the Economic and Social Council had adopted resolution 1503 which enabled the UNCHR to investigate cases 'which appear to reveal a consistent pattern of gross and reliably attested violations of human rights and fundamental freedoms.' Cases are initially discussed in the Sub-Commission on the Protection of Minorities and the Prevention of Discrimination and later forwarded to the main Commission. The procedure was confidential until human rights NGOs pressured the Commission in 1978 to release a list of states under investigation.
2. A.B.K. Kasozi provides a detailed list of massacres committed between 1971 and 1979 (Kasozi 1994: 249–253).
3. Despite well-attested reports about atrocities committed by the Ugandan regime, Amin had been earlier elected as the head of the Organization of African Unity (OAU) and was backed by all African member states. Member states elected to the UNCHR are not scrutinized with regard to their human rights record.
4. See also the statement of Whitney Elsworth, former Chairman of the Board, US section of AI at a US Senate hearing in 1978 (Committee on Foreign Relations 1978: 25).
5. Lule fled to Tanzania and later formed, together with Yoweri Museveni, the NRM. He died in January 1985 in London, one year before the NRM came to power.
6. The British press criticized the 'dubious triumph' (*The Times*, 15 December 1980) of Obote. The *Sunday Telegraph* titled on 14 December 'Observers Quit in Disgust as Obote "Wins".' The *Daily Telegraph* wrote in an editorial on 13 December that Obote was returned to power 'by whatever means.'
7. A.B.K. Kasozi provides a detailed list of massacres committed between 1981 and 1984 (Kasozi 1994: 240–248).

8. Despite a bias in favor of the second Obote regime, the African Contemporary Record confirmed gross human rights violations committed in Uganda in 1981/82: 'Wherever they (Museveni's rebels, HPS) struck, [. . .] the army was routinely send in to deal with them; this sometimes brought innocent villagers and peasants into conflict with the security forces, who did not always behave well and, on occasion, behaved very badly indeed. Obote might be held responsible for sending soldiers, not notable for their discipline in troubled areas, but what was his alternative?' (see ACR, Vol. XIV, B 298–308, 302).

9. Powers had previously been detained in Uganda and claimed that he was beaten by army personnel.

10. 'Malcom Rifkind, le secrétaire d'État britannique aux Affaires africaines qui se rendit à Kampala peu après, contena d'exprimer sa "préoccupation." Ceci n'empêcha pas le renouvellement de l'aide britannique, y compris de l'aide militaire, l'argument en faveur de cette mesure étant que, si les Occidentaux ne le faisaient pas, le président Obote s'adrasserait de manière croissante au bloc communiste' (Prunier 1994: 144).

11. For the details of the six rounds of negotiations, see ACR, Vol. XVIII, B 468–471.

12. During the KANU primaries the number of candidates was, in principle, not limited. However, only KANU members were allowed to vote. If someone gained 70 percent of the votes during this queue-voting procedure, he or she was returned as MP unopposed. In all other cases the candidates reaching at least 30 percent were allowed to contest the seat in the general elections and under secret ballot procedures. In 70 out of 188 constituencies the 70 percent rule led to the election of a candidate prior to election day.

13. On the day of Moi's return, Blaine Harden was notified that he had to leave Kenya within 48 hours. After protests of the US embassy and a personal meeting, Moi agreed to extend his license for another two years (see Harden 1990: 256).

14. Moi's speeches are usually in Swahili. English-spoken words and sentences are quoted in italics.

15. Muge was the first Anglican Bishop from Moi's Kalenjin community. The CPK had always been dominated by Kikuyus, because the christianization of its predecessor missionary organization was most successful in Kikuyu areas. Despite the ascendancy of a Kalenjin, the new bishop did not bring the church more in line with the government, but became one of the strongest critics of Moi. The disagreements originated on the local level, when Muge and the CPK became involved in an intra-KANU struggle for the local leadership. One of the main participants in this feud was a former diocesan development coordinator and MP, Samuel Pogishio, who was expelled from KANU in June 1988 (see Throup 1995: 157).

16. For examples of executive interference in judicial affairs, see African Rights (1996); Days *et al.* (1992); International Bar Association (1997); Kibwana (1992); and Nowrojee (1995)

17. One year later, Kuria was awarded another human rights prize by the American Bar Association for his work in 'promoting respect and observance of the rule of law.' Again, he was refused a passport to travel to the United States.

Chapter 5: Diverging paths of regime change: Electoralist and participatory reforms

1. According to the new NRC statute, the expanded NRC consisted of 38 historical members (from the guerrilla war period), 149 elected members (by RC III representatives), 10 army representatives, 20 presidential nominees, 34 women, 19 municipality, 5 youth, and 3 workers representatives (Tumusiime 1991: 19–23).

2. 'The legal and political conditions for the organization of RCs were uniform throughout the country. Yet, RCs tended to mean different things in different parts of the country' (Ddungu 1994: 402).

3. The proposed time table included a completion of the constitution-making process by 1992, prison reform, police and civil service reform, professionalization of the army, basic infrastructure rehabilitation, and reform of the judiciary (Museveni 1992: 64).

4. During the mid-1990s, regular round-table meetings between interested donor representatives, domestic and international NGOs and officials from the Prisons Department were held (mostly at ICRC headquarters in Kampala). In return for the donor support, the Ugandan government agreed to take control of all prisons in the country, including many local prison facilities infamous for persistent human rights violations.

5. Bigombe later gave in interviews a flavor of those negotiations. 'Before I met them I had to be sprayed with a mixture of holy water and shea nut oil to purify me' (quoted by Barrow 1996).

6. Human Rights Watch began only in 1999 to cover the general human rights situation in Uganda.

7. Lafargue lists and evaluates the major street demonstrations from 1987 to 1994 (Lafargue 1996: 250–253, 307–309).

8. In the following years, the opposition movement used days with symbolic meanings to call for demonstrations. In Kiswaheli, *Saba Saba* is the seventh day of the seventh month in the year.

9. Based on her interviews, Widner wrote, 'upon his return (from the United States, HPS) Moi was so furious with Ouko that he ordered his assassination' (Widner 1992b: 193). Hempstone even discussed accounts of the events, which described a direct participation of the president in the torture and subsequent death of Ouko (Hempstone 1997: 66–70). See also the recently published account of Jonah Anguka, a former District Commissioner who was initially charged with the murder and was later granted political asylum in the United States (Anguka 1998).

10. According to an embassy official interviewed, the Kenyan foreign ministry inquired in November 1995, if Norway would be willing to return aid programs to Kenya in case the Koigi affair ended 'well.'

11. The US Congress asked the Kenyan government to 'charge and try or release all prisoners, including detainees, stop the mistreatment of prisoners, restore the independence of the judiciary and permit freedom of expression' (Human Rights Watch 1991: 42) However, Kenya continued to receive unconditional military aid amounting to $5 Mio. in 1991, and $3,73 Mio. in 1993 (Robinson 1993).

12. When the US journalist Bill Berkeley later asked Attorney General Amos Wako in 1995, why Ntimama or others were never charged in court for the

incitements to violence, he replied: 'If you arrest Ntimama, there would be riots' (Berkeley 1996).

13. Already existing land conflicts between the tribes served as a cover for the attacks. Land conflicts emerged as a result of the discriminatory colonial policies of the white settlers and the sharp increase of population after independence, intensifying pressure on existing land.

14. The confrontation with the 'external enemy' glossed over possible internal dissent and bribed potentially dissatisfied 'poorer members of the Kalenjin community [...] to support the Kalenjin ruling elite' (Throup and Hornsby 1997: 199).

15. 'Tomkys confessed that he had lost the battle over the direction of British policy towards Kenya when he visited London the week of November 16–23. [...] He said he had delivered a list of steps to Moi on his return to Nairobi' (Hempstone 1997: 256).

16. A detective from Scotland Yard identified Biwott as one of two prime suspects in the murder case. Shortly before his death Ouko had challenged Biwott and other Cabinet Ministers alleging misappropriation of foreign aid (including the total Swedish aid package of 1989) for private use (Widner 1992b: 196). Biwott was briefly detained and lost his position in the Cabinet. He returned as Minister in the Office of the President in January 1997 (*Daily Nation*, 16 January 1997).

Chapter 6: How transnational activism undermines democratization

1. Buganda had 55 percent more seats in the CA than in the NRC (59 instead of 38 seats), the West and the East gained about 25 percent seats, while the North rose only from 42 to 44 seats. This bias against the North created additional domestic tensions (Kasfir 1995: 160).

2. Voter registration and turnout were above 80 percent across Uganda. Registration levels tended to be even higher in opposition areas (North and parts of the East) than in Western Uganda and Buganda. In Gulu and Kitgum 93 percent of the eligible population registered and 89 percent voted, in Apac and Lira the same numbers stood at 91 and 94 percent, while in Kumi and Soroti they were as high as 97 and 90 percent, respectively (Kasfir 1995: 157).

3. The exceptional local interest in the CA elections was enabled by the remarkable effort of the Odoki Commission to reach as many Ugandans as possible in collecting popular views on the new constitution. The CA Statute (Section 7b) also encouraged voter participation by allowing voters to register at their birth place, their current home, or at work.

4. The CA Statute encouraged candidacies and the majority of candidates were first-time nominees for a political office. Candidates ran unopposed in only three constituencies (Kasfir 1995: 159).

5. Eighty-five percent of the elected NRC members (a total of 140) competed also for CA seats. None of the NRC army representatives and only one-third of the historical members took the risk of running in popular elections.

6. 'It is true that the army had problems with honoring writs of *habeas corpus*. [...] The army simply did not understand what *habeas corpus* is all about. They did not know how to draw a return on writ of *habeas corpus* to present to court' (Republic of Uganda 1995c: 45).

7. The Ugandan government argued that it is unfair to judge, as AI does, Uganda and the United States against the same standards, because the latter, has experienced two hundred years of strong economy, political stability and human rights observance. [...] AI gives real credit when perfection is achieved and not when genuine efforts are being made as in the case of Uganda... (Republic of Uganda 1995c: 23).

8. A few weeks later, the Minister of Justice, Joseph K. Ekemu, demanded in a speech at the second extraordinary session of the African Commission on Human and Peoples' Rights the creation of a 'supra-national court of human rights' in Africa, 'a court whose decisions will be binding on individual governments' (Ekemu 1995: 4).

9. Amendments to the existing draft constitution required a two-third majority in the CA.

10. Articles 43 and 44 define freedom from 'political persecution,' 'detention without trial,' 'torture,' 'slavery,' and the right to *habeas corpus* and fair hearing as non-derogative rights under any circumstances, including a state of emergency. In Article 48, the UHRC is charged with reviewing detentions under emergency law 'no later than 21 days after the commencement' and thereafter 'at intervals of not more than thirty days.' UHRC is empowered to release a person after it reviewed the case (Art. 48, Sect. 3).

11. Press Release by the United States Information Service (USIS), 13 October 1995.

12. Rwanda supported the rebellion against Mobutu because the late dictator had provided refuge for Hutu rebels after the genocide in Rwanda in 1994.

13. The World Bank, News Release 97/1324-S. Total foreign assistance rose again from $622 million in 1995/96 to $720 million in 1996/97. This was four times more than the total debt service in that period.

14. See for example the telling headline: 'Shaking up Africa. From the Great Lakes Highlands to the Red Sea to the revolution-racked Zaire, Ugandan President Museveni's Disciples are transforming the Lost Continent'; *Time* Magazine, 14 April 1997.

15. In an earlier interview with BBC journalist Anna Borzello at his Gulu headquarters, Museveni sought to convince his counterpart of his standpoint. Borzello admits in her article that 'after one hour of discussion [...] I am exhausted by the relentlessness of the president's argument' and quotes him finally saying: 'Well, my daughter, [...] now do you agree with my attitude to the North?' (Borzello 1998).

16. All Africa News Agency, 28 September 1998.

17. The use of the KANU youth wings can be traced back to Jomo Kenyatta's presidency, where they served the same purpose of intimidating the political opposition (Throup and Hornsby 1997: 14–16).

18. In 1997, Moi promoted Chesoni to the position of Chief Justice.

19. The Kikuyu account for about 21 percent of the Kenyan population, the Luhya for 14 percent, the Luo for 13 percent, the Kamba and Kalenjin for about 11 percent each. The Kisii and Meru follow with between 5 and 6 percent. Most of these groups emerged during the 1940s and as a result

of political struggles. The Kalenjin consist of seven ethnic groups (Elegyo, Kipsigi, Marakwet, Nandi, Ndorobo, Pokot, and Tugen (Moi's ethnic group)), which were brought together during the independence struggle to strengthen their position in national politics.

20. From 1993 to 1997 financial support by the Ford Foundation for KHRC grew from $50,000 to $200,000 annually. The other major recipient in Kenya was the ICJ (Kenya Section), which received a grant totaling $250,000 in 1997. Human Rights Watch received between one and two million US$ from the Ford Foundation during that time period.

21. The Kenyan government responded only to cases involving prominent opposition figures such as Richard Leakey. In his case, the government claimed that he was beaten by 'unruly criminal elements' and not by Special Branch Officers.

22. Oginga Odinga created the NDP in October 1990, but later joined other opposition members to form the umbrella organization FORD and later FORD-Kenya.

23. Biwott had been dropped from government in November 1991, after being implicated in the murder of Foreign Minister Robert Ouko.

24. The diplomats represented Canada, France, Germany, Italy, Japan, the Netherlands, the United Kingdom, and the United States.

25. On 4 August, Kipkorir was removed from his ambassadorial position. It turned out, that the NCEC document bore Attorney General Amos Wako's name, because the NCEC hoped Wako would approve and simply forward the document to parliament.

26. For an overview, see the special sections in the *Daily Nation*, 12 September 1997.

27. This more optimistic reading of the IPPG deal contrasts with Ndegwa's verdict that the reform pact 'actually undermined the possibility for democratic consolidation' (Ndegwa 1998: 193). Similar pessimism is expressed by Rok Ajulu, who claimed that 'Kenya demonstrates that it is possible to have multiparty elections every five years without changing anything' (Ajulu 1998: 283).

28. On 19 November the state dropped all charges against wa Wamwere. He ran for president and gained 0.14 percent of the national vote.

29. For an in-depth review of the state of journalism in Uganda, see Mwesige (2004).

30. A study by the Kampala-based Community Development Research Network (CDRN) concluded that '[civil society] primarily sees itself as apolitical, in tune with the Government's development agenda, and at the receiving end of political processes' (De Coninck 2004). The study was funded by The British Department for International Development.

31. For Kenya, the specific interaction between foreign aid and ethnicity is highlighted by Cohen (1995).

Chapter 7: The limits of multipartyism

1. Museveni sacked Byanyima in February 1999 because she continued to speak up on corruption (see Charles Onyango-Obbo, 'With Byanyima's Ouster, NRM Hardliners are in the rise,' East African, 22–28 February 1999).

2. For an overview of the ICC's activities in Uganda, see the website of the International Criminal Court, at http://www.icc-cpi.int/cases/current_situations/Uganda.html.

3. In February 1999, Moi removed Nyachae from his post. Nyachae declined to take over a lower-level ministry and quit the government (*East African*, 25 February 1999).

4. On 21 December 1998, *Nation* reporters were temporarily banned from the hearings after it had printed a highly government-critical story based on a NCCK report about the ethnic clashes.

5. Additional information on the commission's work can be found on its website: http://www.kenyaconstitution.org/enter.htm.

6. In 2001, Ugandan NGOs received almost 75 percent of their revenue from external sources, primarily from international NGOs (43 percent) and bilateral donors (28 percent); see Angey and Nilsson (2004).

Bibliography

Adar, K.G., 'The Interface between Elections and Democracy: Kenya's Search for a Sustainable Democratic System, 1960s to 1990s', in Hyslop, J. (ed.), *African Democracy in the Era of Globalization*, Johannesburg: Witwatersrand University Press, 1999, pp. 344–346.

Africa Contemporary Record (ACR), edited by Colin Legum, various editions.

Africa Watch/Human Rights Watch, *Kenya Taking Liberties*, New York: Human Rights Watch, 1991.

Africa Watch/Human Rights Watch, *State-Sponsored Ethnic Violence in Kenya*, New York: Human Rights Watch, 1993.

African Rights, *Kenya Shadow Justice*, London: African Rights, 1996.

Aidoo, A., 'Africa. Democracy without Human Rights?', *Human Rights Quarterly*, 15 (1993), pp. 703–715.

Ajulu, R., 'Kenya's Democracy Experiment: The 1997 Elections', *Review of African Political Economy*, 25/76 (1998), pp. 275–288.

Ajulu, R., 'One step forward – Three steps back – The succession dilemma', *Review of African Political Economy*, 88 (2001), pp. 197–210.

Amisi, B.K., *A Crisis in the Making: Conflict in the Rift Valley and Western Kenya*, Notre Dame: The Joan B. Kroc Institute for International Peace Studies, 1997.

Amnesty International, *Jahresbericht 1975/76*, Bonn: Amnesty International, 1976.

Amnesty International, *Human Rights in Uganda*, London: Amnesty International, 1978.

Amnesty International, *Jahresbericht 1978*, Baden-Baden: Nomos, 1979.

Amnesty International, *Jahresbericht 1982*, Frankfurt am Main: Fischer, 1983.

Amnesty International, *Jahresbericht 1984*, Frankfurt am Main: Fischer, 1985.

Amnesty International, *Jahresbericht 1986*, Frankfurt am Main: Fischer, 1987a.

Amnesty International, *Kenya. Torture, Political Detentions and Unfair Trials*, London: Amnesty International, 1987b.

Amnesty International, *Jahresbericht 1987*, Frankfurt am Main: Fischer, 1988.

Amnesty International, *Uganda. The Human Rights Record 1986–1989*, London: Amnesty International, 1989.

Amnesty International, *Kenya: Silencing Opposition to One-Party Rule*, London: Amnesty International, 1990a.

Amnesty International, *Uganda. Death in the Countryside. Killings of Civilians by the Army in 1990*, London: Amnesty International, 1990b.

Amnesty International, *Uganda. Human Rights Violations by the National Resistance Army*, London: Amnesty International, 1991.

Amnesty International, *Uganda. Der Alptraum ist noch nicht zu Ende*, Bonn: Amnesty International, 1992a.

Amnesty International, *Uganda. The Failure to Safeguard Human Rights*, London: Amnesty International, 1992b.

Amnesty International, *Uganda. Detentions of Suspected Government Opponents without Charge or Trial in the North*, London: Amnesty International, 1994.

Amnesty International, *Kenya, Tanzania, Uganda, Zambia and Zimbabwe. Attacks on Human Rights through the Misuse of Criminal Charges*, London: Amnesty International, 1995a.

Amnesty International, *Kenya: Detention, Torture, and Health Professionals*, London: Amnesty International, 1995b.

Amnesty International, *Kenya: Torture compounded by the Denial of Medical Care*, London: Amnesty International, 1995c.

Amnesty International, *Jahresbericht 1995*, Frankfurt am Main: Fischer, 1996.

Amnesty International, *'Breaking God's Commands': The Destruction of Childhood by the Lord's Resistance Army*, London: Amnesty International, 1997.

Amor, M., 'Violent Ethnocentrism: Revisiting the Economic Interpretation of the Expulsion of Ugandan Asians', *Identity*, 3/1 (2003), pp. 53–66.

Anderson, D., *Histories of the Hanged. The Dirty War in Kenya and the End of Empire*, New York: W.W. Norton, 2005.

Anderson, D.M., 'Kenya's Elections 2002 – Dawning of a New Era?', *African Affairs*, 102 (2003), pp. 331–342.

Anderson, K., 'The Ottawa Convention Banning Landmines, the Role of International Non-Governmental Organizations, and the Idea of International Civil Society', *European Journal of International Law*, 11/1 (2000), pp. 91–120.

Andreassen, B.-A., 'Kenya', in Andreassen, B.-A. and T. Swinehart (ed.), *Human Rights in Developing Countries 1993*, Oslo, 1993, pp. 180–233.

Angey, S. and C. Nilsson, 2004. 'The Financial Sustainability of Ugandan NGOs: Are we no better than Government?', in *Civil Society Reviews, Paper No. 7*. Kampala: Community Development Research Network.

Anguka, J., *Absolute Power. The Ouko Murder Mystery*, London: Pen Press, 1998.

Anonymous, 'Uganda: 'The Pearl of Africa' loses its lustre', *The World Today*, 40/5 (1984a), pp. 213–220.

Anonymous, 'Uganda: A Postscript', *The World Today*, 40/12 (1984b), pp. 527–531.

Anonymous, 'Arrest and Detention in Kenya', *Index on Censorship*, 16/1 (1987), pp. 23–28.

Apter, D.E., 'Democracy for Uganda. A Case for Comparison', *Daedalus*, 124/3 (1995), pp. 155–190.

Article 19, *Censorship in Kenya. Government Critics Face the Death Sentence*, London: Article 19, 1995.

Baehr, P., H. Selbervik and A. Tostensen, 'Responses to Human Rights Criticism: Kenya–Norway and Indonesia–The Netherlands', in Baehr, P., H. Hey, J. Smith and T. Swinehart (ed.), *Human Rights in Developing Countries Yearbook 1995*, Den Haag/Oslo: Kluwer Law International, 1995, pp. 57–87.

Barkan, J.D., 'The Rise and Fall of the Governance Realm in Kenya', in Hydén, G. and M. Bratton (ed.), *Governance and Politics in Africa*, Boulder: Lynne Rienner, 1992, pp. 167–192.

Barkan, J.D., 'Kenya. Lessons from a Flawed Election', *Journal of Democracy*, 4/3 (1993), pp. 85–99.

Barkan, J.D., 2003. 'New Forces Shaping Kenyan Politics'. Washington DC: Center for Strategic and International Studies.

Barrow, G., 1996. 'The Lord Be With You'. London: BBC.

Behrend, H., *Alice und die Geister. Krieg im Norden Ugandas*, München: Trickster, 1993.

Berkeley, B., 'An Encore for Chaos?', *The Atlantic Monthly*, 277/2 (1996), pp. 30–36.

Berman, S.E., 'Modernization in Historical Perspective. The Case of Imperial Germany', *World Politics*, 53 (2001), pp. 431–462.

Bermeo, N., *Ordinary People in Extraordinary Times. The Citizenry and the Breakdown of Democracy*, Princeton: Princeton University Press, 2003.

Bob, C., *The Marketing of Rebellion: Insurgents, Media, and International Activism*, Cambridge: Cambridge University Press, 2005.

Boix, C. and S.C. Stokes, 'Endogenous Democratization', *World Politics*, 55/4 (2003), pp. 517–549.

Boli, J. and G.M. Thomas, 'INGOs and the Organization of World Culture', in Boli, J. and G.M. Thomas (ed.), *Constructing World Culture. International Non-Governmental Organizations Since 1875*, Stanford: Stanford University Press, 1999, pp. 13–49.

Bollen, K.A., 'Liberal Democracy: Validity and Method Factors in Cross-National Measures', *American Journal of Political Science*, 37/4 (1993), pp. 1207–1230.

Borstelmann, T., *The Cold War and the Color Line: American Race Relations in the Global Arena*, Cambridge: Harvard University Press, 2001.

Borzello, A., 1998. 'The Charmer'. London: BBC.

Bos, E., 'Die Rolle von Eliten und kollektiven Akteuren in Transitionsprozessen', in Merkel, W. (ed.), *Systemwechsel 1: Theorien, Ansatze und Konzepte der Transitionsforschung*, Opladen: Leske + Budrich, 1994, pp. 81–109.

Bratton, M. and N. van de Walle, *Democratic Experiments in Africa: Regime Transitions in Comparative Perspective*, Cambridge: Cambridge University Press, 1997.

Brown, S., 'Authoritarian Leaders and Multiparty Elections in Africa: How International Donors Help to Keep Kenya's Daniel arap Moi in Power', *Third World Quarterly*, 22/5 (2001), pp. 725–739.

Brown, S., 'Quiet Diplomacy and Recurring 'Ethnic Clashes' in Kenya', in Sriram, C.L. and K. Wermester (ed.), *From Promise to Practice: UN Capacities for the Prevention of Violent Conflict*, Boulder: Lynne Rienner, 2003, pp. 69–100.

Brysk, A., 'From Above and Below: Social Movements, the International System, and Human Rights in Argentina', *Comparative Political Studies*, 26/3 (1993), pp. 259–285.

Bunce, V., 'Comparative Democratization: Big and Bounded Generalizations', *Comparative Political Studies*, 33/6 (2000), pp. 703–734.

Burgerman, S., *Moral Victories. How Activists Provoke Multilateral Action*, Ithaca: Cornell University Press, 2001.

Bwengye, F.A.W., *The Agony of Uganda. From Idi Amin to Obote*, London: Regency Press, 1985.

Carothers, T., 'The End of the Transition Paradigm', *Journal of Democracy*, 13/1 (2002), pp. 5–21.

Charnovitz, S., 'Two Centuries of Participation: NGOs and International Governance', *Michigan Journal of International Law*, 18/2 (1997), pp. 183–286.

Checkel, J.T., 'The Constructivist Turn in International Relations Theory. A Review Essay', *World Politics*, 50/2 (1998), pp. 324–348.

Clapham, C., *Africa and the International System*, Cambridge: Cambridge University Press, 1996.

Clark, J., 'Explaining Uganda's Intervention in the Congo: Evidence and Explanations', *Journal of Modern African Studies*, 39/2 (2001), pp. 261–287.

Clough, M., *Free at last? US Policy toward Africa and the End of the Cold War*, New York: Council on Foreign Relations Press, 1992.

Cohen, J.M., *Ethnicity, Foreign Aid, and Economic Growth in Sub-Saharan Africa: The Case of Kenya*, Cambridge: Harvard Institute for International Development, 1995.

Collier, D. and D.L. Norden, 'Strategic Choice Models of Political Change in Latin America', *Comparative Politics*, 24/2 (1992), pp. 229–243.

Colomer, J.M., 'Transition by Agreement: Modeling the Spanish Way', *American Political Science Review*, 85/4 (1991), pp. 1283–1302.

Committee on Foreign Relations, *Uganda: The Human Rights Situation. Hearings before the Subcommittee on Foreign Economic Policy of the Committee on Foreign Relations/US Congress, June 15, 21, 26, 1978*, Washington, D.C., 1978.

Commonwealth Observer Group, *The Presidential, Parliamentary and Civic Elections in Kenya, 29 December 1992*, London: Commonwealth Secretariat, 1993.

Cook, H.M., 'The Role of Amnesty International in the Fight Against Torture', in Cassese, A. (ed.), *The International Fight Against Torture*, Baden-Baden: Nomos, 1991, pp. 172–186.

Cook, H.M., 'International Human Rights Mechanisms. The Role of the Special Procedures in the Protection of Human Rights', *International Commission for Jurists Review*, 50 (1993), pp. 31–55.

Cooley, A. and J. Ron, 'The NGO Scramble. Organizational Insecurity and the Political Economy of Transnational Action', *International Security*, 27/1 (2002), pp. 5–39.

Dahl, R.A., *Polyarchy: Participation and Opposition*, New Haven: Yale University Press, 1971.

Dahl, R.A., *Democracy and Its Critics*, New Haven: Yale University Press, 1989.

Darwin, J., *Britain and Decolonization. The Retreat of Empire in the Post-War World*, London: Palgrave Macmillan, 1988.

Days, D.S.I., N.R. Jones, M.-R. Blanchard, and J. Klaaren, *Justice Enjoined. The State of the Judiciary in Kenya*, New York: Robert F. Kennedy Memorial Centre for Human Rights, 1992.

Ddungu, E., 'Popular Forms and the Question of Democracy. The Case of Resistance Councils in Uganda', in Mamdani, M. and J. Oloka-Onyango (ed.), *Uganda. Studies in Living Conditions, Popular Movements, and Constitutionalism*, Vienna: JEP, 1994, pp. 365–404.

Ddungu, E. and A.A. Wabwire, *Electoral Mechanisms and the Democratic Process: The 1989 RC-NRC Elections*, Kampala: Center for Basic Research, 1991.

De Coninck, J., *'Politics is [best] left to the politicians'. Civil society in a period of transition in Uganda*, Kampala: Community Development Research Network, 2004.

de Schweinitz, K., 'Industrialization, Labor Controls and Democracy', *Economic Development and Cultural Change*, 7 (1959), pp. 385–404.

de Waal, A., 'Democratizing the aid encounter in Africa', *International Affairs*, 73/4 (1997), pp. 623–639.

Democratic Development Group, *Communique: Observations on Political Violence in Kenya*, Nairobi: Democratic Development Group, 2000.

Desfor Edles, L., 'Rethinking Democratic Transition: A Culturalist Critique and the Spanish Case', *Theory and Society*, 24/3 (1995), pp. 355–384.

Deutsch, K.W., 'Social Mobilization and Political Development', *American Political Science Review*, 55/3 (1961), pp. 493–514.

Di Palma, G., *To Craft Democracies. An Essay on Democratic Transitions*, Berkeley: University of California Press, 1990.

Dicklitch, S. and D. Lwanga, 'The Politics of Being Non-Political: Human Rights Organizations and the Creation of Positive Human Rights Culture in Uganda', *Human Rights Quarterly*, 25/2 (2003), pp. 482–509.

DiMaggio, P. and W. Powell, ' The Iron Cage Revisited. Institutional Isomorphism and Collective Rationality in Organizational Fields', *American Sociological Review*, 48 (1983), pp. 147–160.

Dimitrova, A. and G. Pridham, 'International Actors and Democracy Promotion in Central and Eastern Europe: The Integration Model and its Limits', *Democratization*, 11/5 (2004), pp. 91–112.

Donnelly, E., 'Proclaiming Jubilee. The Debt and Structural Adjustment Network', in Khagram, S., J.V. Riker and K. Sikkink (ed.), *Restructuring World Politics. Transnational Social Movements, Networks, and Norms*, Minneapolis: University of Minnesota Press, 2002, pp. 155–180.

Dudziak, M.L., *Cold War Civil Rights. Race and the Image of American Democracy*, Princeton: Princeton University Press, 2000.

Edgerton, R., *Mau Mau. An African Crucible*, New York: Free Press, 1989.

Ekemu, J.K., *Address on the Occasion Marking the Closing of the 2nd extra-ordinary Session of the African Commission on Human and Peoples' Rights*, Kampala, 1995.

Elkins, C., *Imperial Reckoning. The Untold Story of Britain's Gulag in Kenya*, New York: Henry Holt, 2005.

Emirbayer, M. and J. Goodwin, 'Network Analysis, Culture, and the Problem of Agency', *American Journal of Sociology*, 99/6 (1994), pp. 1411–1454.

Evangelista, M., *Unarmed Forces. The Transnational Movement to End the Cold War*, Ithaca: Cornell University Press, 1999.

Finnemore, M., *National Interests in International Society*, Ithaca: Cornell University Press, 1996.

Finnemore, M. and K. Sikkink, 'International Norm Dynamics and Political Change', *International Organization*, 52/4 (1998), pp. 887–917.

Florini, A.M., *The Third Force. The Rise of Transnational Civil Society*, Tokyo: Japan Center for International Change and Carnegie Endowment for International Peace, 1999.

Foreign Broadcast Information Service (FBIS), FBIS Daily Reports MEA and AFR, published by the U.S. Government Central Intelligence Agency (CIA), various years.

Forsythe, D.P., *Human Rights and U.S. Foreign Policy. Congress Reconsidered*, Gainesville: University of Florida Press, 1988.

Fox, R., 'Bleak Future for Multi-Party Elections in Kenya', *Journal of Modern African Studies*, 34/4 (1996), pp. 597–607.

Franck, T.M., 'The Emerging Right to Democratic Governance', *American Journal of International Law*, 86/1 (1992), pp. 46–91.

Furley, O., 'Britain and Uganda from Amin to Museveni: Blind Eye Diplomacy', in Rupesinghe, K. (ed.), *Conflict Resolution in Uganda*, Oslo: International Peace Research Institute, 1989, pp. 275–294.

Furley, O. and J. Katalikawe, 'Constitutional Reform in Uganda: The New Approach', *African Affairs*, 96 (1997), pp. 243–260.

Geist, J., 'Political Significance of the Constituent Assembly Elections', in Hansen, H.B. and M. Twaddle (ed.), *From Chaos to Order. The Politics of Constitution-Making in Uganda*, Kampala: Fountain Press, 1995, pp. 90–113.

Githongo, J., 1998. 'Kenya's Radical Wing Looses Political Steam', in *East African*, Nairobi.

Glasius, M., 'Expertise in the Cause of Justice. Global Civil Society Influence on the Statute for an International Criminal Court', in Glasius, M., Kaldor M. and H. Anheier (ed.), *Global Civil Society 2002*: Oxford University Press, 2002, pp. 137–168.

Goetz, A.M., 'No Shortcuts to Power. Constraints on Women's Political Effectiveness in Uganda ', *Journal of Modern African Studies*, 40/4 (2002), pp. 549–575.

Grugel, J., 'Democratization Studies Globalization: The Coming of Age of a Paradigm', *British Journal of Politics and International Relations*, 5 (2003), pp. 258–283.

Haas, P.M., 'Introduction: Epistemic Communities and International Policy Coordination', *International Organization*, 46/1 (1992), pp. 1–35.

Hadenius, A., *Democracy and Development*, Cambridge: Cambridge University Press, 1992.

Haggard, S. and R.R. Kaufman, *The Political Economy of Democratic Transition*, Princeton: Princeton University Press, 1995.

Harden, B., *Africa: Dispatches From a Fragile Continent*, New York: HarperCollins, 1990.

Haugerud, A., *The Culture of Politics in Modern Kenya 1890s to 1990s*, Cambridge: Cambridge University Press, 1995.

Hawkins, D.G., *International Human Rights and Authoritarian Rule in Chile*, Lincoln: University of Nebraska Press, 2002.

Helliwell, J.F., 'Empirical Linkages between Democracy and Economic Growth', *British Journal of Political Science*, 24 (1994), pp. 225–248.

Hempstone, S., *Rogue Ambassador. An African Memoir*, Sewanee: University of the South Press, 1997.

Henderson, S., 'Selling Civil Society. Western Aid and the NGO Sector in Russia', *Comparative Political Studies*, 35/2 (2002), pp. 139–167.

Henstridge, M., 'Stabilization Policy & Structural Adjustment in Uganda, 1987–1990', in van der Geest, W. (ed.), *Negotiating Structural Adjustment in Africa*, London: James Currey, 1994, pp. 47–68.

Hills, D., *Tyrants and Mountains. A Reckless Life*, London: Murray, 1992.

Hirschman, A.O., *A Bias for Hope. Essays on Development and Latin America*, New Haven: Yale University Press, 1972.

Hook, S.W., '"Building Democracy" through Foreign Aid: The Limitations of United States Political Conditionalities, 1992–1996', *Democratization*, 5/3 (1998), pp. 156–180.

Howard, R.E., 'Repression and State Terror in Kenya 1982–1988', in Bushnell, P.T., V. Shlapentokh, C.K. Vanderpool and J. Sundram (ed.), *State Organized Terror. The Case of Violent Internal Repression*, Boulder: Westview Press, 1991, pp. 77–98.

Huber, E., D. Rueschemeyer and J.D. Stephens, 'The Impact of Economic Development on Democracy', *Journal of Economic Perspectives*, 7/3 (1993), pp. 71–85.

Human Rights Watch, *Human Rights Watch World Report 1991. Events of 1990*, New York: Human Rights Watch, 1991.

Human Rights Watch, *Human Rights Watch World Report 1995. Events of 1994*, New York: Human Rights Watch, 1995.

Human Rights Watch, *Not a Level Playing Field. Government Violations in the Lead-up to the Election*, New York: Human Rights Watch, 2001a.

Human Rights Watch, *Protectors or Pretenders? Government Human Rights Commissions in Africa*, New York: Human Rights Watch, 2001b.

Human Rights Watch, *Playing with Fire. Weapons Proliferation, Political Violence, and Human Rights in Kenya*, New York: Human Rights Watch, 2002.

Human Rights Watch, *Abducted and Abused. Renewed Conflict in Northern Uganda*, New York: Human Rights Watch, 2003.

Human Rights Watch, *State of Pain. Torture in Uganda*, New York: Human Rights Watch, 2004.

Human Rights Watch, *Concerns Regarding Torture and Other Cruel, Inhumane and Degrading Treatment or Punishment in Uganda*, New York: Human Rights Watch, 2005.

Human Rights Watch/Africa, *Failing the Internally Displaced: The UNDP Displaced Persons Program in Kenya*, New York: Human Rights Watch, 1997a.

Human Rights Watch/Africa, *The Scars of Death. Children Abducted by the Lord's Resistance Army in Uganda*, New York: Human Rights Watch, 1997b.

Huntington, S.P., *Political Order in Changing Societies*, New Haven: Yale University Press, 1968.

Huntington, S.P., *The Third Wave. Democratization in the Late Twentieth Century*, Norman: University of Oklahoma Press, 1991.

Huntington, S.P. and J.M. Nelson, *No Easy Choice. Political Participation in Developing Countries*, Cambridge: Harvard University Press, 1976.

International Bar Association, *Report on the Legal System and Independence of the Judiciary in Kenya*, London: International Bar Association, 1997.

International Commission of Jurists, *Uganda and Human Rights. Reports to the UN Commission on Human Rights*, Geneva: International Commission of Jurists, 1977.

International Commission of Jurists, 'The UN Commission on Human Rights and the New Working Group on Arbitrary Detention', *International Commission of Jurists Review*, 46 (1991), pp. 23–32.

International Commission of Jurists (Kenya Chapter), *State of the Rule of Law*, Nairobi: International Commission of Jurists, 1996.

International Crisis Group, *Northern Uganda. Understanding and Solving the Conflict*, Nairobi/Brussels, 2004.

Jackson, R.H., *Quasi-States: Sovereignty, International Relations, and the Third World*, Cambridge: Cambridge University Press, 1990.

Joseph, R., 'Africa, 1990–1997: From Abertura to Closure', *Journal of Democracy*, 9/2 (1998), pp. 3–17.

Kannyo, E., 'Change in Uganda. A New Opening?', *Journal of Democracy*, 15/2 (2004), pp. 125–139.

Karimi, J. and P. Ochieng, *The Kenyatta Succession*, Nairobi: Transafrica, 1980.

Karl, T.L., 'Imposing Consent? Electoralism vs. Democratization in El Salvador', in Drake, P.W. and E. Silva (ed.), *Elections and Democratization in Latin America, 1980–1985*, San Diego: Center for Iberian and Latin American Studies, 1986, pp. 9–36.

Karl, T.L., 'Petroleum and Political Pacts. The Transition to Democracy in Venezuela', *Latin American Political Review*, 22/1 (1987), pp. 63–94.

Karl, T.L. and P.C. Schmitter, 'Modes of Transition in Latin America, Southern and Eastern Europe', *International Social Science Journal*, 128 (1991), pp. 269–284.

Kasfir, N., 'The Ugandan Elections of 1989: Power, Populism and Democratization', in Hansen, H.B. and M. Twaddle (ed.), *Changing Uganda. The Dilemmas of*

Structural Adjustment and Revolutionary Change, London: James Currey, 1991, pp. 248–278.

Kasfir, N., 'Ugandan Politics and the Constituent Assembly Elections', in Hansen, H.B. and M. Twaddle (ed.), *From Chaos to Order. The Politics of Constitution-Making in Uganda*, Kampala: Fountain Press, 1995, pp. 148–179.

Kasfir, N., '"No-Party Democracy" in Uganda', *Journal of Democracy*, 9/2 (1998), pp. 49–63.

Kasozi, A.B.K., *The Social Origins of Violence in Uganda, 1964–1985*, Montreal: McGill-Queen's University Press, 1994.

Keck, M.E. and K. Sikkink, *Activists Beyond Borders. Advocacy Networks in International Politics*, Ithaca: Cornell University Press, 1998.

Kenya Human Rights Commission, *Independence without Freedom. The Legitimisation of Repressive Laws and Practices in Kenya*, Nairobi: Kenya Human Rights Commission, 1994.

Kenya Human Rights Commission, *Licensed to Kill: Police Shootings In Kenya*, Nairobi: Kenya Human Rights Commission, 1995.

Kenya Human Rights Commission, *Kayas of Deprivation, Kayas of Blood: Violence and the State in Coastal Kenya*, Nairobi: Kenya Human Rights Commission, 1997.

Keohane, R.O. and J.S. Nye Jr., 'Introduction', in Keohane, R.O. and J.S. Nye Jr. (ed.), *Transnational Relations and World Politics*, Cambridge: Harvard University Press, 1971, pp. xii–xvi.

Khadiagala, G.M., 'State Collapse and Reconstruction in Uganda', in Zartman, I.W. (ed.), *Collapsed States. The Disintegration and Restoration of Legitimate Authority*, Boulder: Westview Press, 1995, pp. 33–48.

Khagram, S., 'Restructuring the Global Politics of Development', in Sikkink, K., J.V. Riker and S. Khagram (ed.), *Restructuring World Politics. Transnational Social Movements, Networks, and Norms*, Minneapolis: University of Minnesota Press, 2002, pp. 206–230.

Khagram, S., J.V. Riker and K. Sikkink, 'From Santiago to Seattle. Transnational Advocacy Groups Restructuring World Politics', in Sikkink, K., J.V. Riker and S. Khagram (ed.), *Restructuring World Politics. Transnational Social Movements, Networks, and Norms*, Minneapolis: University of Minnesota Press, 2002, pp. 3–23.

Kibwana, K., *Law and the Administration of Justice in Kenya*, Nairobi: International Commission of Jurists (Kenya Section), 1992.

Kirby, D., 2004. 'What Reduced HIV Prevalence in Uganda?', in *XV International AIDS Conference*. Bangkok, Thailand: (posted at: http://www.synergyaids.com/announce/Bangkok_Presentations.htm).

Kirschke, L., 'Informal Repression, Zero-Sum Politics and Late Third Wave Transitions', *Journal of Modern African Studies*, 38/3 (2000), pp. 383–405.

Kjaer, A.M., 'Fundamental Change or No Change? The Process of Constitutionalizing Uganda', *Democratization*, 6/4 (1999), pp. 93–113.

Klopp, J., '"Ethnic Clashes" and Winning Elections: The Case of Kenya's Electoral Despotism', *Canadian Journal of African Studies*, 35/3 (2001), pp. 473–517.

Klug, H., *Constituting Democracy: Law, Globalism, and South Africa's Political Reconstruction*, New York: Cambridge University Press, 2000.

Krasner, S.D., 'Power Politics, Institutions, and Transnational Relations', in Risse-Kappen, T. (ed.), *Bringing Transnational Relations Back In. Non-State Actors, Domestic Structures and International Institutions*, Cambridge: Cambridge University Press, 1995, pp. 257–279.

Kratochwil, F., *Rules, Norms, and Decisions. On the Conditions of Practical and Legal reasoning in International Relations and Domestic Affairs*, Cambridge: Cambridge University Press, 1989.

Kuria, G.K., *Majimboism, Ethnic Cleansing and Constitutionalism in Kenya*, Nairobi: Kenya Human Rights Commission, 1994.

Kyemba, H., *State of Blood. The Inside Story of Idi Amin's Reign of Fear*, London: Corgi Books, 1977.

Lafargue, J., *Contestations démocratiques en Afrique. Sociologie de la protestations au Kenya et en Zambie*, Paris: Éditions Karthala, 1996.

Layton, A.S., *International Politics and Civil Rights Policies in the United States, 1941–1960*, Cambridge: Cambridge University Press, 2000.

Leftwich, A., 'Two Cheers for Democracy?', *The Political Quarterly*, 67/4 (1996), pp. 334–339.

Lerner, D., *The Passing of Traditional Society. Modernizing the Middle East*, New York: Free Press, 1958.

Lijphart, A., *Democracy in Plural Societies. A Comparative Exploration*, New Haven: Yale University Press, 1977.

Lindberg, S.I., '"It's Time to Chop": Do Elections in Africa Feed Neo-Patrimonialism rather than Counter-Act it?', *Democratization*, 10/2 (2003), pp. 121–140.

Lipset, S.M., *Political Man. The Social Bases of Politics*, New York: Anchor Books, 1960.

Lipset, S.M., S. Kyoung-Ryung and J.C. Torres, 'A Comparative Analysis of the Social Requisites of Democracy', *International Social Science Journal*, 136 (1993), pp. 155–175.

Lonsdale, J., S. Booth-Clibborn and A. Hake, 'The Emerging Pattern of Church and State Cooperation in Kenya', in Fasholé-Luke, E., R. Gray, A. Hastings and G. Tasie (ed.), *Christianity in Independent Africa*, Bloomington: Indiana University Press, 1978, pp. 267–284.

Low, D.A., *Political Parties in Uganda, 1949–1962*, London: University of London Institute of Commonwealth Affairs, 1962.

Lule, G., 'Foreword', in Kyemba, H. (ed.), *State of Blood. The Inside Story of Idi Amin's Reign of Fear*, London: Corgi Books, 1977, pp. 5–8.

Lynch, D.C., 'International "Decentering" and Democratization: The Case of Thailand', *International Studies Quarterly*, 48/2 (2004), pp. 339–362.

Macy, M.W. and A. Flache, 'Beyond Rationality in Models of Choice', *Annual Review of Sociology*, 21 (1995), pp. 73–91.

Mainwaring, S. and A. Pérez-Liñán, 'Level of Development and Democracy: Latin American Exceptionalism, 1945–1996', *Comparative Political Studies*, 36/3 (2003), pp. 1031–1067.

Mair, S., *Kenias Weg in die Mehrparteiendemokratie. Von Uhuru über Harambee und Nyayo erneut zur Uhuru*, Baden-Baden: Nomos, 1994.

Mamdani, M., *Citizen and Subject. Contemporary Africa and the Legacy of Late Colonialism*, Princeton: Princeton University Press, 1996.

Martin, D., *General Amin*, London: Faber and Faber, 1974.

McNeely, C.L., *Constructing the Nation-State. International Organization and Prescriptive Action*, Westport: Greenwood Press, 1995.

Mendelson, S.E. and J.K. Glenn, *The Power and Limits of NGOs*, New York: Columbia University Press, 2002.

Merkel, W., 'Theorien der Transformation. Die demokratische Konsolidierung postautoritärer Gesellschaften', in von Beyme, K. and C. Offe (ed.), *Politische*

Theorien in der Ära der Transformation, Opladen: Westdeutscher Verlag, 1996, pp. 30–58.

Meyer, J.W., J. Boli and G.M. Thomas, 'Ontology and Rationalization in the Western Cultural Account', in Thomas, G.M., J.W. Meyer, F.O. Ramirez and J. Boli (ed.), *Institutional Structure. Constituting the State, Society, and the Individual*, Newbury Park: Sage, 1987, pp. 12–37.

Meyer, J.W., J. Boli, G.M. Thomas, and F.O. Ramirez, 'World Society and the Nation-State', *American Journal of Sociology*, 103/1 (1997), pp. 144–181.

Moore, M., 'Is Democracy Rooted in Material Prosperity?', in Luckham, R. and G. White (ed.), *Democratization in the South: the Jagged Wave*, Manchester: Manchester University Press, 1996, pp. 37–68.

Mughisa, A., 'Museveni's Machinations', *Journal of Democracy*, 15/2 (2004), pp. 140–144.

Muhumuza, R. (ed.), *Shattered Innocence. Testimonies of Children Abducted in Northern Uganda*, Kampala: World Vision/UNICEF, 1997.

Munck, G.L. and J. Verkuilen, 'Conceptualizing and measuring democracy. Evaluating alternative indices', *Comparative Political Studies*, 35/1 (2002), pp. 5–34.

Museveni, Y.K., *What is Africa's Problem?*, Kampala: NRM Publications, 1992.

Muthoga, L., 'Why the I.B.A. Conference was moved from Nairobi', *Nairobi Law Monthly*, 24 (1990), pp. 8–9.

Mwesige, P.G., 'Disseminators, Advocates, and Watchdogs. A Profile of Ugandan Journalists in the New Millennium', *Journalism*, 5/1 (2004), pp. 69–96.

Nairobi Law Monthly, 'Uproar Over the Kennedy's Human Rights Visit', *Nairobi Law Monthly*, 15 (1989), pp. 14–24.

Nairobi Law Monthly, 'Bishop Muge's Death Shocks', *Nairobi Law Monthly*, 24 (1990), pp. 11–12.

National Resistance Movement, *Towards a Free and Democratic Uganda. The Basic Principles and Policies of the National Resistance Movement*, Kampala: National Resistance Movement, 1985.

Ndegwa, S.N., *The Two Faces of Civil Society. NGOs and Politics in Africa*, West Hartford: Kumarian Press, 1996.

Ndegwa, S.N., 'Citizenship and Ethnicity: An Examination of Two Transition Moments in Kenyan Politics', *American Political Science Review*, 91/3 (1997), pp. 599–616.

Ndegwa, S.N., 'The Incomplete Transition: The Constitutional and Electoral Context in Kenya', *Africa Today*, 45/2 (1998), pp. 193–212.

Ndegwa, S.N., 'Kenya: Third Time Lucky?', *Journal of Democracy*, 14/3 (2003), pp. 145–158.

Neubauer, D., 'Some Conditions of Democracy', *American Political Science Review*, 61/4 (1967), pp. 1002–1009.

Ngunyi, M., H. Kithinji and S. Matsvai, 2004. 'Review of Swedish Support to Human Rights and Democracy through Partnership with CSOs in Kenya.' Stockholm: Swedish International Development Cooperation Agency.

Nowrojee, P., 'Being Nobody's Darling. The Independence of the Bar', *University of Nairobi Law Journal*, 2/3 (1995), pp. 79–85.

Nsibambi, A.R., 'La crise ougandaise de 1966', in Prunier, G. and B. Calas (ed.), *L'Ouganda Contemporain*, Paris: Éditions Karthala, 1994, pp. 89–104.

O'Brien, R., A.M. Goetz, J.A. Scholte, and M. Williams, *Contesting Global Governance. Multilateral Economic Institutions and Global Social Movements*, Cambridge: Cambridge University Press, 2000.

O'Donnell, G., 'Illusions about Consolidation', *Journal of Democracy*, 7/2 (1996), pp. 34–51.

O'Donnell, G. and P.C. Schmitter, *Transitions from Authoritarian Rule. Tentative Conclusions about Uncertain Democracies*, Baltimore: Johns Hopkins University Press, 1986.

O'Donnell, G., P.C. Schmitter and L. Whitehead, *Transitions from Authoritarian Rule. Prospects for Democracy*, Baltimore: Johns Hopkins University Press, 1986.

Odoki Commission, *The Report of the Uganda Constitutional Commission. Analysis and Recommendations*, Entebbe: Government Printer, 1992.

Ofcansky, T.P., *Uganda. Tarnished Pearl of Africa*, Boulder: Westview Press, 1996.

Offe, C., *Der Tunnel am Ende des Lichts. Erkundungen der politischen Transformation im Neuen Osten*, Frankfurt am Main: Campus, 1994.

Oloka-Onyango, J., 'Law, "Grassroots Democracy", and the National Resistance Movement in Uganda', *International Journal of the Sociology of Law*, 17 (1989), pp. 465–480.

Oloka-Onyango, J., 'The Dynamics of Corruption Control and Human Rights Enforcement in Uganda: The Case of the Inspector General of Government', *East African Journal of Peace and Human Rights*, 1/1 (1993), pp. 23–51.

Olsen, G.R., 'Europe and the Promotion of Democracy in Post Cold War Africa: How serious is Europe and for what Reason?', *African Affairs*, 97 (1998), pp. 343–367.

Olson, M., 'Dictatorship, Democracy, and Development', *American Political Science Review*, 87/3 (1993), pp. 567–576.

Omara-Otunnu, A., *Politics and the Military in Uganda, 1890–1985*, New York: St. Martin's Press, 1987.

Omara-Otunnu, A., 'The Struggle for Democracy in Uganda', *The Journal of Modern African Studies*, 30/3 (1992), pp. 443–463.

Orvis, S., 'Kenyan Civil Society. Bridging the Urban-Rural Divide?', *Journal of Modern African Studies*, 41/2 (2003), pp. 247–268.

Peters, R.-M., *Zivile und politische Gesellschaft in Kenya*, Hamburg: Institut für Afrikakunde, 1996.

Philpott, D., *Revolutions in Sovereignty. How Ideas Shaped Modern International Relations*, Princeton: Princeton University Press, 2001.

Price, R., 'Reversing the Gun Sights: Transnational Civil Society Targets Land Mines', *International Organization*, 52/3 (1998), pp. 613–644.

Price, R., 'Transnational Civil Society and Advocacy in World Politics', *World Politics*, 55/4 (2003), pp. 579–606.

Pridham, G., E. Herring and G. Sanford, *Building Democracy: The International Dimension of Democratization in Eastern Europe*, London: Routledge, 1994.

Pridham, G. and T. Vanhanen (ed.), *Democratization in Eastern Europe. Domestic and International Perspectives*, London: Routledge, 1994.

Prunier, G., 'La recherche de la normalisation (1979–1994)', in Prunier, G. and B. Calas (ed.), *L'Ouganda Contemporain*, Paris: Éditions Karthala, 1994, pp. 131–158.

Prunier, G., 'Kenya. Des habits neufs pour un vieux despote', *Le Monde Diplomatique*, 514 (1997), 9 pp.

Przeworski, A., 'Some Problems in the Study of the Transition to Democracy', in O'Donnell, G., P.C. Schmitter and L. Whitehead (ed.), *Transition from Authoritarian Rule. Prospects for Democracy*, Baltimore: Johns Hopkins University Press, 1986, pp. 47–63.

Przeworski, A., *Democracy and the Market. Political and Economic Reforms in Eastern Europe and Latin America*, Cambridge: Cambridge University Press, 1991.

Przeworski, A., 'The Games of Transition', in Mainwaring, S., G. O'Donnell and J.S. Valenzuela (ed.), *Issues in Democratic Consolidation: The New South American Democracies in Comparative Perspective*, Notre Dame: University of Notre Dame Press, 1992, pp. 105–152.

Przeworski, A., M.E. Alvarez, J.A. Cheibub, and F. Limongi, *Democracy and Development. Political Institutions and Well-Being in the World, 1950–1990*, Cambridge: Cambridge University Press, 2000.

Przeworski, A. and F. Limongi, 'Political Regimes and Economic Growth', *Journal of Economic Perspectives*, 7/3 (1993), pp. 51–69.

Przeworski, A. and F. Limongi, 'Modernization: Theories and Facts', *World Politics*, 49/2 (1997), pp. 155–183.

Remmer, K.L., 'New Theoretical Perspectives on Democratization', *Comparative Politics*, 28/1 (1995), pp. 103–122.

Republic of Kenya, *Nailing Lies*, Nairobi: The Ministry of Foreign Affairs and International Cooperation, 1991.

Republic of Kenya, *Report of the Parliamentary Select Committee to Investigate Ethnic Clashes in Western and Other Parts of Kenya 1992*, Nairobi: The National Assembly, 1992.

Republic of Kenya, *Human Rights Situation in Kenya. The Way It Is*, Nairobi: Government of Kenya, 1996.

Republic of Uganda, *The Report of The Commission of Inquiry into Violations of Human Rights. Findings, Conclusions, and Recommendations*, Kampala: The Government of Uganda, 1994.

Republic of Uganda, *Constitution of the Republic of Uganda*, Kampala: Government Printer, 1995a.

Republic of Uganda, *Instrument of Accession to the First Optional Protocol of the International Covenant on Civil and Political Rights, 22 September 1995*, Kampala: Government of Uganda, 1995b.

Republic of Uganda, *Observations by the Government of Uganda on Communication No. 92/4/6,719 in Respect of Human Rights Violations to the United Nations by Amnesty International*, Geneva, 1995c.

Reus-Smit, C., 'The Constitutional Structure of International Society and the Nature of Fundamental Institutions', *International Organization*, 51/4 (1997), pp. 555–589.

Risse-Kappen, T. (ed.), *Bringing Transnational Relations Back In. Non-State Actors, Domestic Structures and International Institutions*, Cambridge: Cambridge University Press, 1995.

Risse, T., '"Let's Argue!" Communicative Action in World Politics', *International Organization*, 54/1 (2000), pp. 1–39.

Risse, T., 'Transnational Actors and World Politics', in Carlsnaes, W., T. Risse and B. Simmons (ed.), *Handbook of International Relations*, London: Sage, 2002, pp. 255–274.

Risse, T. and K. Sikkink, 'The Socialization of International Human Rights Norms into Domestic Practices', in Risse, T., S. Ropp and K. Sikkink (ed.), *The Power of Human Rights. International Norms and Domestic Change*, Cambridge: Cambridge University Press, 1999, pp. 1–38.

Risse, T., S.C. Ropp and K. Sikkink (ed.), *The Power of Human Rights. International Norms and Domestic Change*, Cambridge: Cambridge University Press, 1999.

Robinson, M., 'Will Political Conditionality Work?', *IDS Bulletin*, 24/1 (1993), pp. 58–65.

Robinson, M. and S. Friedman, 2005. 'Civil Society, Democratization, and Foreign Aid in Africa', in *IDS Discussion Paper 383*. Brighton, Sussex: Institute of Development Studies.

Roessler, P.G., 'Donor-Induced Democratization and Privatization of State Violence in Kenya and Rwanda', *Comparative Politics*, 37/2 (2005), pp. 207–227.

Ross, M.L., 'Does Oil Hinder Democracy?', *World Politics*, 53/3 (2001), pp. 325–361.

Rubin, E., 'Our Children are Killing Us', *The New Yorker*, 74/5 (1998), pp. 56–64.

Rueschemeyer, D., E. Huber Stephens and J.D. Stephens, *Capitalist Development and Democracy*, Cambridge: Polity Press, 1992.

Rustow, D.A., 'Transitions to Democracy. Toward a Dynamic Model', *Comparative Politics*, 2/3 (1970), pp. 337–363.

Sabar-Friedmann, G., 'Church and State in Kenya, 1986–1992: The Churches' Involvement in the 'Game of Change', *African Affairs*, 96 (1997), pp. 25–52.

Sathyamurthy, T.V., *The Political Development of Uganda: 1900–1986*, Aldershot: Gower, 1986.

Saulnier, B., 'Prisoner of Conscience', *Cornell Magazine*, 99/7 (1997), pp. 27–31.

Schmitter, P.C., 'The Proto-Science of Consolidology: Can it Improve the Outcome of Contemporary Efforts at Democratization?', *Politikon*, 21/2 (1994), pp. 15–27.

Schmitter, P.C., 'The Influence of the International Context upon the Choice of National Institutions and Policies in Neo-Democracies', in Whitehead, L. (ed.), *The International Dimensions of Democratization. Europe and the Americas*, New York: Oxford University Press, 2001, pp. 26–54.

Schmitz, H.P. and K. Sikkink, 'International Human Rights', in Carlsnaes, W., T. Risse and B. Simmons (ed.), *Handbook of International Relations*, London: Sage, 2002, pp. 517–537.

Schofield, D., 'Why I Left Kenya – Speech to the Cayman Bar Association by the Hon. Mr Justice Derek Schofield', *Nairobi Law Monthly*, 41 (1992), pp. 49–50.

Schraeder, P.J., S.W. Hook and H. Taylor, 'Clarifying the Foreign Aid Puzzle. A Comparison of American, Japanese, French and Swedish Aid Flows', *World Politics*, 50/2 (1998), pp. 294–323.

Schumpeter, J.A., *Capitalism, Socialism, and Democracy*, London: George Allen & Unwin, 1942.

Seftel, A. (ed.), *Uganda. The Bloodstained Pearl of Africa and its Struggle for Peace. From the Pages of Drum Magazine*, Kampala: Fountain Press, 1994.

Shapiro, I., 'Democratic Innovation. South Africa in Comparative Context', *World Politics*, 46/1 (1993), pp. 121–150.

Sirowy, L. and A. Inkeles, 'The Effects of Democracy on Economic Growth and Inequality: A Review', *Studies in Comparative International Development*, 25/1 (1990), pp. 126–157.

Ssekandi, F. and C. Gitta, 'Protection of Fundamental Rights in the Uganda Constitution', *Columbia Human Rights Law Review*, 26/1 (1994), pp. 191–213.

Stiles, K.W., 'International Support for NGOs in Bangladesh: Some Unintended Consequences', *World Development*, 30/5 (2002), pp. 835–846.

Tangri, R. and A.M. Mwenda, 'Military Corruption and Ugandan Politics since the late 1990s', *Review of African Political Economy*, 30 (2003), pp. 539–552.

Tarrow, S., 'Transnational Politics: Contention and Institutions in International Politics', *Annual Review of Political Science*, 4 (2001), pp. 1–20.

Tarrow, S., *The New Transnational Activism*, Cambridge: Cambridge University Press, 2005.

Thomas, D., *The Helsinki Effect. International Norms, Human Rights, and the Demise of Communism*, Princeton: Princeton University Press, 2001.

Thompson, K.B., 'Women's Rights are Human Rights Institutionalizing Global Norms about Women Rights', in Khagram, S., J.V. Riker and K. Sikkink (ed.), *Restructuring World Politics. Transnational Social Movements, Networks, and Norms*, Minneapolis: University of Minnesota Press, 2002, pp. 96–122.

Throup, D., *Economic and Social Origins of Mau Mau, 1945–53*, London: James Currey, 1987.

Throup, D., 'Elections and Political Legitimacy in Kenya', *Africa*, 63/3 (1993), pp. 371–396.

Throup, D., 'Render unto Caesar the Things that are Caesar's', in Hansen, H.B. and M. Twaddle (ed.), *Religion & Politics in East Africa. The Period Since Independence*, London: James Currey, 1995, pp. 143–176.

Throup, D.W. and C. Hornsby, *Multi-Party Politics in Kenya*, Oxford: James Currey, 1997.

Tolley Jr., H.B., *The International Commission of Jurists. Global Advocates for Human Rights*, Philadelphia: University of Pennsylvania Press, 1994.

Tostensen, A., B.-A. Andreassen and K. Tronvoll, *Kenya's Hobbled Democracy Revisited. The 1997 General Elections in Retrospect and Prospect*, Oslo: Norwegian Institute of Human Rights, 1998.

Tripp, A.M., 'The Changing Face of Authoritarianism in Africa: The Case of Uganda', *Africa Today*, 50/3 (2004), pp. 3–26.

Tumusiime, J., *Uganda 1986–1991: An Illustrated Review*, Kampala: Fountain Press, 1991.

Tumusiime, J., *Uganda 30 Years: 1962–1992*, Kampala: Fountain Press, 1992.

U.S. Department of State, *Kenya Country Report on Human Rights Practices for 1993*, Washington, D.C.: General Press Office, 1994a.

U.S. Department of State, *Uganda Country Report on Human Rights Practices for 1993*, Washington, D.C.: General Press Office, 1994b.

U.S. Department of State, *Kenya Country Report on Human Rights Practices for 1997*, Washington D.C.: U.S. Department of State, 1998.

U.S. Department of State, *Kenya Country Report on Human Rights Practices for 2001*, Washington, D.C.: General Press Office, 2002a.

U.S. Department of State, *Uganda Country Report on Human Rights Practices for 2001*, Washington, D.C.: General Press Office, 2002b.

U.S. Department of State, *Kenya Country Report on Human Rights Practices for 2002*, Washington, D.C.: General Press Office, 2003.

U.S. Department of State, *Kenya Country Report on Human Rights Practices for 2003*, Washington, D.C.: General Press Office, 2004.

UN Commission on Human Rights, *Report of the Special Rapporteur on Torture*, Geneva: United Nations, 1996.

Vanhanen, T., *The Process of Democratization. A Comparative Study of 147 States, 1980–88*, New York/London: Crane Russak, 1990.

wa Wamwere, K., *The People's Representative and the Tyrants*, Nairobi: New Concept Typesetters, 1992.

Waliggo, J.M., 'Constitution-Making and the Politics of Democratization in Uganda', in Hansen, H.B. and M. Twaddle (ed.), *From Chaos to Order. The Politics of Constitution-Making in Uganda*, Kampala/London: Fountain Press/James Currey, 1995, pp. 18–40.

Waltz, K.N., *Theory of International Politics*, Reading: Addison-Wesley, 1979.

Ward, K., 'The Church of Uganda amidst Conflict. The Interplay between Church and Politics in Uganda since 1962', in Hansen, H.B. and M. Twaddle (ed.), *Religion & Politics in East Africa. The Period Since Independence*, London: James Currey, 1995, pp. 72–105.

Weiner, M., 'Empirical Democratic Theory', in Weiner, M. and E. Özbudun (ed.), *Competitive Elections in Developing Countries*, Durham: Duke University Press, 1987, pp. 3–34.

Wendt, A., *Social Theory of International Politics*, Cambridge: Cambridge University Press, 1999.

Weyel, V., 'Uganda', in Büttner, V. and J. Krause (ed.), *Rüstung statt Entwicklung? Sicherheitspolitik, Militärausgaben und Rüstungskontrolle in der Dritten Welt*, Baden-Baden: Nomos, 1995, pp. 554–572.

Whitehead, L., *The International Dimensions of Democratization: Europe and the Americas*, Oxford: Oxford University Press, 2001.

Widner, J.A., 'Kenya's Slow Progress towards Multiparty Politics', *Current History*, 91 (1992a), pp. 214–218.

Widner, J.A., *The Rise of the One-Party-State in Kenya: From 'Harambee' to 'Nyayo'*, Berkeley: University of California Press, 1992b.

Willetts, P. (ed.), *Pressure Groups in the Global System: The Transnational Relations of Issue-Oriented Non-Governmental Organizations*, New York: St. Martin's Press, 1982.

Young, C., 'Africa. An Interim Balance Sheet', *Journal of Democracy*, 7/3 (1996), pp. 53–68.

Youngs, R., *International Democracy and the West: The Roles of Government, Civil Society, and Multinational Business*, Oxford: Oxford University Press, 2004.

Zakaria, F., 'The Rise of Illiberal Democracy', *Foreign Affairs*, 76/6 (1997), pp. 22–43.

Index

Notes: Page numbers in *italics* refers to figures and **bold** refers to tables.